A PERFECT UNDERSTANDING

OF ALL THINGS FROM THE VERY FIRST

A walk with Dr. Luke through his Gospel

FRED A. KUYPERS

PREFACE

Jesus Christ said to all who would listen:

John 14:6 ...I am the way, the truth, and the life: no man cometh unto the Father, but by me.

It's very simple. If we don't find the way, how can we know the truth? And if we don't know the truth, how can we have the life? Jesus Christ brought this to light during His last supper as a man. That's right, as a man. Jesus wanted His followers to know about life. That is, eternal life. He said in no uncertain terms:

John 10:10 ...I am come that they might have life, and that they might have *it* more abundantly.

As a man, Jesus wanted all to have an understanding that abundant life was free. But it would not come easy. Souls would come hard to bow to Jesus Christ. There would be roadblocks. There would be obstacles. There would be those desiring to prevent a person from having this abundant life. However, as a man, Jesus declared the reason He came into this world. And as God, He could perform it! Abundant life that has alluded man from the beginning of time. From Adam and Eve.

God declared that there is only one thing that man can do. God said that this one thing can only come one way. God said this is the only way to approach Him as the Almighty. This one way, one truth, one life to have it is:

BELIEF!

John 3:15 That whosoever believeth in him should not perish, but have eternal life.

Matthew, Mark, Luke, and John are four books in the Holy Bible. They are called the Gospels. The word "Gospel simply means "Good News." Four different accounts of Good News have been presented by God so that there will be no doubt that God's plan is real. I have used the Gospel of John to give the introduction to this study about Luke. But Matthew and Mark could have given the same introduction but in their own specific way. Matthew was very straight forward and held nothing back. His introduction might have gone something like this:

Matthew 18:6 But whoso shall offend one of these little ones which believe in me, it were better for him that a millstone were hanged about his neck, and that he were drowned in the depth of the sea.

Mark on the other hand would write so that he would be understood by anyone from any walk of life as he quotes Jesus saying:

Mark 1:15 And saying, The time is fulfilled, and the kingdom of God is at hand: repent ye, and believe the gospel.

The last thing I want is for this to be just another commentary on the Gospel of Luke. I want the reader to be able to quickly locate the situation in question and learn what the rest of the Bible has to say. I chose to use statements by John, because his view of Christ is Deity, to introduce the reader to the book of Luke, because his view of Christ is as a man. I will use other Bible verses to elaborate on any point that is made. Over the course of the next 24 chapters of the book of Luke, it will be seen that Luke presented the same idea of what it *takes* for man to understand what it is that God *wants*. Believing God does not come easy for a man. To believe with nothing added by man. That is only believe! In chapter 8 of Luke, there are three points about what it takes to be saved from hell and have eternal life with God. They agree with what John said above:

1. You must discover the way. That is God's way. His way is to believe in the work of Jesus Christ at the cross.

2. You must hear the truth. That is the truth of the death, burial, and resurrection of Jesus Christ explained in this study.

3. You must believe this to have eternal life.

Luke 8:12 Those by the way side are they that hear; then cometh the devil, and taketh away the word out of their hearts, lest they should believe and be saved.

Luke 8:13 They on the rock are they, which, when they hear, receive the word with joy; and these have no root,

which for a while believe, and in time of temptation fall away.

Luke 8:14 And that which fell among thorns are they, which, when they have heard, go forth, and are choked with cares and riches and pleasures of this life, and bring no fruit to perfection.

Luke 8:15 But that on the good ground are they, which in an honest and good heart, having heard the word, keep it, and bring forth fruit with patience.

CONTENTS

INTRODUCTION TO LUKE

Many have wondered why there are four gospels, especially if three of the four, (*known as the synoptic gospels*) have much in common. The number four is a key number in understanding God. Four is the number of creation completeness. Four is the number of earthly completeness. Four is the number of spiritual completeness. God loves the number four!

The creation started with God creating the four heavenly objects, The earth was created first. Then the Sun, Moon, and Stars were created. By the way they were created on the fourth day. God creates four types of animals, reptiles, mammals, fowl, and fish. God completes His creation with the basic four elements needed to supply man with his needs. They are Carbon, Nitrogen, Oxygen, and Hydrogen.

Next God moves to instruction for man. Man needs the four directions of movement, left, right, up, down. However, there are four directions of the earth; north, south, east, and west. The earth has the four seasons of a year; winter, summer, autumn and spring. The four parts of a day, that is the day, night, dawn, and dusk.

God then moved into the spiritual realm of His creation. There were four colors for the tabernacle, four faces in Ezekiel's image, four faces in John's image and four gospels.

There are four primary answers why God gave us four Gospels Matthew, Mark, Luke, and John. The all-important spiritual work of four gospels can have the question asked, why four gospels? Here are four reasons:

1. **Fulfilling God's design in the Old Testament**
    Many accounts in the Old Testament point to four distinct and different ways of describing the coming of the Messiah.

2. **Fulfilling Gods legal requirement with Multiple Witnesses and First-hand accounts.**

Multiple independent eyewitness or first-hand accounts establishes the reliability of the testimony concerning the life and ministry of Jesus.

3. **Announcing four varied Perspectives of Christ as King, Servant, Son of Man, and Son of God**
    Each author recorded the events of Jesus' life and ministry from a different perspective with different goals and objectives.

4. **Resolving the Old Testament Mystery of the "name" of the "Son" that God promised by giving four prominent names to Christ.**
    Each author records the name of Jesus Christ that was a Mystery in the Old Testament. This includes Jesus, Christ, Emanuel in Matthew, and Word in John.

1. Fulfilling God's design in the Old Testament

Requires a look at the Tabernacle.

The tabernacle building: the coverings were of four items, fine linen, goats hair, rams skins, and badgers skins:
Exodus 25:4 And blue, and purple, and scarlet, and fine linen, and goats' *hair,*
Exodus 25:5 And rams' skins dyed red, and badgers' skins, and shittim wood,

Notice the four colors of the curtains, (Fine Linen (White), Blue, Purple, and Scarlet) and the direction of each "leading tribe" around the tabernacle.
Exodus 26:1 Moreover thou shalt make the tabernacle *with* ten curtains *of* fine twined linen, and blue, and purple, and scarlet: *with* cherubims of cunning work shalt thou make them.

Purple- Kingly color represented by the Gospel of Matthew who is presenting Jesus as King of kings and the tribe of Judah to the east of the tabernacle along with Issachar and Zebulun. The

first group had Judah as their lead tribe. This camp was always to the East.

> Numbers 2:3 And on the east side toward the rising of the sun shall they of the standard of the camp of Judah pitch throughout their armies: and Nahshon the son of Amminadab *shall be* captain of the children of Judah.

Scarlet- Sacrifice of blood represented by the Gospel of Mark, that is, presenting Jesus as the servant, willing to go to the cross. Red representing blood and sacrifice and service, seen as the ox serving mankind. The tribe of Reuben to the south of the tabernacle was the lead tribe along with Simeon and Gad.

> Numbers 2:10 On the south side *shall be* the standard of the camp of Reuben according to their armies: and the captain of the children of Reuben *shall be* Elizur the son of Shedeur.

Linen, white- Symbol of purity represented by the Gospel of Luke who presents Jesus as the sinless "Son of Man." White representing sinless and serving to mankind by Jesus and the tribe of Ephraim to the west of the tabernacle. Manasseh, Ephraim's brother, and Benjamin joined Ephraim to the west.

> Numbers 2:18 On the west side *shall be* the standard of the camp of Ephraim according to their armies: and the captain of the sons of Ephraim *shall be* Elishama the son of Ammihud.

Blue- Symbol of deity represented by the Gospel of John who presents Jesus as the Son of God. The eagle being a Godly symbol of that which dwells in the heavens above, is the tribe of Dan to the north of the tabernacle. Asher and Naphtali join Dan.

> Numbers 2:25 The standard of the camp of Dan *shall be* on the north side by their armies: and the captain of the children of Dan *shall be* Ahiezer the son of Ammishaddai.

There are four directions for man to instruct, up, down, right, and left. North on a map is always up. The direction of "up" is the location of where God dwells:

Psalms 75:6 For promotion *cometh* neither from the east, nor from the west, nor from the south.

Every time someone went to Jerusalem he would be told to go up. If a person was walking from the north to the south, he would be going down as on a map. However, traveling in this direction or from any direction one would always be going "up to Jerusalem." Even if they were on a higher mountain such as the Mount of Olives, they were told to go "up to Jerusalem."

Luke 2:42 And when he was twelve years old, they went "up" to Jerusalem after the custom of the feast.

The faces of the beast that both Ezekiel and John saw in their prophecies were four-sided. Ezekiel describes his vision:

Ezekiel 1:3 The word of the LORD came expressly unto Ezekiel the priest, the son of Buzi, in the land of the Chaldeans by the river Chebar; and the hand of the LORD was there upon him.

Ezekiel 1:4 And I looked, and, behold, a whirlwind came out of the north, a great cloud, and a fire infolding itself, and a brightness *was* about it, and out of the midst thereof as the colour of amber, out of the midst of the fire.

Ezekiel 1:5 Also out of the midst thereof *came* the likeness of four living creatures. And this *was* their appearance; they had the likeness of a man.

Ezekiel 1:6 And every one had four faces, and every one had four wings.

Ezekiel 1:7 And their feet *were* straight feet; and the sole of their feet *was* like the sole of a calf's foot: and they sparkled like the colour of burnished brass.

Ezekiel 1:8 And *they had* the hands of a man under their wings on their four sides; and they four had their faces and their wings.

Ezekiel 1:9 Their wings *were* joined one to another; they turned not when they went; they went every one straight forward.

Ezekiel 1:10 As for the likeness of their faces, they four had the face of a man, and the face of a lion, on the right side: and they four had the face of an ox on the left side; they four also had the face of an eagle.

Ezekiel 1:11 Thus *were* their faces: and their wings *were* stretched upward; two *wings* of every one *were* joined one to another, and two covered their bodies.

Ezekiel confirms this vision in chapter 10. However in this vision Ezekiel sees a cherub instead of an ox. Both are creations of God and were created to serve and both still point to Christ as the great Servant to man:

Ezekiel 10:14 And every one had four faces: the first face *was* the face of a cherub, and the second face *was* the face of a man, and the third the face of a lion, and the fourth the face of an eagle.

Ezekiel 10:15 And the cherubims were lifted up. This *is* the living creature that I saw by the river of Chebar.

And John describes his vision with four beasts in Revelation:

Revelation 4:6 And before the throne *there was* a sea of glass like unto crystal: and in the midst of the throne, and round about the throne, *were* four beasts full of eyes before and behind.

Revelation 4:7 And the first beast *was* like a lion, and the second beast like a calf, and the third beast had a face as a man, and the fourth beast *was* like a flying eagle.

Revelation 4:8 And the four beasts had each of them six wings about *him;* and *they were* full of eyes within: and they rest not day and night, saying, Holy, holy, holy, Lord God Almighty, which was, and is, and is to come.

Now notice the four standards or flags representing the camp around the tabernacle. The first group of three tribes had Judah as their leader with Issachar and Zebulun following. The banner they assembled under was a lion. This camp was always to the east. Representing Matthew:

Genesis 49:9 Judah *is* a lion's whelp: from the prey, my son, thou art gone up: he stooped down, he couched as a lion, and as an old lion; who shall rouse him up?

Lion- The tribe of Judah to the east of the tabernacle had a Lion as its standard.

Next came Reuben to the south leading Simeon and Gad bearing their banner of an ox. An ox is known as a servant. An animal that will suffer through hard labor to continue to serve. This is Leah's expression as she gave birth to Reuben in affliction or misery of hard labor, what a servant would do. Representing Mark:

> Genesis 29:32 And Leah conceived, and bare a son, and she called his name Reuben: for she said, Surely the LORD hath looked upon my affliction; now therefore my husband will love me.

Ox- The tribe of Reuben to the south of the tabernacle had an ox as its standard.

Next came Ephraim with Manasseh and Benjamin having the face of a man as their standard. Joseph was blessed with a double portion of his two sons receiving a blessing. Salvation of all men was to come through Jesus Christ becoming man to pay for all of man's salvation.

> Genesis 49:22 Joseph *is* a fruitful bough, *even* a fruitful bough by a well; *whose* branches run over the wall:

Man- The tribe of Ephraim to the west of the tabernacle had a face of a man as its standard. Representing Luke.

The last group was Dan leading Asher and Naphtali with their banner of an eagle. What is the one thing God must do to keep His word? He must judge the wicked and the good. This is not an easy thing to do; and to do it PERFECTLY! An eagle must make a very fast and correct judgement as he descends to catch his prey. The eagle is a divine symbol of God to judge righteously and quickly.

> Genesis 49:16 Dan shall judge his people, as one of the tribes of Israel.

Eagle- The tribe of Dan to the north of the tabernacle had a face of an eagle as its standard. Representing John.

God's design in the Old Testament always points to the coming of the Christ, the Messiah, that is Shiloh. God declares He will judge righteously. This righteous judgement will be by His Son, the Lord Jesus Christ. Presented in the Old Testament:

Psalms 67:4 O let the nations be glad and sing for joy: for thou shalt judge the people righteously, and govern the nations upon earth. Selah.

Explained in the New Testament:

John 5:22 For the Father judgeth no man, but hath committed all judgment unto the Son:

2. God's legal requirement of Multiple Witnesses.

Multiple independent eyewitnesses would be the Apostles and perhaps Jesus' half brothers and sisters. The two eye-witnesses writing gospels are Matthew and John. Both were Apostles and were with Jesus during His public ministry. This fulfills the Biblical requirement for legality:

Deuteronomy 19:5 One witness shall not rise up against a man for any iniquity, or for any sin, in any sin that he sinneth: at the mouth of two witnesses, or at the mouth of three witnesses, shall the matter be established.

First-hand accounts definitely establish the reliability of the testimony concerning the life and ministry of Jesus. The two first-hand accounts are from Mark and Luke. They were both alive at the time of Christ but may not have always been eyewitnesses.

3. Four varied Perspectives.

Each author recorded the events of Jesus' life and ministry from a different perspective with different goals and objectives. Each Gospel is different in their unique way of writing thus showing no collaboration or collusion. Matthew, Mark, and Luke are called synoptic gospels with John being different, however, many times all four gospels say the same thing and many times all four gospel's testimonies are completely different.

Matthew has the "Kingdom of Heaven" in his writings, and it appears 32 times. This phrase appears in no other book in the Bible. Matthew discusses Jesus as the King.

Mark has the miracles of Jesus spelled out in the most compelling accounts. Mark has no lineage as a bond-slave. Mark gets right to the work of Christ in repentance and believing.

Mark 1:15 And saying, The time is fulfilled, and the kingdom of God is at hand: repent ye, and believe the gospel.

Luke, the beloved physician, reveals the best account of Jesus Christ's birth, His death, His agony in the garden (sweating great drops of blood only in the Gospel of Luke) and Christ's physical healing as only a physician can describe.

Last is John who gives the lineage of Jesus Christ as clear as is possible in human understanding. In the beginning was the "Word" and the "Word" was with God, and the "Word" was God. No human lineage at all.

John 1:1 In the beginning was the Word, and the Word was with God, and the Word was God.

As far as lineage goes, this word, "Word" became Jesus Christ in the flesh:

John 1:14 And the Word was made flesh, and dwelt among us, (and we beheld his glory, the glory as of the only begotten of the Father,) full of grace and truth.

The Gospel of John portrays Christ as truly God come down in the flesh.

4. Resolving the Mystery of the Name of the Promised Redeemer.

Each author records the name of Jesus Christ which was a Mystery in the Old Testament. Matthew and Mark speak of "Jesus Christ" becoming the earliest time in the New Testament the word "Christ" is used.

Matthew 1:1 The book of the generation of Jesus Christ, the son of David, the son of Abraham.

Mark 1:1 The beginning of the gospel of Jesus Christ, the Son of God;

The word "Christ means the "Annointed one" and the Old Testament has only one word from Daniel for this meaning. It is the word "Messiah."

Daniel 9:27 Know therefore and understand, *that* from the going forth of the commandment to restore and to build Jerusalem unto the Messiah the Prince *shall be* seven weeks, and threescore and two weeks: the street shall be built again, and the wall, even in troublous times.

Daniel 9:27 And after threescore and two weeks shall Messiah be cut off, but not for himself: and the people of the prince that shall come shall destroy the city and the sanctuary; and the end thereof *shall be* with a flood, and unto the end of the war desolations are determined.

Mary and Joseph were instructed to name the child "Jesus" given in Matthew and Luke. This instruction given to one eye-witness (Matthew) and one first-hand account (Luke):

Matthew 1:21 And she shall bring forth a son, and thou shalt call his name JESUS: for he shall save his people from their sins.

Luke 1:31 And, behold, thou shalt conceive in thy womb, and bring forth a son, and shalt call his name JESUS.

Matthew confirms the naming of Jesus to be correct as he calls upon the name of Emmanuel from the Old Testament. Emmanuel (Greek), Immanuel (Hebrew) being descriptive meaning "God with Us".

Matthew 1:22 Now all this was done, that it might be fulfilled which was spoken of the Lord by the prophet, saying,
Matthew 1:23 Behold, a virgin shall be with child, and shall bring forth a son, and they shall call his name Emmanuel, which being interpreted is, God with us.

This justifies the Old Testament name "Immanuel" of the promised one given in Isaiah:

Isaiah 7:14 Therefore the Lord himself shall give you a sign; Behold, a virgin shall conceive, and bear a son, and shall call his name Immanuel.

John uses an even more unique yet simple name of Christ. The name "WORD" (John 1:1). This is spoken of in the Old Testament, that the word "Word" would be to Him for a name:

Isaiah 55:11 So shall my word be that goeth forth out of my mouth: it (Word) shall not return unto me void, but it (Word) shall accomplish that which I please, and it (Word) shall prosper *in the thing* whereto I sent it (Word).
Isaiah 55:12 For ye shall go out with joy, and be led forth with peace: the mountains and the hills shall break forth before you into singing, and all the trees of the field shall clap *their* hands.
Isaiah 55:13 Instead of the thorn shall come up the fir tree, and instead of the brier shall come up the myrtle tree: and it (Word) shall be to the LORD for a name, for an everlasting sign *that* shall not be cut off.

These are the only comments I will endeavor to make with each chapter.

a. **Historically only those that speak to the history of the era being talked about.**
b. **I will strive to direct the reader to other verses in the Bible, particularly the Old Testament, that will reinforce what the Holy Spirit is saying.**
c. **Also to make it evident what is strictly written by Luke and what is written by the other three Gospel writers which makes many passages synoptical.**

As chapter one begins, instructions will be given as to what part of Luke stands alone, what part of Luke is synoptic with other gospels and what part of Luke is in all four of the gospels. Luke will become an interesting friend to you for eternity if you are born again. By the way, are you born again? Jesus said you must be.

John 3:3 Jesus answered and said unto him, Verily, verily, I say unto thee, Except a man be born again, he cannot see the kingdom of God.

Jesus said you must be born physically (mothers water breaking) and you must be born spiritually:

John 3:5 Jesus answered, Verily, verily, I say unto thee, Except a man be born of water and *of* the Spirit, he cannot enter into the kingdom of God.

Jesus told the most intelligent Pharisee of the day, Nicodemus that this is exactly what he needed to do:

John 3:6 That which is born of the flesh is flesh; and that which is born of the Spirit is spirit.

John 3:7 Marvel not that I said unto thee, Ye must be born again.

God loves you and gave you a gift:

John 3:16 For God so loved the world, that he gave his only begotten Son, that whosoever believeth in him should not perish, but have everlasting life.

God's view of this born-again command is pretty strong. In fact, God says that if you are not born again you are already condemned. We are born condemned.

John 3:18 He that believeth on him is not condemned: but he that believeth not is condemned already, because he hath not believed in the name of the only begotten Son of God.

This gift is God himself. He always gives Himself to a man who wants Him.

John 3:17 For God sent not his Son into the world to condemn the world; but that the world through him might be saved.

LUKE CHAPTER 1

Highlights:

Every chapter is about Jesus Christ. Chapter one introduces the writer, Luke, and his decision to write this Gospel about Jesus Christ. Luke is the writer, not the author. The Author is God. The writer addresses this Gospel to Theophilus, which means "love of God", or "Friend of God". Theophilus can represent anyone who wants to draw closer to God. It can mean you! However, Theophilus himself remains unknown.

Main Participants:

Herod, king of Judaea v.5,
Zacharias and Elisabeth v.5,
An Angel v.11,
John the Baptist v.13,
The angel Gabriel v.26,
Joseph and Mary v.27,
JESUS v.31.

In Brief:

Luke writes to Theophilus and wants him to have a "perfect understanding" of all things from the very first. Zacharias seeks a sign from God and is made a mute. He has doubts, but his wife, Elisabeth believes. They host Mary for three months without Joseph. Mary humbly acknowledges who she is and that she needs a Savior. She returns to Joseph pregnant! Going back to Zacharias and Elisabeth, John is born, and his parents tell all his name will not be Zacharias Jr. but John. They are told that he will prepare the way for Messiah.

Only in Luke's Gospel

Who was Luke?

Luke 1:1 Forasmuch as many have taken in hand to set forth in order a declaration of those things which are most surely believed among us,
Luke 1:2 Even as they delivered them unto us, which from the beginning were eyewitnesses, and ministers of the word;
Luke 1:3 It seemed good to me also, having had perfect understanding of all things from the very first, to write unto thee in order, most excellent Theophilus,
Luke 1:4 That thou mightest know the certainty of those things, wherein thou hast been instructed.

Luke was not an Apostle to Jesus Christ's ministry. However, he lived during that time. According to his own writings, he carefully listened to those who "were eyewitnesses, and ministers of the word." God also gave him a "perfect understanding of all things from the very first." He was commanded by God to "write unto thee in order." In so doing he made the story of the human life of Jesus Christ to be instruction for all mankind and according to his gospel, certain that it is correct and right. This is what God means when He says All scripture is given by His inspiration:
2Timothy 3:16 All scripture *is* given by inspiration of God, and *is* profitable for doctrine, for reproof, for correction, for instruction in righteousness:
2Timothy 3:17 That the man of God may be perfect, throughly furnished unto all good works.

A PERFECT UNDERSTANDING
LUKE CHAPTER 1

Luke who is also known as Luke the evangelist, Luke the physician, and Luke the writer, is the penman of both the Gospel of Luke and the Book of Acts. Notice he is not the author. The Author is God Himself:

> Hebrews 12:2 Looking unto Jesus the author and finisher of *our* faith; who for the joy that was set before him endured the cross, despising the shame, and is set down at the right hand of the throne of God.

Luke wrote more words of the New Testament than anyone else; even the Apostle Paul. He also assisted Paul when Paul, who was moved by the Holy Spirit, had Luke and Titus pen 2 Corinthians:

> 2Corinthians 13:14 The grace of the Lord Jesus Christ, and the love of God, and the communion of the Holy Ghost, *be* with you all. Amen. The second epistle to the Corinthians was written from Philippi, a city of Macedonia, by Titus and Lucas.

Luke the evangelist was a constant traveling companion of Paul. He would be there to give the Gospel out just as Paul did:

> Philemon 1:24 Marcus, Aristarchus, Demas, Lucas, my fellowlabourers.

There were some individuals who were not profitable for Paul to assist with Evangelizing:

> 2Timothy 4:10 For Demas hath forsaken me, having loved this present world, and is departed unto Thessalonica; Crescens to Galatia, Titus unto Dalmatia.
> 2Timothy 4:11 Only Luke is with me. Take Mark, and bring him with thee: for he is profitable to me for the ministry.

However, Luke was profitable and always by Paul's side. Luke now describes what he had a perfect understanding of.

Luke 1:5 There was in the days of Herod, the king of Judaea, a certain priest named Zacharias, of the course of Abia: and his wife *was* of the daughters of Aaron, and her name *was* Elisabeth. Luke 1:6 And they were both righteous before God, walking in all the commandments and ordinances of the Lord blameless.

3

Zacharias was of the course of Abia. Abia (Greek or New Testament) or Abijah (Hebrew or Old Testament) was one of the Levites that had a "lot" or a "course" assigned to them by David.

> 1Chronicles 24:3 And David distributed them, both Zadok of the sons of Eleazar, and Ahimelech of the sons of Ithamar, according to their offices in their service.
>
> 1Chronicles 24:4 And there were more chief men found of the sons of Eleazar than of the sons of Ithamar; and *thus* were they divided. Among the sons of Eleazar *there were* sixteen chief men of the house of *their* fathers, and eight among the sons of Ithamar according to the house of their fathers.
>
> 1Chronicles 24:5 Thus were they divided by lot, one sort with another; for the governors of the sanctuary, and governors *of the house* of God, were of the sons of Eleazar, and of the sons of Ithamar.

Zacharias had served for many years in the temple of the Lord as it is revealed that he was childless in all the years of his service.

Luke 1:7 And they had no child, because that Elisabeth was barren, and they both were *now* well stricken in years.

Zacharias was faithful in his service. We need to be as faithful as he was. If you never see a single bit of fruit come from your witness understand that faithfulness is what God requires:

> 1Corinthians 4:1 Let a man so account of us, as of the ministers of Christ, and stewards of the mysteries of God.
>
> 1Corinthians 4:2 Moreover it is required in stewards, that a man be found faithful.

Luke 1:8 And it came to pass, that while he executed the priest's office before God in the order of his course,

Luke 1:9 According to the custom of the priest's office, his lot was to burn incense when he went into the temple of the Lord.

Zacharias' lot was to burn incense when he went into the temple of the Lord. He was of the eighth course or the eighth lot of Levitical priests.

> 1Corinthians 24:10 The seventh to Hakkoz, the eighth to Abijah,

These priests descended from Aaron the first high priest:
>1Corinthians 24:19 These were the orderings of them in their service to come into the house of the LORD, according to their manner, under Aaron their father, as the LORD God of Israel had commanded him.

Luke 1:10 And the whole multitude of the people were praying without at the time of incense.

Remember that the altar of incense is one of the three pieces of furniture in the Holy Place. In fact, this altar had a very special location in the Holy Place just before the Holiest of all or the most holy place.
>Exodus 40:1 And the LORD spake unto Moses, saying,
>Exodus 40:2 On the first day of the first month shalt thou set up the tabernacle of the tent of the congregation.
>Exodus 40:3 And thou shalt put therein the ark of the testimony, and cover the ark with the vail.
>Exodus 40:4 And thou shalt bring in the table, and set in order the things that are to be set in order upon it; and thou shalt bring in the candlestick, and light the lamps thereof.
>Exodus 40:5 And thou shalt set the altar of gold for the incense before the ark of the testimony, and put the hanging of the door to the tabernacle.

Seeing an angel in the Holy Place must have been a real shock to Zacharias. Matthew says that an angel appeared to Joseph also.
>Matthew 1:20 But while he thought on these things, behold, the angel of the Lord appeared unto him in a dream, saying, Joseph, thou son of David, fear not to take unto thee Mary thy wife: for that which is conceived in her is of the Holy Ghost.

There was no name given for this angel in Matthew. However, Zacharias will hear the name of this angel.

Luke 1:11 And there appeared unto him an angel of the Lord standing on the right side of the altar of incense.
Luke 1:12 And when Zacharias saw *him,* he was troubled, and fear fell upon him.

Luke 1:13 But the angel said unto him, Fear not, Zacharias: for thy prayer is heard; and thy wife Elisabeth shall bear thee a son, and thou shalt call his name John.

God will answer prayer but not always in the time or manner that we would want. Zacharias prayer is heard just as Isaac's prayer was heard.

> Genesis 25:21 And Isaac intreated the LORD for his wife, because she *was* barren: and the LORD was intreated of him, and Rebekah his wife conceived.

The word "intreat" means to pray and the only way for your prayer to be heard is because you asked of the Lord;

> 1Sa 1:20 Wherefore it came to pass, when the time was come about after Hannah had conceived, that she bare a son, and called his name Samuel, *saying,* Because I have asked him of the LORD.

Zacharias and Elisabeth were indeed excited about having a child at such an age. Many looked at this as a miracle and watched with rejoicing as God answered their prayer.

Luke 1:14 And thou shalt have joy and gladness; and many shall rejoice at his birth.
Luke 1:15 For he shall be great in the sight of the Lord, and shall drink neither wine nor strong drink; and he shall be filled with the Holy Ghost, even from his mother's womb.

Those who ministered in the Holy Place were already held to a higher standard, in that they could not drink wine or strong drink. This almost sounds like a Nazarite vow to be taken. However, there is no record of John taking a Nazarite vow as the book of Numbers so describes.

> Numbers 6:1 And the LORD spake unto Moses, saying,
> Numbers 6:2 Speak unto the children of Israel, and say unto them, When either man or woman shall separate *themselves* to vow a vow of a Nazarite, to separate *themselves* unto the LORD:

God tells Zacharias through His angel that his son, John, will turn many (to "turn from" is what repentance means). Turn from disobedience to wisdom of the just. God says to "turn to the Lord their God". This is what happens with belief and faith to the Lord.

Luke 1:16 And many of the children of Israel shall he turn to the Lord their God.

Luke 1:17 And he shall go before him in the spirit and power of Elias, to turn the hearts of the fathers to the children, and the disobedient to the wisdom of the just; to make ready a people prepared for the Lord.

Who is this "him" in verse 17? It refers to the last-mentioned name which is "the Lord their God" from verse 16. John was going to go before the "Lord their God." This Lord their God is none other than our Lord Jesus Christ, who will be conceived in the womb of Elisabeth's cousin, Mary.

The angel said he was going to go in the spirit and power of Elias. This brought the final scripture of the Old Testament to mind from Malachi, that all Israel had waited for. The Glass of Wine and empty place at the Seder meal even today is still set at the Passover meal for Elijah (Greek form Elias) waiting for him to come:

Malachi 4:5 Behold, I will send you Elijah the prophet before the coming of the great and dreadful day of the LORD:

Malachi 4:6 And he shall turn the heart of the fathers to the children, and the heart of the children to their fathers, lest I come and smite the earth with a curse.

God later says that Elias, that is Elijah (Hebrew) already came. He is John the Baptist.

Matthew 17:11 And Jesus answered and said unto them, Elias truly shall first come, and restore all things.

Matthew 17:12 But I say unto you, That Elias is come already, and they knew him not, but have done unto him whatsoever they listed. Likewise shall also the Son of man suffer of them.

Matthew 17:13 Then the disciples understood that he spake unto them of John the Baptist.

Zacharias does not believe the angel and questions him. Now this angel appeared to Zacharias while he was in the temple. There should have been no mistaking him. There should have been no doubt.

Luke 1:18 And Zacharias said unto the angel, Whereby shall I know this? for I am an old man, and my wife well stricken in years.

This angel that appeared to Zacharias is Gabriel. Angels come in the appearance of a man just as God described in Daniel. This is the same angel that appeared to Daniel to announce the time frame of the first and second appearance of the Messiah.

Daniel 8:15 And it came to pass, when I, *even* I Daniel, had seen the vision, and sought for the meaning, then, behold, there stood before me as the appearance of a man.

Daniel 8:16 And I heard a man's voice between *the banks of* Ulai, which called, and said, Gabriel, make this *man* to understand the vision.

Gabriel speaks here and he will be heard from again in six months when he speaks to Mary.

Luke 1:19 And the angel answering said unto him, I am Gabriel, that stand in the presence of God; and am sent to speak unto thee, and to shew thee these glad tidings.

Luke 1:20 And, behold, thou shalt be dumb, and not able to speak, until the day that these things shall be performed, because thou believest not my words, which shall be fulfilled in their season.

Because Zacharias doubted the angel, God struck him with not being able to speak. Zacharias, doubting the statement of the angel Gabriel was not a good thing to do. Paul gives some instruction in Romans concerning doubting:

Romans 14:22 Hast thou faith? have *it* to thyself before God. Happy *is* he that condemneth not himself in that thing which he alloweth.

Romans 14:23 And he that doubteth is damned if he eat, because *he eateth* not of faith: for whatsoever *is* not of faith is sin.

James has something to say about this also:

James 1:5 If any of you lack wisdom, let him ask of God, that giveth to all *men* liberally, and upbraideth not; and it shall be given him.

James 1:6 But let him ask in faith, nothing wavering. For he that wavereth is like a wave of the sea driven with the wind and tossed.

We have a sure word from God, and it needs to be followed down to the jot and tittle.

Zacharias had friends who cared for him probably because of his age. Perhaps they grew concerned with the amount of time he was spending in the holy place.

Luke 1:21 And the people waited for Zacharias, and marvelled that he tarried so long in the temple.

The people marveled? They still do today! The world has no idea of God's plans for the second coming. When God has an angel speak, rest assured it will come to pass! God gives the sign:

Luke 1:22 And when he came out, he could not speak unto them: and they perceived that he had seen a vision in the temple: for he beckoned unto them, and remained speechless.

Luke 1:23 And it came to pass, that, as soon as the days of his ministration were accomplished, he departed to his own house.

Elisabeth Conceives a baby whom we will come to know as John the Baptist:

Luke 1:24 And after those days his wife Elisabeth conceived, and hid herself five months, saying,

Luke 1:25 Thus hath the Lord dealt with me in the days wherein he looked on *me,* to take away my reproach among men.

God took away Elisabeth's reproach. God did not have to strike Elisabeth with any dumbness for she believed. It was considered a bad thing for a woman who was married not to

conceive a baby. Rachel spoke of the same thing when God allowed her to become pregnant;

> Genesis 30:22 And God remembered Rachel, and God hearkened to her, and opened her womb.
> Genesis 30:23 And she conceived, and bare a son; and said, God hath taken away my reproach:

God worked this special miracle with the angel Gabriel for one specific reason. His Son, the Lord Jesus Christ was about to be announced at the first coming.

Luke 1:26 And in the sixth month the angel Gabriel was sent from God unto a city of Galilee, named Nazareth,

The angel Gabriel appears to be God's favored angel to reveal special messages about the coming "Christ" to mankind. The two times that it was important enough to use Gabriel was to Zacharias and to Mary, in the New Testament, to announce God's Son at His first coming and in the Old Testament, to Daniel and his vision of the time frame that God would use to bring His Son to the throne at His second coming. This angelic foretelling is to deal with the Jews, Daniels People, called "thy people":

> Daniel 9:21 Yea, whiles I *was* speaking in prayer, even the man Gabriel, whom I had seen in the vision at the beginning, being caused to fly swiftly, touched me about the time of the evening oblation.
> Daniel 9:22 And he informed *me,* and talked with me, and said, O Daniel, I am now come forth to give thee skill and understanding.
> Daniel 9:23 At the beginning of thy supplications the commandment came forth, and I am come to shew *thee;* for thou *art* greatly beloved: therefore understand the matter, and consider the vision.
> Daniel 9:24 Seventy weeks are determined upon thy people and upon thy holy city, to finish the transgression, and to make an end of sins, and to make reconciliation for iniquity, and to bring in everlasting righteousness, and to seal up the vision and prophecy, and to anoint the most Holy.

Daniel 9:25 Know therefore and understand, *that* from the going forth of the commandment to restore and to build Jerusalem unto the Messiah the Prince *shall be* seven weeks, and threescore and two weeks: the street shall be built again, and the wall, even in troublous times.

Daniel 9:26 And after threescore and two weeks shall Messiah be cut off, but not for himself: and the people of the prince that shall come shall destroy the city and the sanctuary; and the end thereof *shall be* with a flood, and unto the end of the war desolations are determined.

Daniel 9:27 And he shall confirm the covenant with many for one week: and in the midst of the week he shall cause the sacrifice and the oblation to cease, and for the overspreading of abominations he shall make *it* desolate, even until the consummation, and that determined shall be poured upon the desolate.

God is looking forward with much anticipation to His Son, the Lord Jesus Christ, sitting on His throne, over all the world. Notice that this first appearance of Gabriel to Daniel spoke of both His first and second coming.

Psalms 2:4 He that sitteth in the heavens shall laugh: the Lord shall have them in derision.

Psalms 2:5 Then shall he speak unto them in his wrath, and vex them in his sore displeasure.

Psalms 2:6 Yet have I set my king upon my holy hill of Zion.

Psalms 2:7 I will declare the decree: the LORD hath said unto me, Thou *art* my Son; this day have I begotten thee.

Psalms 2:8 Ask of me, and I shall give *thee* the heathen *for* thine inheritance, and the uttermost parts of the earth *for* thy possession.

In Luke's and Matthew's Gospel:

Gabriel the heralding angel is sent to Mary, a virgin.

Luke 1:27 To a virgin espoused to a man whose name was Joseph, of the house of David; and the virgin's name *was* Mary.

In Matthew, the angel appears to Joseph. This heralding angel tells Joseph not to fear as Mary will have a baby and His name shall be Jesus.

Matthew 1:20 But while he thought on these things, behold, the angel of the Lord appeared unto him in a dream, saying, Joseph, thou son of David, fear not to take unto thee Mary thy wife: for that which is conceived in her is of the Holy Ghost.

Matthew 1:21 And she shall bring forth a son, and thou shalt call his name JESUS: for he shall save his people from their sins.

Only in Luke's Gospel

Again, God is going to keep His word. He is going to reveal something that was predicted over 700 years earlier.

Isaiah 7:10 Moreover the LORD spake again unto Ahaz, saying,

Isaiah 7:11 Ask thee a sign of the LORD thy God; ask it either in the depth, or in the height above.

Isaiah 7:12 But Ahaz said, I will not ask, neither will I tempt the LORD.

Isaiah 7:13 And he said, Hear ye now, O house of David; *Is it* a small thing for you to weary men, but will ye weary my God also?

Isaiah 7:14 Therefore the Lord himself shall give you a sign; Behold, a virgin shall conceive, and bear a son, and shall call his name Immanuel.

God is going to address the one who will bring His Son into the world.

Luke 1:28 And the angel came in unto her, and said, Hail, *thou that art* highly favoured, the Lord *is* with thee: blessed *art* thou among women.

When Catholics pray the "Hail Mary" it is conceived from this passage. The first half of the "Hail Mary" is basically quoting this scripture.

"Hail, Mary, full of grace, the Lord is with thee. Blessed art thou amongst women and blessed is the fruit of thy womb, Jesus."

They even use good old King James pronouns such as thee, thou, and thy. This is quoted from the "Douay-Rheims Version" of scripture translated from the Latin to English at approximately the same time as the King James Bible was translated. Both versions use the singular personal pronouns beginning with "TH" However, it's the second part of this prayer that is blasphemy. Calling Mary "the mother of God" and asking Mary to "pray for us sinners" is total blasphemy! We will expand on this in the next few verses.

Mary was not sure how to take this announcement by Gabriel, but God knew in her heart that she did not question the Angel as Zacharias did.

Luke 1:29 And when she saw *him,* she was troubled at his saying, and cast in her mind what manner of salutation this should be.

The angel Gabriel would pronounce this very carefully. The angel cannot say that Mary would be the "mother of God." God is eternal and therefore cannot have a mother.
Genesis explains it best by just saying God was already there at the beginning:
Genesis 1:1 In the beginning God created the heaven and the earth.
God declares another name for Jesus in the Gospel of John.
John 1:1 In the beginning was the Word, and the Word was with God, and the Word was God.
John 1:2 The same was in the beginning with God.
John 1:3 All things were made by him; and without him was not any thing made that was made.
And it becomes clear when just a few verses later, John the Apostle describes the Word as becoming flesh.
John 1:14 And the Word was made flesh, and dwelt among us, (and we beheld his glory, the glory as of the only begotten of the Father,) full of grace and truth.

Gabriel gives us exactly what God wants to say to describe His Son coming into the world.

Luke 1:30 And the angel said unto her, Fear not, Mary: for thou hast found favour with God.
Luke 1:31 And, behold, thou shalt conceive in thy womb, and bring forth a son, and shalt call his name JESUS.

This is what God meant in Genesis 3:15 when He declared for the very first time how the redeemer, Jesus Christ His Son, unknown by name throughout the Old Testament, but known as the promise of God was announced.

Genesis 3:15 And I will put enmity between thee and the woman, and between thy seed and her seed; it shall bruise thy head, and thou shalt bruise his heel.

The woman does not have the seed. The man has the seed. For "her seed" to exist would take a miracle. This miracle of virgin birth! A core belief in Christianity is the virgin birth of our Lord. Satan would begin his work at trying to destroy this conception, this embryo, this fetus, this seed of the woman. God the Son, Jesus, unknown by name for 4 millennium until this moment, when the mystery of the Kinsman Redeemer is finally revealed.

Mary listens to Gabriel and questions the fact that how is this possible to be a pregnant virgin?

Luke 1:32 He shall be great, and shall be called the Son of the Highest: and the Lord God shall give unto him the throne of his father David:

The throne of his father David sounds like Isaiah which spoke of this promised one:

Isaiah 9:6 For unto us a child is born, unto us a son is given: and the government shall be upon his shoulder: and his name shall be called Wonderful, Counsellor, The mighty God, The everlasting Father, The Prince of Peace.
Isaiah 9:7 Of the increase of *his* government and peace *there shall be* no end, upon the throne of David, and upon his kingdom, to

order it, and to establish it with judgment and with justice from henceforth even for ever. The zeal of the LORD of hosts will perform this.

Luke will announce the same events that Isaiah predicted some eight hundred years earlier.

Luke 1:33 And he shall reign over the house of Jacob for ever; and of his kingdom there shall be no end.
Luke 1:34 Then said Mary unto the angel, How shall this be, seeing I know not a man?

The Angel Gabriel also must be very articulate not to say that Jesus began here, at Mary's pregnancy carrying Jesus. If this were so, Jesus cannot be eternal and could have His beginning here at His conception. The Angel chooses the words carefully:

Luke 1:35 And the angel answered and said unto her, The Holy Ghost shall come upon thee, and the power of the Highest shall overshadow thee: therefore also that holy thing which shall be born of thee shall be called the Son of God.

"that holy thing which shall be born of thee"

Some have described this term as derogatory. Calling the fetus in Mary a "holy thing" does not sound very flattering. God gave this promise at the beginning in Genesis to Adam and Eve by saying it was "her seed":

Genesis 3:15 And I will put enmity between thee and the woman, and between thy seed and her seed; it shall bruise thy head, and thou shalt bruise his heel.

God selected Luke the physician to discuss this medical miracle. And Luke used the term "holy thing" for as a doctor, he had no other way to describe this miracle. Luke did not have the terms that we have today such as embryos and then the fetus that would have developed in Mary's womb. In Hebrews we read that a body was prepared for Him:

Hebrews 10:5 Wherefore when he cometh into the world, he saith, Sacrifice and offering thou wouldest not, but a body hast thou prepared me:

Hebrews 10:6 In burnt offerings and *sacrifices* for sin thou hast had no pleasure.

Hebrews 10:7 Then said I, Lo, I come (in the volume of the book it is written of me,) to do thy will, O God.

Hebrews 10:8 Above when he said, Sacrifice and offering and burnt offerings and *offering* for sin thou wouldest not, neither hadst pleasure *therein;* which are offered by the law;

Hebrews 10:9 Then said he, Lo, I come to do thy will, O God. He taketh away the first, that he may establish the second.

Hebrews 10:10 By the which will we are sanctified through the offering of the body of Jesus Christ once *for all.*

Let's take a closer look. In Psalms chapter two, God said that His Son would be begotten.

Psalms 2:6 Yet have I set my king upon my holy hill of Zion.

Psalms 2:7 I will declare the decree: the LORD hath said unto me, Thou *art* my Son; this day have I begotten thee.

God was looking forward a thousand years to this exact moment in time for His Son to be begotten. The plan of the ages which was established by a determinate counsel, by those present in eternity past, God the Father, God the Son, and God the Holy Spirit. A counsel or the decision that was to determine the roles that each of the Godhead would play in the redemption of mankind.

Acts 2:23 Him, being delivered by the determinate counsel and foreknowledge of God, ye have taken, and by wicked hands have crucified and slain:

Acts 2:24 Whom God hath raised up, having loosed the pains of death: because it was not possible that he should be holden of it.

Acts 2:25 For David speaketh concerning him, I foresaw the Lord always before my face, for he is on my right hand, that I should not be moved:

God the Father and God the Son and God the Holy Spirit's plan is revealed to us in this determinate counsel. As Paul says, God spared not His own Son:

Romans 8:32 He that spared not his own Son, but delivered him up for us all, how shall he not with him also freely give us all things?

The set up of this determinate counsel is of His Son going to the cross. This was established, as Jesus indicated, when He said in the garden of Gethsemane;

Luke 22:42 Saying, Father, if thou be willing, remove this cup from me: nevertheless not my will, but thine, be done.

God said His counsel would stand. This counsel is advice or words spoken with authority.

Isaiah 46:9 Remember the former things of old: for I *am* God, and *there is* none else; *I am* God, and *there is* none like me,

Isaiah 46:10 Declaring the end from the beginning, and from ancient times *the things* that are not *yet* done, saying, My counsel shall stand, and I will do all my pleasure:

When Isaiah wrote this, the pleasure God spoke of still needed to be done. That is why it is future "I will do all my pleasure." This took place over 700 years in the future from Isaiah. But it says to do His pleasure? How can Jesus Christ the Son of God who is truly God, being born in the next few months from the time of Luke chapter one, only to die a horrific death on the cross, be pleasurable to God the Father? Isaiah speaks more about this time of pleasure in Isaiah 53:

Isaiah 53:1 Who hath believed our report? and to whom is the arm of the LORD revealed?

Isaiah 53:2 For he shall grow up before him as a tender plant, and as a root out of a dry ground: he hath no form nor comeliness; and when we shall see him, *there is* no beauty that we should desire him.

Isaiah 53:3 He is despised and rejected of men; a man of sorrows, and acquainted with grief: and we hid as it were *our* faces from him; he was despised, and we esteemed him not.

Isaiah 53:4 Surely he hath borne our griefs, and carried our sorrows: yet we did esteem him stricken, smitten of God, and afflicted.

Isaiah 53:5 But he *was* wounded for our transgressions, *he was* bruised for our iniquities: the chastisement of our peace *was* upon him; and with his stripes we are healed.

Isaiah 53:6 All we like sheep have gone astray; we have turned every one to his own way; and the LORD hath laid on him the iniquity of us all.

Isaiah 53:7 He was oppressed, and he was afflicted, yet he opened not his mouth: he is brought as a lamb to the slaughter, and as a sheep before her shearers is dumb, so he openeth not his mouth.

Isaiah 53:8 He was taken from prison and from judgment: and who shall declare his generation? for he was cut off out of the land of the living: for the transgression of my people was he stricken.

Isaiah 53:9 And he made his grave with the wicked, and with the rich in his death; because he had done no violence, neither *was any* deceit in his mouth.

Isaiah 53:10 Yet it pleased the LORD to bruise him; he hath put *him* to grief: when thou shalt make his soul an offering for sin, he shall see *his* seed, he shall prolong *his* days, and the pleasure of the LORD shall prosper in his hand.

How can this torture of His Son Jesus Christ please God? He gives the answer right here; right now! You and I are justified because of the travail of His soul. Because of God's knowledge established at a counsel held in eternity past, when it was decreed that Jesus would bear the iniquities (sin) of the whole world:

1John 2:2 And he is the propitiation for our sins: and not for ours only, but also for *the sins of* the whole world.

And those who accept Him as their Savior, He now applies justification to their souls.

Isaiah 53:11 He shall see of the travail of his soul, *and* shall be satisfied: by his knowledge shall my righteous servant justify many; for he shall bear their iniquities.

Isaiah 53:12 Therefore will I divide him *a portion* with the great, and he shall divide the spoil with the strong; because he hath poured out his soul unto death: and he was numbered with the transgressors; and he bare the sin of many, and made intercession for the transgressors.

The Angel Gabriel had already described what would be taking place in the womb of Mary. Back in verse 31, God says He will bring forth a Son. You are going to call His name Jesus. He shall be called the Son of the Highest. Proof of this is with your cousin, Elisabeth:

Luke 1:36 And, behold, thy cousin Elisabeth, she hath also conceived a son in her old age: and this is the sixth month with her, who was called barren.

Luke gives what every saved believer wants to know and believe. That nothing is too hard for God.

Luke 1:37 For with God nothing shall be impossible.

The world loves to argue this point and take it totally out of context. In so doing Satan takes the entire focus from the saving work of God thru Jesus Christ His Son. He does all he can to lead a follower of God into a trap by asking irrelevant questions.

Mary does not doubt the angel as Zacharias did. She is entirely submissive to the will of God. This is an excellent example of how a young woman, or anyone should react upon hearing from God through His word the Bible, submissive to the will of God. If we all would say "be it unto me according to thy word."

Luke 1:38 And Mary said, Behold the handmaid of the Lord; be it unto me according to thy word. And the angel departed from her.

Gabriel did not have to say another word. Mary understood and claimed it. Gabriel was able to depart. After the proclamation of Gabriel to Mary, Mary decides to depart and heads to Elisabeth's house. A young woman who is seeking advice from the much older Elisabeth.

Luke 1:39 And Mary arose in those days, and went into the hill country with haste, into a city of Juda;

From Nazareth to Jerusalem is about a four day walk. Mary heads for Elisabeth's house.

Luke 1:40 And entered into the house of Zacharias, and saluted Elisabeth.

Elisabeth heard the salutation, but it is the babe, in Elisabeth's womb, who understands what Mary is saying.

Luke 1:41 And it came to pass, that, when Elisabeth heard the salutation of Mary, the babe leaped in her womb; and Elisabeth was filled with the Holy Ghost:

Elisabeth needed to be filled with the Holy Ghost to understand the role of Mary and her pregnancy. Elisabeth then announces a blessing upon her.

Luke 1:42 And she spake out with a loud voice, and said, Blessed *art* thou among women, and blessed *is* the fruit of thy womb.

Here now is the first half of the "Hail Mary". To start, the Hail Mary quotes some of these scriptures. If you want to memorize scripture there is no problem with that. We should all work on memorizing all the scriptures we can. But don't forget to say chapter and verse for location. Remember that praying in vain repetition is not pleasing to God.

Matthew 6:7 But when ye pray, use not vain repetitions, as the heathen *do:* for they think that they shall be heard for their much speaking.

If you want, you can quote the Lord 's Prayer from memory just remember its location, Matthew chapter 6:

Matthew 6:9 After this manner therefore pray ye: Our Father which art in heaven, Hallowed be thy name.

Matthew 6:10 Thy kingdom come. Thy will be done in earth, as *it is* in heaven.

Matthew 6:11 Give us this day our daily bread.

Matthew 6:12 And forgive us our debts, as we forgive our debtors.

Matthew 6:13 And lead us not into temptation, but deliver us from evil: For thine is the kingdom, and the power, and the glory, for ever. Amen.

It is important that Elisabeth, by the Holy Spirit chose the word "Lord" at this point. Not the name "God."

Luke 1:43 And whence *is* this to me, that the mother of my Lord should come to me?

If Elisabeth used the name "God" here it would set Mary on a pedestal like many churches have done, making Mary the mother of God and equal to Jesus or a co-redeemer. Choosing the word Lord (Kyrios) here is a title. It can mean master or as the title "Shiloh means "He to whom it belongs." That "Holy thing" from verse 35 is described as nonother than the Lord Jesus Christ. In a body prepared by God himself and implanted in Mary by the Holy Ghost. Elisabeth describes her joy in having a full understanding of what is about to take place confirmed as John the Baptist leaped in her womb.

Luke 1:44 For, lo, as soon as the voice of thy salutation sounded in mine ears, the babe leaped in my womb for joy.

Elisabeth says Mary is blessed in the same manner we are blessed. She believed.

Luke 1:45 And blessed *is* she that believed: for there shall be a performance of those things which were told her from the Lord.

Mary now delivers her statement of belief. It is called today "The Magnificat." She says that all she wants to do is magnify the Lord. She wants to do this in spirit, soul, and body. This is a great speech, and Christians should say the same thing.

Luke 1:46 And Mary said, My soul doth magnify the Lord,

Here, Mary sounds a lot like Hannah of Samuel's fame as she prayed and exalted the Lord!

1Samuel 2:1 And Hannah prayed, and said, My heart rejoiceth in the LORD, mine horn is exalted in the LORD: my mouth is enlarged over mine enemies; because I rejoice in thy salvation.

1Samuel 2:2 *There is* none holy as the LORD: for *there is* none beside thee: neither *is there* any rock like our God.

Both Mary and Hannah have a good understanding of God and His plans for them as God's chosen.

Luke 1:47 And my spirit hath rejoiced in God my Saviour.

Mary says she needs a Saviour. She says God is her Saviour. She must be like us. Because she is like the rest of us, only a sinner, she needs a Saviour.

Romans 3:23 For all have sinned, and come short of the glory of God;

This slaps in the face of Roman Catholicism. Catholicism holds Mary up as a sinless, immaculately conceived, a perpetual virgin and co-redeemer with Jesus Christ. The only two high holy days in the Catholic Church that do not fall on a Sunday are Christmas and the Immaculate Conception of Mary. A person is required to go to mass, no matter what day of the week they fall on, Christmas and the Immaculate Conception, December 8th when Mary, as the Catholic Church says, not Jesus, was conceived.

"The Feast of the Immaculate Conception (December 8)."

This is pure Blasphemy! Mary was not a perpetual virgin. In fact, Joseph and Mary went on to have at least six more children:

Matthew 13:55 Is not this the carpenter's son? is not his mother called Mary? and his brethren, James, and Joses, and Simon, and Judas?

Matthew 13:56 And his sisters, are they not all with us? Whence then hath this *man* all these things?

Mary herself would deny all the blasphemy taking place today in her honor. She was very humble. God could use someone humble like her for this one-time event.

Luke 1:48 For he hath regarded the low estate of his handmaiden: for, behold, from henceforth all generations shall call me blessed.

Mary knew something special was about to happen. She knew that something was happening to her that would change the world. She knew that she was blessed by God. And she would hold up the name of God:

Luke 1:49 For he that is mighty hath done to me great things; and holy *is* his name.
Luke 1:50 And his mercy *is* on them that fear him from generation to generation.

Knowing the scriptures, Mary held up the name of God as Psalms tells us to do:
> Psalms 69:29 But I *am* poor and sorrowful: let thy salvation, O God, set me up on high.
> Psalms 69:30 I will praise the name of God with a song, and will magnify him with thanksgiving.

Mary also knew from Psalms that there is one thing that God holds up higher than His name. That is His Word!
> Psalms 138:2 I will worship toward thy holy temple, and praise thy name for thy lovingkindness and for thy truth: for thou hast magnified thy word above all thy name.

Mary knew her scriptures as she recites back promises made and kept by "God her Saviour."

Luke 1:51 He hath shewed strength with his arm; he hath scattered the proud in the imagination of their hearts.

Mary quotes from Jeremiah:
> Jeremiah 11:8 Yet they obeyed not, nor inclined their ear, but walked every one in the imagination of their evil heart: therefore

I will bring upon them all the words of this covenant, which I commanded them to do; but they did them not.

Luke 1:52 He hath put down the mighty from *their* seats, and exalted them of low degree.

Mary quotes from Isaiah:
Isaiah 2:17 And the loftiness of man shall be bowed down, and the haughtiness of men shall be made low: and the LORD alone shall be exalted in that day.

Luke 1:53 He hath filled the hungry with good things; and the rich he hath sent empty away.

Mary quotes from Proverbs:
Proverbs 13:7 There is that maketh himself rich, yet *hath* nothing: *there is* that maketh himself poor, yet *hath* great riches.

Luke 1:54 He hath holpen his servant Israel, in remembrance of *his* mercy;

Mary quotes from all of Psalms 136:
Psalms 136:1 O give thanks unto the LORD; for *he is* good: for his mercy *endureth* for ever.

Luke 1:55 As he spake to our fathers, to Abraham, and to his seed for ever.

Mary even quotes from Genesis:
Genesis 13:14 And the LORD said unto Abram, after that Lot was separated from him, Lift up now thine eyes, and look from the place where thou art northward, and southward, and eastward, and westward:
Genesis 13:15 For all the land which thou seest, to thee will I give it, and to thy seed for ever.

This is all a part of Mary's Magnificat. Mary declares how God keeps His Word to us. Since He spoke to Abraham and his seed, God has done all He has said He would do. And now the promise of the Kinsman Redeemer is upon her. Surely Mary

knew of the "kinsman" God had promised to Naomi, Ruth's mother-in-law:

> Ruth 4:14 And the women said unto Naomi, Blessed *be* the LORD, which hath not left thee this day without a kinsman, that his name may be famous in Israel.
>
> Ruth 4:15 And he shall be unto thee a restorer of *thy* life, and a nourisher of thine old age: for thy daughter in law, which loveth thee, which is better to thee than seven sons, hath born him.

And she knew of this promise of God called a redeemer first by Job:

> Job 19:25 For I know *that* my redeemer liveth, and *that* he shall stand at the latter *day* upon the earth:

Also called "Redeemer" repeatedly by Isaiah and other prophets:

> Isaiah 44:6 Thus saith the LORD the King of Israel, and his redeemer the LORD of hosts; I *am* the first, and I *am* the last; and beside me *there is* no God.

The Redeemer that formed thee from the womb:

> Isaiah 44:24 Thus saith the LORD, thy redeemer, and he that formed thee from the womb, I *am* the LORD that maketh all *things;* that stretcheth forth the heavens alone; that spreadeth abroad the earth by myself;

That Jeremiah calls the Lord of Hosts!

> Jeremiah 50:34 Their Redeemer *is* strong; the LORD of hosts *is* his name: he shall throughly plead their cause, that he may give rest to the land, and disquiet the inhabitants of Babylon.

The Redeemer is mighty:

> Proverbs 23:11 For their redeemer *is* mighty; he shall plead their cause with thee.

Mary uses what she learned from her studies of the scriptures:

> Psalms 19:14 Let the words of my mouth, and the meditation of my heart, be acceptable in thy sight, O LORD, my strength, and my redeemer.

Luke 1:56 And Mary abode with her about three months, and returned to her own house.

Mary stays with Elisabeth up till the time of the birth of John and then goes home. She has been with Elisabethfor three months now. Mary is about three months pregnant when she comes home to Nazareth. Joseph can do the math also as Matthew explains.

Matthew 1:18 Now the birth of Jesus Christ was on this wise: When as his mother Mary was espoused to Joseph, before they came together, she was found with child of the Holy Ghost.

Matthew 1:19 Then Joseph her husband, being a just *man,* and not willing to make her a publick example, was minded to put her away privily.

Matthew 1:20 But while he thought on these things, behold, the angel of the Lord appeared unto him in a dream, saying, Joseph, thou son of David, fear not to take unto thee Mary thy wife: for that which is conceived in her is of the Holy Ghost.

Matthew 1:21 And she shall bring forth a son, and thou shalt call his name JESUS: for he shall save his people from their sins.

Luke's narrative now switches back to Elisabeth as she gives birth to John the Baptist:

Luke 1:57 Now Elisabeth's full time came that she should be delivered; and she brought forth a son.

Luke 1:58 And her neighbours and her cousins heard how the Lord had shewed great mercy upon her; and they rejoiced with her.

Elisabeth and Zacharias obey scripture. On the 8th day the male child is to be circumcised:

Genesis 17:11 And ye shall circumcise the flesh of your foreskin; and it shall be a token of the covenant betwixt me and you.

Genesis 17:12 And he that is eight days old shall be circumcised among you, every man child in your generations, he that is born in the house, or bought with money of any stranger, which *is* not of thy seed.

So on the 8th day the noisy neighbors seek to name the child Zacharias after his father.

Luke 1:59 And it came to pass, that on the eighth day they came to circumcise the child; and they called him Zacharias, after the name of his father.

Luke 1:60 And his mother answered and said, Not so; but he shall be called John.

Today we name our babies after athletes and movie stars. The Godly tradition was to name a baby after an honored person in the family or after the names of God Himself. They knew this tradition and spoke of it.

Luke 1:61 And they said unto her, There is none of thy kindred that is called by this name.

Zacharias did not want a woman scorned! Even though this is not a biblical phrase, he better back her up. He asks for a writing tablet and obeys God.

Luke 1:62 And they made signs to his father, how he would have him called.

Luke 1:63 And he asked for a writing table, and wrote, saying, His name is John. And they marvelled all.

Zacharias at this time has his speech return as he obeys God and keeps his marriage intact:

Luke 1:64 And his mouth was opened immediately, and his tongue loosed, and he spake, and praised God.

Zacharias received his speech back and this meant very much to the people who were familiar with him in the Temple. Fear came on all that dwelt around them. This fear is the Greek word Phobeo or Phobes. It is not the fear of a coward but more the fear of the unknown. This fear in many cases generates respect and is the fear of one who fears the Lord.

Luke 1:65 And fear came on all that dwelt round about them: and all these sayings were noised abroad throughout all the hill country of Judaea.

The fear that describes a coward appears very rarely in the New Testament. In fact only one time does fear refer to that of a coward.
2Timothy 1:7 For God hath not given us the spirit of fear; but of power, and of love, and of a sound mind.

Luke 1:66 And all they that heard *them* laid *them* up in their hearts, saying, What manner of child shall this be! And the hand of the Lord was with him.
Luke 1:67 And his father Zacharias was filled with the Holy Ghost, and prophesied, saying

Zacharias now is filled with the Holy Ghost. This happened to John in the womb (Luke 1:15) and Elisabeth (Luke 1:41). Zacharias begins to quote and reveals promises from the scriptures. Little did the people know that Zacharias was about to reveal the first and second coming of the Messiah.

Luke 1:68 Blessed *be* the Lord God of Israel; for he hath visited and redeemed his people,
Luke 1:69 And hath raised up an horn of salvation for us in the house of his servant David;
Luke 1:70 As he spake by the mouth of his holy prophets, which have been since the world began:

Zacharias makes two statements that the Jews have believed on for years and have never really seen come to reality. The first promise is from the house of David, a horn of salvation, which the prophets have spoken, which is our Lord's first coming. The very first couple, Adam and Eve, were given a promise of the woman's seed to come. This is about to take place. However, the first sign to all that were present at the temple is the birth of this one called John. The sign is the restoration of Zacharias' voice.

The second oath that God swore was to Abraham. This oath that delivered the Jews out of the hand of their oppressors will not come to pass until the second coming, which would not become evident for two thousand years, in the future.

Luke 1:71 That we should be saved from our enemies, and from the hand of all that hate us;
Luke 1:72 To perform the mercy *promised* to our fathers, and to remember his holy covenant;
Luke 1:73 The oath which he sware to our father Abraham,
Luke 1:74 That he would grant unto us, that we being delivered out of the hand of our enemies might serve him without fear,
Luke 1:75 In holiness and righteousness before him, all the days of our life.

Zacharias said that the Jews wanted to serve God without fear. They have not been able to do that until recently. The dream of Nebuchadnezzar was still not fulfilled. The world powers in the dream had to move down the statue to the legs of iron (legs which represent Roman control) to the feet and the ten toes that would be struck by the stone cut without hands. Jesus, the stone or rock, coming in power and great glory at His second coming.

Zacharias now prophecies about his son, John:

Luke 1:76 And thou, child, shalt be called the prophet of the Highest: for thou shalt go before the face of the Lord to prepare his ways;

He quotes from the prophet Isaiah.
Isaiah 40:3 The voice of him that crieth in the wilderness, Prepare ye the way of the LORD, make straight in the desert a highway for our God.
And from the prophet Malachi:
Malachi 3:1 Behold, I will send my messenger, and he shall prepare the way before me: and the Lord, whom ye seek, shall suddenly come to his temple, even the messenger of the covenant, whom ye delight in: behold, he shall come, saith the LORD of hosts.

The Jews knew the scriptures called for a special someone to prepare the way before the "Anointed One" the "Messiah" the "Christ" would come. But they read in Malachi that it was Elijah.
> Malachi 4:5 Behold, I will send you Elijah the prophet before the coming of the great and dreadful day of the LORD:

Zacharias again declares the knowledge of salvation would only come by the remission of sins. All the sacrifices of the Old Testament never took away this sin problem. The Jews had a problem with sin, and they knew it.

Luke 1:77 To give knowledge of salvation unto his people by the remission of their sins,

God had revealed this sin problem in the past through the sin offerings that forgave nothing:
> 1Samuel 15:22 And Samuel said, Hath the LORD *as great* delight in burnt offerings and sacrifices, as in obeying the voice of the LORD? Behold, to obey *is* better than sacrifice, *and* to hearken than the fat of rams.

The coming of this promised one should have instructed His people to obey instead of offer:
> Hebrews 10:4 For *it is* not possible that the blood of bulls and of goats should take away sins.
> Hebrews 10:5 Wherefore when he cometh into the world, he saith, Sacrifice and offering thou wouldest not, but a body hast thou prepared me:
> Hebrews 10:6 In burnt offerings and *sacrifices* for sin thou hast had no pleasure.

Knowledge of salvation comes by the revealing of the Messiah, the day spring or rising light about to come and be received by those who know the scriptures.

Luke 1:78 Through the tender mercy of our God; whereby the dayspring from on high hath visited us,

A PERFECT UNDERSTANDING
LUKE CHAPTER 1

Luke 1:79 To give light to them that sit in darkness and *in* the shadow of death, to guide our feet into the way of peace.

Isaiah spoke of this one who would give light, this dayspring, this Branch:
> Isaiah 11:1 And there shall come forth a rod out of the stem of Jesse, and a Branch shall grow out of his roots:
> Isaiah 11:2 And the spirit of the LORD shall rest upon him, the spirit of wisdom and understanding, the spirit of counsel and might, the spirit of knowledge and of the fear of the LORD;

The Old Testament prophet Zechariah spoke of this also:
> Zechariah 3:8 Hear now, O Joshua the high priest, thou, and thy fellows that sit before thee: for they *are* men wondered at: for, behold, I will bring forth my servant the BRANCH.

Zacharias, Elisabeth and John are now filled with the Holy Ghost. John became strong in spirit and lived a life as far from sin as he could.

Luke 1:80 And the child grew, and waxed strong in spirit, and was in the deserts till the day of his shewing unto Israel.

Luke is the only Gospel that gives us the full account of John the Baptist. It is so very important to see all the passages of the Old Testament come to light that reveal this forerunner of Christ. He came before Christ to prepare Christ's way. Hiss baptism was that of repentance. The only way you can prepare your heart for Christ to enter is by repentance. In today's churches repentance is called a work. However, Jesus points out how important this repentance is. He declared it is a requirement to believe in Him.
> Mark 1:15 And saying, The time is fulfilled, and the kingdom of God is at hand: repent ye, and believe the gospel.

31

LUKE CHAPTER 2

Highlights:

Chapter two has the birth of Jesus Christ. Later, He is described as a twelve-year old desiring to start His public ministry and follow His Father's will. He returns to Nazareth with His earthly mother and Joseph.

Main Participants:

Caesar Augustus v.1,
Joseph v.4,
Mary v.5,
Shepherds v.8,
Angel of the Lord v.9,
Christ the Lord v.11,
Simeon v.25,
Anna v.36.

In Brief:

Jesus Christ comes into this world as a baby. He is humbly born in an animal area and laid in a manger as frail as could be. Angels appeared to shepherds in the field. They came and adored Him. Mom and Joseph circumcised Him on the eighth day. He was also adored by Simeon and Anna. Joseph and Mary went back to Nazareth with Jesus to rear Him up. Later, after twelve years of upbringing and having more children, the family finds itself in Jerusalem for the Passover that year. Jesus is "left behind" OH

NO! and then found by Mary and Joseph who return to Nazareth with the family to raise Jesus up to manhood.

Only in Luke's Gospel

Luke 2:1 And it came to pass in those days, that there went out a decree from Caesar Augustus, that all the world should be taxed.

Luke is the only Gospel that gives an incredibly detailed account of the birth of Jesus Christ. The only other Gospel that touches on the birth of Jesus Christ is Matthew which gives a very short narrative from Joseph's viewpoint. Only one verse gives the prenatal view of the birth of Christ in Matthew:

Matthew 1:23 Behold, a virgin shall be with child, and shall bring forth a son, and they shall call his name Emmanuel, which being interpreted is, God with us.

Luke names the reason for the trip from Nazareth to Bethlehem. Luke discusses why the trip was made, when the trip was made, the problems finding a place to stay, and the actual birth of baby Jesus. The view of Christ's birth, that is God becoming man is evident in Luke. No other Gospel has this. As discussed, Matthew is the only other account in the bible speaking about this event and he gives no detailed information. Stated above, Matthew describes the birth from the father's side or lineage, the line of the King of kings as Joseph is mentioned in the Kings lineage back to David.

Luke 2:2 (*And* this taxing was first made when Cyrenius was governor of Syria.)

Luke includes a time frame of world events so that this period may be narrowed down. This allows for historians to gauge when this taxation took place. Augustus in verse one is more of a title than a name. It means majestic, or great, or venerable. Caesar Augustus' real name was, Gaius Julius Caesar Octavianus. Known simply as Octavianus, the adopted son of Julius Caesar, Augustus reigned from 31BC till 14AD. The title of Augustus was given to him and followed by many successors including Diocletian and later Charlemagne of the Holy Roman Empire.

Many historians say a conflict occurs with this statement. Cyrenius was governor of Syria where no census is mentioned until 6AD. But Mary and Joseph went to Bethlehem for taxation and not a census. The Westcott and Hort developers of the revised text, the standard for modern versions changed this word "taxing" to "enrolled" which some versions viewed as a "census." This created much confusion. The first known historical information about Cyrenius is around 12BC. His name at that time was Quirinius. He was a military leader who fought against tribes of the mountainous region of Galatia and Cilicia. Sometime around 5–3 BC, he was appointed as legate of Galatia which perhaps was understood as a governor of this territory. Taxation could have occurred at this point for Joseph and Mary who were from the area of Galilee.

The first chapter of Luke speaks of Herod as the king of Judaea who lived at the time of Zacchaeus and Elisabeth. This would be Herod the 1st who was a very evil dictator. Historians have narrowed the time of this Herod's reign to end with his death between 4BC and 1BC. Before his death, Herod the 1st had ordered the killing of all infants born in Bethlehem two years old and younger. This would mean that Jesus would have a birth year of between 6BC and 2BC as the child was taken by Joseph and Mary to Egypt until the death of Herod occurred.

Luke 2:3 And all went to be taxed, every one into his own city.

Notice it is a taxation and not a census. In this case the word taxed means to write off.

Luke 2:4 And Joseph also went up from Galilee, out of the city of Nazareth, into Judaea, unto the city of David, which is called Bethlehem; (because he was of the house and lineage of David:)

From the Old Testament in 1Samuel it is written that the house of David was in the family of Ephrathite of Bethlehemjudah.

1Samuel 17:12 Now David *was* the son of that Ephrathite of Bethlehemjudah, whose name *was* Jesse; and he had eight sons: and the man went among men *for* an old man in the days of Saul.

This city named Bethlehem had to be called out because there are two Bethlehem's in Israel. One in the north of Israel just a few kilometers west of Nazareth and one to the south about ten kilometers south of Jerusalem. During the days of the prophet Micah, he calls the city that is to have the ruler of Israel come from Bethlehem Ephratah to the south.

Micah 5:2 But thou, Bethlehem Ephratah, *though* thou be little among the thousands of Judah, *yet* out of thee shall he come forth unto me *that is* to be ruler in Israel; whose goings forth *have been* from of old, from everlasting.

Joseph, even though he was not the biological father of Jesus, was still of the house of David the promised King. God fulfilled many prophesies about David through Joseph and Mary.

2Samuel 7:8 Now therefore so shalt thou say unto my servant David, Thus saith the LORD of hosts, I took thee from the sheepcote, from following the sheep, to be ruler over my people, over Israel:

David who was ruler over Israel:

2Samuel 7:12 And when thy days be fulfilled, and thou shalt sleep with thy fathers, I will set up thy seed after thee, which shall proceed out of thy bowels, and I will establish his kingdom.

David who had the kingdom established with his seed:

2Samuel 7:16 And thine house and thy kingdom shall be established for ever before thee: thy throne shall be established for ever.

David who had the throne forever.

Jeremiah 23:5 Behold, the days come, saith the LORD, that I will raise unto David a righteous Branch, and a King shall reign and prosper, and shall execute judgment and justice in the earth.

Jeremiah 23:6 In his days Judah shall be saved, and Israel shall dwell safely: and this *is* his name whereby he shall be called, THE LORD OUR RIGHTEOUSNESS.

This righteous Branch raised unto the house of David is known as:

THE LORD OUR RIGHTEOUSNESS, JESUS CHRIST!

Luke 2:5 To be taxed with Mary his espoused wife, being great with child.

Mary was at this time full term nine months pregnant. She had left Elisabeth 6 months earlier. Joseph had to be convinced that Mary was faithful and so Matthew describes how Joseph dealt with this. He decided he would put her away privily.

Matthew 1:19 Then Joseph her husband, being a just *man,* and not willing to make her a publick example, was minded to put her away privily.

Joseph could not be that privily with Mary. She was moving close to her due date and now would have to go out on the road, pregnant and in full view for the tax mandate.

Luke 2:6 And so it was, that, while they were there, the days were accomplished that she should be delivered.

Joseph, six months after discovering that Mary was pregnant, is traveling approximately one whole week with his wife Mary who is nearing full term. They arrive in Bethlehem from Nazareth where she will now go into labor.

Luke 2:7 And she brought forth her firstborn son, and wrapped him in swaddling clothes, and laid him in a manger; because there was no room for them in the inn.

Since there was no "Airbnb," Joseph could not find a place at the inn. So, God took over and provided a humble place for His Son's entry into the world. This place would be as humble as possible. Joseph and Mary must decide on the only place they

could find cover and that was near an animal feeding trough known as a manger.

Luke 2:8 And there were in the same country shepherds abiding in the field, keeping watch over their flock by night.

Shepherds are the first outsiders to hear of this birth. Mary was to be used as the mother. And He became known as the Saviour, Christ the Lord.

Luke 2:9 And, lo, the angel of the Lord came upon them, and the glory of the Lord shone round about them: and they were sore afraid.
Luke 2:10 And the angel said unto them, Fear not: for, behold, I bring you good tidings of great joy, which shall be to all people.

"Afraid" and "fear" in verses 9 and 10 come from the same Greek word "phobeo". One way "phobeo" can be understood is to be "in awe of" or to revere or have reverence. Some modern versions have changed the word afraid to terrified. The shepherds were not terrified for if they were they would not have decided to go to Bethlehem to see the babe. The angel or "messenger" brings the message of good tidings of great joy to all people. Even today it is a great message. However, tonight the message goes to those closest so that witnesses are available to come and see the babe lying in the manger.

Luke 2:11 For unto you is born this day in the city of David a Saviour, which is Christ the Lord.
Luke 2:12 And this *shall be* a sign unto you; Ye shall find the babe wrapped in swaddling clothes, lying in a manger.

Mary has given birth to baby Jesus. There are no newborn baby clothes, no Pampers, no formulas nor any baby bottles, and the baby's crib is the animal's food trough, a manger. But there were heavenly hosts! There were angels! And they were praising God:

Luke 2:13 And suddenly there was with the angel a multitude of the heavenly host praising God, and saying,
Luke 2:14 Glory to God in the highest, and on earth peace, good will toward men.

The angels depart and the shepherds are left alone to determine what just happened to them.

Luke 2:15 And it came to pass, as the angels were gone away from them into heaven, the shepherds said one to another, Let us now go even unto Bethlehem, and see this thing which is come to pass, which the Lord hath made known unto us.
Luke 2:16 And they came with haste, and found Mary, and Joseph, and the babe lying in a manger.

The shepherds came with haste, proving they were not terrified, to see the child as they had received divine instruction. They were not terrified when they saw the babe lying in a manger, they knew the vision was confirmed.

Luke 2:17 And when they had seen *it,* they made known abroad the saying which was told them concerning this child.
Luke 2:18 And all they that heard *it* wondered at those things which were told them by the shepherds.

The hard thing to believe was not a mother giving birth. And it was not that the inn was so full that the only place to have a baby was in a barn? But the hard thing to believe was that the innkeeper could not make room for a pregnant lady and told her to go to a barn to have the baby. An angel had declared this to them, and it was exactly as the angel had said.

Luke 2:19 But Mary kept all these things, and pondered *them* in her heart.
Luke 2:20 And the shepherds returned, glorifying and praising God for all the things that they had heard and seen, as it was told unto them.

Both Mary and the shepherds realized that something special had just occurred. Angels do not always appear and say what was spoken this night. But this night was a special night!

In Luke's and Matthew's Gospel:

Luke 2:21 And when eight days were accomplished for the circumcising of the child, his name was called JESUS, which was so named of the angel before he was conceived in the womb.

Before He was conceived in the womb? Yes! Mary was told this immediately before conception took place. Going back to the first chapter of Luke:

Luke 1:31 And, behold, thou shalt conceive in thy womb, and bring forth a son, and shalt call his name JESUS.

Just as God had instructed Joseph when Mary was found to be pregnant they followed through with the name Jesus. Joseph was told also to name the baby "JESUS":

Matthew 1:21 And she shall bring forth a son, and thou shalt call his name JESUS: for he shall save his people from their sins.

Only in Luke's Gospel

Luke 2:22 And when the days of her purification according to the law of Moses were accomplished, they brought him to Jerusalem, to present *him* to the Lord;
Luke 2:23 (As it is written in the law of the Lord, Every male that openeth the womb shall be called holy to the Lord;)

Joseph and Mary are now residing somewhere near Jerusalem. The eight days have been accomplished and Jesus was circumcised according to the law. Mary now had to fulfill her days of purification. For a male child that would be forty-one days, seven days before the circumcision and thirty-three after. A mother who has a baby girl had to remain unclean and purify herself for a total of eighty days.

Leviticus 12:1 And the LORD spake unto Moses, saying,

Leviticus 12:2 Speak unto the children of Israel, saying, If a woman have conceived seed, and born a man child: then she shall be unclean seven days; according to the days of the separation for her infirmity shall she be unclean.

Leviticus 12:3 And in the eighth day the flesh of his foreskin shall be circumcised.

Leviticus 12:4 And she shall then continue in the blood of her purifying three and thirty days; she shall touch no hallowed thing, nor come into the sanctuary, until the days of her purifying be fulfilled.

Leviticus 12:5 But if she bear a maid child, then she shall be unclean two weeks, as in her separation: and she shall continue in the blood of her purifying threescore and six days.

Leviticus 12:6 And when the days of her purifying are fulfilled, for a son, or for a daughter, she shall bring a lamb of the first year for a burnt offering, and a young pigeon, or a turtledove, for a sin offering, unto the door of the tabernacle of the congregation, unto the priest:

Leviticus 12:7 Who shall offer it before the LORD, and make an atonement for her; and she shall be cleansed from the issue of her blood. This *is* the law for her that hath born a male or a female.

Mary could now offer her sacrifice. The acceptable sacrifice for this cleansing was a lamb of the first year. Or if they could not afford a lamb a pair of turtle doves or two young pigeons were acceptable. Joseph is not wealthy, so Mary brings the birds:

Luke 2:24 And to offer a sacrifice according to that which is said in the law of the Lord, A pair of turtledoves, or two young pigeons.

God is about to give several signs to others that the Christ is born. Simeon has a sign:

Luke 2:25 And, behold, there was a man in Jerusalem, whose name *was* Simeon; and the same man *was* just and devout, waiting for the consolation of Israel: and the Holy Ghost was upon him.
Luke 2:26 And it was revealed unto him by the Holy Ghost, that he should not see death, before he had seen the Lord's Christ.

There are two that will herald the arrival of the Messiah. Simeon and Anna the Prophetess are blessed and allowed to announce the arrival of the Baby. Simeon will speak first.

Luke 2:27 And he came by the Spirit into the temple: and when the parents brought in the child Jesus, to do for him after the custom of the law,
Luke 2:28 Then took he him up in his arms, and blessed God, and said,

Simeon declares that he had been waiting for this child; and announces the salvation of the Lord!

Luke 2:29 Lord, now lettest thou thy servant depart in peace, according to thy word:

Simeon says it's OK for him to depart in peace; that is to die. Why? Salvation has appeared.

Luke 2:30 For mine eyes have seen thy salvation,
Luke 2:31 Which thou hast prepared before the face of all people;
Luke 2:32 A light to lighten the Gentiles, and the glory of thy people Israel.

The quote Simeon spoke has ended. And now a very important statement by the narrator takes place. The Holy Spirit speaking through Luke now makes no errors.

Luke 2:33 And Joseph and his mother marvelled at those things which were spoken of him.

What is said about Jesus in verse 33 is not a quote. It is a narrative given to Luke by the Holy Spirit. Joseph and Mary were

marveling at the things that were spoken. It is a very important way of phrasing this sentence by the narrator, who is The Holy Spirit, speaking through the Gospel writer, Luke. Simeon had just spoken and both Joseph and Mary marvel at what he is saying. Notice the King James Bible does not refer to "Joseph" as the child's father. However, it does refer to Mary as the child's "mother". It is very important to realize here that all scripture needs to be correct and exact. The writer, Luke, who is just the vessel God used to bring His words about uses the term Joseph instead of father. The narrator, who is the Holy Ghost, did not make any mistakes. All modern versions do not pick up on this. They changed the word Joseph to the word father. Joseph is not the child's father! It is important to understand what the Bible says about statements such as this one.

2Peter 1:21 For the prophecy came not in old time by the will of man: but holy men of God spake *as they were* moved by the Holy Ghost.

Do you need proof that the Holy Ghost is God? That all scripture is given by God? Peter says here is proof. Paul makes it much clearer:

2Timothy 3:16 All scripture *is* given by inspiration of God, and *is* profitable for doctrine, for reproof, for correction, for instruction in righteousness:

2Timothy 3:17 That the man of God may be perfect, throughly furnished unto all good works.

Luke 2:34 And Simeon blessed them, and said unto Mary his mother, Behold, this child is set for the fall and rising again of many in Israel; and for a sign which shall be spoken against;

Luke 2:35 (Yea, a sword shall pierce through thy own soul also,) that the thoughts of many hearts may be revealed.

Simeon describes what must take place in a man's heart. He must first admit he is lost. A man must realize that there is no hope at all in his own idea of salvation. A man must realize that he is fallen as one whose own soul has been pierced with a killer sword with no chance of going to heaven. This killer sword is the Bible, the Word of God! The thoughts and intents of the heart must be revealed that are in the heart of the sinner. Hebrews speaks of this exposure of fallen man from God. How God exposes his sin of unbelief.

Hebrews 4:11 Let us labour therefore to enter into that rest, lest any man fall after the same example of unbelief.

Hebrews 4:12 For the word of God *is* quick, and powerful, and sharper than any twoedged sword, piercing even to the dividing asunder of soul and spirit, and of the joints and marrow, and *is* a discerner of the thoughts and intents of the heart.

Luke 2:36 And there was one Anna, a prophetess, the daughter of Phanuel, of the tribe of Aser: she was of a great age, and had lived with an husband seven years from her virginity;

Anna was from the family of Phanuel who was of the tribe of Asher. Asher was one of the ten tribes who were taken captive by the Assyrians and dispersed throughout the world. Anna is part of a remnant that returned. One day soon, God will have twelve thousand from each tribe return to the land.

Revelation 7:4 And I heard the number of them which were sealed: *and there were* sealed an hundred *and* forty *and* four thousand of all the tribes of the children of Israel.

Asher's land was to the north up in Galilee. We know that most Jews back in this day thought nothing good could come out of this area:

Mark 1:9 And it came to pass in those days, that Jesus came from Nazareth of Galilee, and was baptized of John in Jordan.

Nothing good, included Jesus in their eyes.

John 1:46 And Nathanael said unto him, Can there any good thing come out of Nazareth? Philip saith unto him, Come and see.

Anna had lived seven years from her virginity with her husband. He dies and now she is a widow. Perhaps her wedding could have taken place at a very early age. However usually by

44

sixteen a young virgin would be betrothed. If she would have lost her virginity at sixteen and seven years have gone by, she is now twenty-three. She has been a widow for eighty- four years. This makes her one hundred and seven years old, a very great age.

Luke 2:37 And she *was* a widow of about fourscore and four years, which departed not from the temple, but served *God* with fastings and prayers night and day.

She also pointed out, as did Simeon that this child is for the redemption by salvation of all those seeking and looking for God's answer to their sin problem.

Luke 2:38 And she coming in that instant gave thanks likewise unto the Lord, and spake of him to all them that looked for redemption in Jerusalem.

These two, Simeon and Anna, make a big impression on everyone present at the temple that this child is very special. Mary has kept these things in her heart as was stated in verse 19 and again in 51. She will need all this reassurance as Jesus begins to grow in wisdom and in stature.

Luke 2:39 And when they had performed all things according to the law of the Lord, they returned into Galilee, to their own city Nazareth. Luke 2:40 And the child grew, and waxed strong in spirit, filled with wisdom: and the grace of God was upon him.

Twelve years go by. Jesus has grown to approximately 90% of full growth. He is capable of being on his own and the Jews have a celebration at this time called Bar Mitzvah. Today it is slightly different with added rules, customs, and traditions.

Luke 2:41 Now his parents went to Jerusalem every year at the feast of the passover. Luke 2:42 And when he was twelve years old, they went up to Jerusalem after the custom of the feast.

Luke 2:43 And when they had fulfilled the days, as they returned, the child Jesus tarried behind in Jerusalem; and Joseph and his mother knew not *of it.*

Jesus stays behind. Jesus alone makes this decision to stay behind. Respect and obedience to God the Father must not be misconstrued as disrespect to our natural parents.

Verse 43 says that they had fulfilled the days. Days of what? The days must be the feast of Passover and the seven days of unleavened bread that immediately follow the day of Passover. Many Jews, during Passover, stay in Jerusalem till the end of the seven-day feast of unleavened bread. The first day of the feast of unleavened bread and the seventh day of unleavened bread are High Sabbath days. A day when they cannot travel nor do servile work. It is just like the first day of unleavened bread, a High Sabbath of no work and no travel. John the Apostle spoke by the Holy Spirit of this first day of unleavened bread as a High Sabbath.

John 19:31 The Jews therefore, because it was the preparation, that the bodies should not remain upon the cross on the sabbath day, (for that sabbath day was an high day,) besought Pilate that their legs might be broken, and *that* they might be taken away.

Jesus was crucified on the 14th of the first month, the day of Passover. The following day, the 15th of the first month would be a High Sabbath, the first day of unleavened bread. The day of the Passover was to be kept on the 14th day of the first month. The seven days to follow, The Feast of Unleavened Bread, was issued to Moses for the keeping of the entire feast of the Passover.

Numbers 28:16 And in the fourteenth day of the first month *is* the passover of the LORD.

Numbers 28:17 And in the fifteenth day of this month *is* the feast: seven days shall unleavened bread be eaten.

Numbers 28:18 In the first day *shall be* an holy convocation; ye shall do no manner of servile work *therein:*

The name of the first month according to Moses was Abib:

Exodus 34:18 The feast of unleavened bread shalt thou keep. Seven days thou shalt eat unleavened bread, as I commanded thee, in the time of the month Abib: for in the month Abib thou camest out from Egypt.

According to Moses the seven days of unleavened bread and the day of Passover were referred to as the "Feast of the Passover"

Exodus 34:25 Thou shalt not offer the blood of my sacrifice with leaven; neither shall the sacrifice of the feast of the passover be left unto the morning.

To be kept during the first month. Moses gave this first month the name Abib.

Deuteronomy 16:1 Observe the month of Abib, and keep the passover unto the LORD thy God: for in the month of Abib the LORD thy God brought thee forth out of Egypt by night.

The name of the first month, Abib, was later changed to Nisan during the Babylonian Captivity:

Esther 3:7 In the first month, that *is,* the month Nisan, in the twelfth year of king Ahasuerus, they cast Pur, that *is,* the lot, before Haman from day to day, and from month to month, *to* the twelfth *month,* that *is,* the month Adar.

Luke 2:44 But they, supposing him to have been in the company, went a day's journey; and they sought him among *their* kinsfolk and acquaintance.

Joseph and Mary must have learned on previous trips to Jerusalem how trustworthy Jesus was. But how could they have traveled for a day and not noticed that Jesus was gone? They must have been consumed with watching their other children. Four boys and at least two girls in the family of Joseph and Mary according to Matthew:

Matthew 13:55 Is not this the carpenter's son? is not his mother called Mary? and his brethren, James, and Joses, and Simon, and Judas?

Matthew 13:56 And his sisters, are they not all with us? Whence then hath this *man* all these things?

For this family to journey a day without checking on Him at the age of twelve years old, shows an incredible amount of trust in the child, Jesus.

Luke 2:45 And when they found him not, they turned back again to Jerusalem, seeking him.
Luke 2:46 And it came to pass, that after three days they found him in the temple, sitting in the midst of the doctors, both hearing them, and asking them questions.

Jesus in His Divine nature could astonish even the very elect.

Luke 2:47 And all that heard him were astonished at his understanding and answers.
Luke 2:48 And when they saw him, they were amazed: and his mother said unto him, Son, why hast thou thus dealt with us? behold, thy father and I have sought thee sorrowing.

Mary now has something to say to Jesus. She knew Joseph was not His biological father. However, Jesus will now correctly use the term "Father." Notice the translators accurately translate the quote by Mary as she calls Joseph His "father". This is a quote and not a narrative proving Mary made mistakes. She could not have been immaculately conceived. Jesus in His humanity who is increasing in stature and wisdom corrects His mother.

Luke 2:49 And he said unto them, How is it that ye sought me? wist ye not that I must be about my Father's business?

This is not disrespectful. Instead, it is a wise way of handling Christ's actual real role in life. He came to do the will of the Father. Paul said it best:

Galatians 1:4 Who gave himself for our sins, that he might deliver us from this present evil world, according to the will of God and our Father:

Here is proof that even Mary and Joseph did not know of the importance of Christ being submissive to the will of the Father. However, Jesus would be submissive to His earthly parents at this time.

Luke 2:50 And they understood not the saying which he spake unto them.

Luke 2:51 And he went down with them, and came to Nazareth, and was subject unto them: but his mother kept all these sayings in her heart.

Luke 2:52 And Jesus increased in wisdom and stature, and in favour with God and man.

This chapter speaks of increasing in wisdom and stature. Every person will increase in wisdom and understanding before God and man. For a Christian to be an effective witness he must first win the lost soul by his actions to a point where his neighbor will believe what you as a Christian have to say. The important advice here is that you have to say it. Faith comes by hearing not doing.

Romans 10:16 But they have not all obeyed the gospel. For Esaias saith, Lord, who hath believed our report?

Romans 10:17 So then faith *cometh* by hearing, and hearing by the word of God.

The wicked will never ask about Christ if he sees no change in you after being saved.

Proverbs 21:10 The soul of the wicked desireth evil: his neighbour findeth no favour in his eyes.

This is done by being truthful and upright and humble and prayerful and setting no wicked thing before the eyes.

Psalms 101:2 I will behave myself wisely in a perfect way. O when wilt thou come unto me? I will walk within my house with a perfect heart.

Psalms 101:3 I will set no wicked thing before mine eyes: I hate the work of them that turn aside; *it* shall not cleave to me.

LUKE CHAPTER 3

Highlights:

Chapter three introduces Jesus Christ. His baptism by John the Baptist. Luke gives Christ's lineage back to Adam through His mother's side.

Main Participants:

Tiberius Caesar,
Pontius Pilate, Herod, Phillip the Tetrarch, Lysanias v.1,
Annas and Caiaphas v.2,
John the Baptist v.2,
Herodias v.19,
Jesus v.21.

In Brief:

John the Baptist was prophesied to say what he said and do what he did by Isaiah. He announces His public ministry. It begins with His baptism by John the Baptist. John has made no friends with the magistrates. He preaches repentance before anything else. His baptism and the message of the Holy Ghost coming upon Jesus becomes evident. Jesus being the first ever to have the Holy Spirit descend upon Him in this manner. It marks the start of all who may be part of the church age which is known as the age of grace.

Only in Luke's Gospel

There is no more information about Jesus until He is thirty years old and about to begin His public ministry. His life up until this age is silent. This chapter will confirm that He was about thirty when He began His public ministry, being baptized by John the Baptist in the Jordan River. Except for what just happened in Luke chapter two, His staying in Jerusalem for His twelfth Passover, no more information of His life is revealed. During the next eighteen years, He was subject to His earthly mother and Joseph as Chapter 2 verse 51 stated. Luke now picks back up with the life of Jesus with His baptism.

Luke 3:1 Now in the fifteenth year of the reign of Tiberius Caesar, Pontius Pilate being governor of Judaea, and Herod being tetrarch of Galilee, and his brother Philip tetrarch of Ituraea and of the region of Trachonitis, and Lysanias the tetrarch of Abilene,

The Bible spells out the time in history as to when the events of Christ's public life are to begin. Jesus will set the requirement for all who wish to follow Him by doing so in a public way. This takes place in the fifteenth year of Tiberious Caesar:
(Taken from Wikipedia)
- ➢ Tiberius Caesar Augustus was the second Roman emperor. He reigned from AD 14 until 37, succeeding his stepfather, the first Roman emperor Augustus. Tiberius was born in Rome in 42 BC. Wikipedia Born: November 16, 42 BC, Rome, Italy Died: March 16, 37 AD, Miseno, Italy
- ➢ Pontius Pilate was the fifth governor of the Roman province of Judaea, serving under Emperor Tiberius from the year 26/27 to 36/37 AD.
- ➢ Herod being tetrarch of Galilee He was a son of Herod the Great. Reign: 4BC – 39AD

> ➤ **Philip tetrarch of Ituraea sometimes called Herod Philip II by modern writers, son of Herod the Great and his fifth wife, Cleopatra of Jerusalem, ruled over the northeast part of his father's kingdom between 4 BCE and 34CE.**
> ➤ **Lysanias the tetrarch of Abilene was the ruler of a small realm on the western slopes of Mount Hermon, mentioned by the Jewish historian Josephus. According to Eusebius, Lysanias was a son of Herod the Great.**

A historian can search and search the annuls of time to prove or disprove dates but let's just accept what the Bible says. That is Jesus being about 30 years old as the end of this chapter says.

Luke 3:2 Annas and Caiaphas being the high priests, the word of God came unto John the son of Zacharias in the wilderness.

Annas and Caiaphas were both the high priests at this time. Today we might say Annas was high priest "Emeritus". As in the past the high priest was to come from the family line of Aaron. Annas and Caiaphas are related by marriage.

John 18:13 And led him away to Annas first; for he was father in law to Caiaphas, which was the high priest that same year.

John the Baptist is about to be introduced now as a full-grown man to the high priests. He also is around thirty years old as he is just 6 months older than Jesus. Most agree that a man enters the prime of his life at around thirty years. His family, his career, his investments, his responsibilities are all on the table. For the next few decades, a man will have success or failure. The Bible gives us the key to having success.

Deuteronomy 8:18 But thou shalt remember the LORD thy God: for *it is* he that giveth thee power to get wealth, that he may establish his covenant which he sware unto thy fathers, as *it is* this day.

A PERFECT UNDERSTANDING
FRED A. KUYPERS

Synoptic in Matthew, Mark, Luke, and John's Gospel

The introduction of John the Baptist comes from all four of the Gospels. It is at this point that all four gospels are chronologically connected. The Bible gives a clear understanding of the ministry of John the Baptist. He came to preach repentance and to baptize.

Luke 3:3 And he came into all the country about Jordan, preaching the baptism of repentance for the remission of sins;

The ministry of John the Baptist presented in Luke above is also in Matthew:

Matthew 3:1 In those days came John the Baptist, preaching in the wilderness of Judaea,

Matthew 3:2 And saying, Repent ye: for the kingdom of heaven is at hand.

And in Mark:

Mark 1:4 John did baptize in the wilderness, and preach the baptism of repentance for the remission of sins.

And in John:

John 1:19 And this is the record of John, when the Jews sent priests and Levites from Jerusalem to ask him, Who art thou?

John 1:20 And he confessed, and denied not; but confessed, I am not the Christ.

John 1:21 And they asked him, What then? Art thou Elias? And he saith, I am not. Art thou that prophet? And he answered, No.

In the Apostle John's gospel, John the Baptist is asked if he is Elias. The Jews were looking for the fulfillment of a prophecy by Malachi that Elijah would have to appear to herald the coming of Messiah. Today the Jews continue to look for the one who will herald in the coming of the Messiah. This takes place every Passover at the Seder meal.

Malachi 4:5 Behold, I will send you Elijah the prophet before the coming of the great and dreadful day of the LORD:

Malachi 4:6 And he shall turn the heart of the fathers to the children, and the heart of the children to their fathers, lest I come and smite the earth with a curse.

The fulfillment of another Old Testament Bible prophecy which came from Isaiah:

Isaiah 40:3 The voice of him that crieth in the wilderness, Prepare ye the way of the LORD, make straight in the desert a highway for our God.

Isaiah 40:4 Every valley shall be exalted, and every mountain and hill shall be made low: and the crooked shall be made straight, and the rough places plain:

Isaiah 40:5 And the glory of the LORD shall be revealed, and all flesh shall see *it* together: for the mouth of the LORD hath spoken *it*.

This fulfillment is captured in all four Gospels. From a standpoint of chronology all four gospels are now at the exact same time in Christ's life.

In Matthew:

Matthew 3:3 For this is he that was spoken of by the prophet Esaias, saying, The voice of one crying in the wilderness, Prepare ye the way of the Lord, make his paths straight.

In Mark:

Mark 1:3 The voice of one crying in the wilderness, Prepare ye the way of the Lord, make his paths straight.

In Luke:

Luke 3:4 As it is written in the book of the words of Esaias the prophet, saying, The voice of one crying in the wilderness, Prepare ye the way of the Lord, make his paths straight.

And in John who explains this very clear also.

John 1:22 Then said they unto him, Who art thou? that we may give an answer to them that sent us. What sayest thou of thyself?

John 1:23 He said, I *am* the voice of one crying in the wilderness, Make straight the way of the Lord, as said the prophet Esaias.

In the Old Testament, Isaiah was very clear of what John the Baptist would have to say. Now, John the Baptist cries out what it will take in God's eyes to bring a man to the point of turning to Christ by faith.

Luke 3:5 Every valley shall be filled, and every mountain and hill shall be brought low; and the crooked shall be made straight, and the rough ways *shall be* made smooth;
Luke 3:6 And all flesh shall see the salvation of God.

God will fill every valley; He will level every hill and mountain; He will straighten the road and smooth out the potholes. To go to hell, a person will have to ignore everything that God will do to aid and assist in your salvation and that person will have to step over the Lord Jesus Christ. John the Baptist was a straight shooter. He did not hold back on declaring "sin" as sin. Later this would get him in trouble with Herod the Tetrarch (Matthew 14). But at this moment in time John the Baptist is directing his speech to the high priests and other religious ones.

Luke 3:7 Then said he to the multitude that came forth to be baptized of him, O generation of vipers, who hath warned you to flee from the wrath to come?
Luke 3:8 Bring forth therefore fruits worthy of repentance, and begin not to say within yourselves, We have Abraham to *our* father: for I say unto you, That God is able of these stones to raise up children unto Abraham.

John the Baptist was stating that because Abraham was your father, (in other words they thought they were above others because they were Jews) does not bring you saving grace. You would still need to have faith the way God spoke through Habakkuk:
Habakkuk 2:4 Behold, his soul *which* is lifted up is not upright in him: but the just shall live by his faith.
John the Baptist brings forth the main part of his message and that is without repentance as your source of turning to God, there

is a punishment of eternal consequences. A man changing his mind (repent by turning from sin and self-righteousness) must take place so that by faith you can turn to the Lord Jesus Christ.

Luke 3:9 And now also the axe is laid unto the root of the trees: every tree therefore which bringeth not forth good fruit is hewn down, and cast into the fire.

When God talks about fire He is talking about Hell and the torment of it. So how can you or I as a sinner bring forth good fruit? John is notifying all who are there that they are in big trouble when he says if you do not bring forth good fruit, you are cast into the fire. However, the Bible says nothing good can come up from a man.

Jeremiah 17:9 The heart *is* deceitful above all *things,* and desperately wicked: who can know it?

Jeremiah 17:10 I the LORD search the heart, *I* try the reins, even to give every man according to his ways, *and* according to the fruit of his doings.

It is the start of understanding God's plan, the Old Testament laid out in the New Testament of the Bible. Most important is that God does the saving. The people still wanted to have some part in their salvation; "all that the Lord hath spoken we will do." (Exodus 19:8) and John the Baptist describes to the people how short they have fallen from doing what the Lord has spoken. About loving your neighbor by doing something good for him.

Luke 3:10 And the people asked him, saying, What shall we do then?
Luke 3:11 He answereth and saith unto them, He that hath two coats, let him impart to him that hath none; and he that hath meat, let him do likewise.

Others came to be baptized by John and he would hit them right in their weakness.

Luke 3:12 Then came also publicans to be baptized, and said unto him, Master, what shall we do?

Luke 3:13 And he said unto them, Exact no more than that which is appointed you.

Luke 3:14 And the soldiers likewise demanded of him, saying, And what shall we do? And he said unto them, Do violence to no man, neither accuse *any* falsely; and be content with your wages.

John was aiming for their hearts, and he was hitting it!

Luke 3:15 And as the people were in expectation, and all men mused in their hearts of John, whether he were the Christ, or not;

Luke 3:16 John answered, saying unto *them* all, I indeed baptize you with water; but one mightier than I cometh, the latchet of whose shoes I am not worthy to unloose: he shall baptize you with the Holy Ghost and with fire:

John would baptize with water. The water was just a symbol. It had no working power or saving efficacy. This is still true today. Water baptism has no saving power. It is a symbol only. But as this verse declares the one who is coming could baptize you in two ways. One is with the Holy Ghost. By the Holy Ghost you are sealed till the day of redemption.

> Ephesians 1:13 In whom ye also *trusted,* after that ye heard the word of truth, the gospel of your salvation: in whom also after that ye believed, ye were sealed with that holy Spirit of promise,

And you are baptized into the body of Christ by that Holy Spirit:

> 1Corinthians 12:12 For as the body is one, and hath many members, and all the members of that one body, being many, are one body: so also *is* Christ.
>
> 1Corinthians 12:13 For by one Spirit are we all baptized into one body, whether *we be* Jews or Gentiles, whether *we be* bond or free; and have been all made to drink into one Spirit.
>
> 1Corinthians 12:14 For the body is not one member, but many.

John says some will be baptized by Christ with the Holy Ghost and some with fire. This fire that is unquenchable. That is forever and ever. This is not good as the next verse explains.

Luke 3:17 Whose fan *is* in his hand, and he will throughly purge his floor, and will gather the wheat into his garner; but the chaff he will burn with fire unquenchable.

When Jesus deals with you, where do you want him to place you (Baptize you)? It sounds so easy. Do I want to be baptized with fire unquenchable as the chaff or do I want to be baptized or placed into the body of Christ as Paul explains in his writings of 1Corinthians 12 above? This is your choice! John the Baptist had no power before Christ to baptize other than for repentance.

Matthew 3:11 I indeed baptize you with water unto repentance: but he that cometh after me is mightier than I, whose shoes I am not worthy to bear: he shall baptize you with the Holy Ghost, and *with* fire:

John could not work the work of repentance in them, but he could direct a person to repentance. It's still your choice!

Mark 1:1 The beginning of the gospel of Jesus Christ, the Son of God;

Mark 1:2 As it is written in the prophets, Behold, I send my messenger before thy face, which shall prepare thy way before thee.

Mark 1:3 The voice of one crying in the wilderness, Prepare ye the way of the Lord, make his paths straight.

The only thing John the Baptist could do is prepare the way for Christ to come into the heart and be the answer to man's biggest problem.

Luke 3:18 And many other things in his exhortation preached he unto the people.

John the Baptist would preach and was greatly respected by the people. He did not have the power of the Savior to save a soul, but still paid the price of imprisonment for his stand against the evil acts of men, and of the politicians of his day.

Luke 3:19 But Herod the tetrarch, being reproved by him for Herodias his brother Philip's wife, and for all the evils which Herod had done,

Luke 3:20 Added yet this above all, that he shut up John in prison.

This passage about John the Baptist going to prison is proof that Luke wrote this not as an eyewitness like John and Matthew were, but as a firsthand account that is historical noting the account of John going to jail. He may not have seen this, but he sure heard about it.

Luke 3:21 Now when all the people were baptized, it came to pass, that Jesus also being baptized, and praying, the heaven was opened,

A view of the trinity now takes place. Luke describes God the Father in heaven, Jesus in the Jordan River and the Holy Ghost coming upon Him. This is the start of the Church. How do we know that? Because Jesus said to the apostles that in the not to distant future, they would have a mighty rushing wind and well, he explained it like this:
John 20:21 Then said Jesus to them again, Peace *be* unto you: as *my* Father hath sent me, even so send I you.
John 20:22 And when he had said this, he breathed on *them,* and saith unto them, Receive ye the Holy Ghost:
John recorded the above after the resurrection, indicating that the Holy Ghost had not yet come upon any of His disciples. Luke says in Acts that it did not happen until Pentecost, fifty days after first fruits or Christ's resurrection. The church which began with Jesus Christ had only one member, Jesus Himself until the feast of Pentecost after His death.

Luke 3:22 And the Holy Ghost descended in a bodily shape like a dove upon him, and a voice came from heaven, which said, Thou art my beloved Son; in thee I am well pleased.

Luke writes a very important genealogy. Luke describes Jesus as the Son of man and will go all the way back to the first man, Adam. This gives a lineage of Jesus coming through Mary's family tree because Jesus, in human form, has His only earthly

ancestry through Mary and not Joseph. Matthew gives the family tree of Joseph as the King who comes through the male side of the genealogy. In Matthew, Joseph comes through Solomon the king, a son of David. Luke meets all the Old Testament prophecies of Messiah, but through Nathan who also was a son of David; then going back to Abraham; then Noah and on to Adam.

Only in Luke's Gospel

Luke 3:23 And Jesus himself began to be about thirty years of age, being (as was supposed) the son of Joseph, which was *the son* of Heli,

Notice it does not say Joseph begat Jesus but rather that Jesus is the son of Joseph (as was supposed). This of course can be by adoption. Matthew 1:16 does not declare that Joseph begat Jesus either. This means that what is given in the Bible is accurate describing both lineages, Joseph in Matthew (as king) and Mary in Luke (as man). In Mark's Gospel there is no lineage. As a servant to man, there is no lineage. John, however, gives the most important lineage, that is that He always existed as the Word; that is God.

Luke 3:24 Which was *the son* of Matthat, which was *the son* of Levi, which was *the son* of Melchi, which was *the son* of Janna, which was *the son* of Joseph,
Luke 3:25 Which was *the son* of Mattathias, which was *the son* of Amos, which was *the son* of Naum, which was *the son* of Esli, which was *the son* of Nagge,
Luke 3:26 Which was *the son* of Maath, which was *the son* of Mattathias, which was *the son* of Semei, which was *the son* of Joseph, which was *the son* of Juda,
Luke 3:27 Which was *the son* of Joanna, which was *the son* of Rhesa, which was *the son* of Zorobabel, which was *the son* of Salathiel, which was *the son* of Neri,

Luke 3:28 Which was *the son* of Melchi, which was *the son* of Addi, which was *the son* of Cosam, which was *the son* of Elmodam, which was *the son* of Er,

Luke 3:29 Which was *the son* of Jose, which was *the son* of Eliezer, which was *the son* of Jorim, which was *the son* of Matthat, which was *the son* of Levi,

Luke 3:30 Which was *the son* of Simeon, which was *the son* of Juda, which was *the son* of Joseph, which was *the son* of Jonan, which was *the son* of Eliakim,

Luke 3:31 Which was *the son* of Melea, which was *the son* of Menan, which was *the son* of Mattatha, which was *the son* of Nathan, which was *the son* of David,

Jesus' family tree now comes together in David as Mary's ancestry is through Nathan and Joseph's ancestry is through Solomon, both sons of David.

Luke 3:32 Which was *the son* of Jesse, which was *the son* of Obed, which was *the son* of Booz, which was *the son* of Salmon, which was *the son* of Naasson,

Luke 3:33 Which was *the son* of Aminadab, which was *the son* of Aram, which was *the son* of Esrom, which was *the son* of Phares, which was *the son* of Juda,

Why do Christians stand against all forms of abortion even an abortion for rape and incest? Because, any abortion can be lied about and declared rape or incest. But secondly, here is proof that God can use for good what man calls evil, that is some of the worst sins committed by men. Juda had a sexual relationship with Tamar his daughter-in-law:

Gen 38:15 When Judah saw her, he thought her *to be* an harlot; because she had covered her face.

Gen 38:16 And he turned unto her by the way, and said, Go to, I pray thee, let me come in unto thee; (for he knew not that she *was* his daughter in law.) And she said, What wilt thou give me, that thou mayest come in unto me?

Tamar set up Judah and he could have cried foul and aborted the baby. But God says;

> Romans 8:28 And we know that all things work together for good to them that love God, to them who are the called according to *his* purpose.

Jesus Christ's family tree came through an incestual act. Phares was born this way. The bible's definition of a bastard child is one born out of incest or out of wedlock, an illegitimate child. God has ordained that a bastard child's heritage will be affected for ten generations:

> Deuteronomy 23:2 A bastard shall not enter into the congregation of the LORD; even to his tenth generation shall he not enter into the congregation of the LORD.

A point of interest is that God held off using the lineage of Jesus as a king, or a judge, or a leader, from Judah to David a total of ten generations. Could this be due to Judah's sin with his daughter-in-law, Tamar (Genesis 38)?

Luke 3:34 Which was *the son* of Jacob, which was *the son* of Isaac, which was *the son* of Abraham, which was *the son* of Thara, which was *the son* of Nachor,

Luke 3:35 Which was *the son* of Saruch, which was *the son* of Ragau, which was *the son* of Phalec, which was *the son* of Heber, which was *the son* of Sala,

Luke 3:36 Which was *the son* of Cainan, which was *the son* of Arphaxad, which was *the son* of Sem, which was *the son* of Noe, which was *the son* of Lamech,

Luke 3:37 Which was *the son* of Mathusala, which was *the son* of Enoch, which was *the son* of Jared, which was *the son* of Maleleel, which was *the son* of Cainan,

Luke 3:38 Which was *the son* of Enos, which was *the son* of Seth, which was *the son* of Adam, which was *the son* of God.

As this lineage of Jesus concludes with Adam, it proves Jesus, on His mother's side, goes back to the same ancestry as all of us. Starting with Adam, a man. Luke continues his Gospel

representing Jesus Christ as 100% man and 100% God. This is a core belief as a Christian. To believe that Jesus Christ was truly man and truly God is called the "hypostatic union" of God and Man in one person. Are you a true Christian? Then this must be truly believed. By you, by faith, and by faith alone!

LUKE CHAPTER 4

Highlights:

Chapter four describes Jesus Christ as He begins His public ministry as God and man. He declares this to Satan. He declares it in the synagogue. And He declares it to all the people.

Main Participants:

Jesus Christ, v.1,
the devil v.2,
known as Satan v.8,
Minister of the Synagogue v.20,
All in the Synagogue v.28,
A man with an unclean spirit v.33
Simon Peter v.38,
Simon's wife's mother v.38.

In Brief:

Tempted by the devil himself, Jesus withstood Satan on three occasions. He goes to His hometown of Nazareth to the synagogue. He then presents Himself to everyone present and opens the scriptures. He declared He is the one Isaiah prophesied about in Isaiah chapter 61. Those of the synagogue thrust Him out of the city. He then goes to Capernaum and casts evil spirits out of a man. While in Capernaum He visits Simon and heals Simon's wife's mother. He continues to heal many.

Only in Matthew and Luke's Gospel

Luke 4:1 And Jesus being full of the Holy Ghost returned from Jordan, and was led by the Spirit into the wilderness,

Jesus always led by example and there is no better example than this.
Romans 8:14 For as many as are led by the Spirit of God, they are the sons of God.

Luke 4:2 Being forty days tempted of the devil. And in those days he did eat nothing: and when they were ended, he afterward hungered.

John has nothing of this temptation and Mark has only two verses and does not elaborate on the events of this temptation.
Mark 1:12 And immediately the Spirit driveth him into the wilderness.
Mark 1:13 And he was there in the wilderness forty days, tempted of Satan; and was with the wild beasts; and the angels ministered unto him.

Well, here we have it! A sure error occurring in the Bible? Matthew and Luke are so different! The Bible must be wrong. Critics have attacked this so much. Jesus is tempted three times, and the two gospels have this in a different order.

Luke:		Matthew:	
	1. Stones be made bread		1. Stones be made bread
	2. Kingdoms of the world		2. Pinnacle of the temple
	3. Pinnacle of the temple		3. Kingdoms of the world

No man was with Christ at this time. But the Holy Spirit breathed out this event so that two of the writers would discuss this. As we have studied Matthew is an eyewitness account.

However, he was not present at the time these events occurred and Matthew has them in the correct order in which they happened. Luke is not an eyewitness to Christ either but has a first-hand account of these events. Being a physician, Luke holds the plunging to death of a man as the last and most important in his view. The order is not the important thing, the reply by Jesus is what is important.

Luke 4:3 And the devil said unto him, If thou be the Son of God, command this stone that it be made bread.

This first temptation has no religious meaning behind it but is just that Jesus was very hungry. Of course, this is where the devil will tempt Jesus. It is where you would think He would be the most vulnerable. But Jesus had just been close to His Father in prayer and in time alone with His Father and with the Word for forty days. He easily defeated Satan with the Words of God!

Luke 4:4 And Jesus answered him, saying, It is written, That man shall not live by bread alone, but by every word of God.

Both Matthew and Luke have this as the first temptation. After not eating for forty days Satan will attack a man at his weakest point. This proves that Satan knew Jesus was 100% man. He attacked Him in the flesh. But Jesus responded with a verse from the chapter of success, Deuteronomy 8:

> Deuteronomy 8:3 And he humbled thee, and suffered thee to hunger, and fed thee with manna, which thou knewest not, neither did thy fathers know; that he might make thee know that man doth not live by bread only, but by every *word* that proceedeth out of the mouth of the LORD doth man live.

Notice what Deuteronomy says that is important.

"BUT BY EVERY WORD THAT PROCEEDETH OUT OF THE MOUTH OF THE LORD"!

Or as Luke states:

"EVERY WORD OF GOD"

Now why would the newer versions drop this part of the verse in Luke? They left it in Matthew but dropped it in Luke. Could it be that they cannot emphatically say that they live by every single Word of God? The new versions are mostly designed around "dynamic equivalence" and by definition this means not by "every word of God," but by every thought.

Matthew uses the words "then" (verse 5) and "again" (verse 8) to address the order of temptations indicating some form of order of sequence.

Matthew 4:5 Then the devil taketh him up into the holy city, and setteth him on a pinnacle of the temple,

Matthew 4:8 Again, the devil taketh him up into an exceeding high mountain, and sheweth him all the kingdoms of the world, and the glory of them;

Luke uses the word "and" meaning this temptation happened but not necessarily in this order.

Luke 4:5 And the devil, taking him up into an high mountain, shewed unto him all the kingdoms of the world in a moment of time.

Luke the physician is addressing his letter to a Gentile audience. He goes to the next temptation that a Gentile would be familiar with. Satan tempting Jesus to personally be willing to sin and that is pride.

Luke 4:6 And the devil said unto him, All this power will I give thee, and the glory of them: for that is delivered unto me; and to whomsoever I will I give it.

Luke 4:7 If thou therefore wilt worship me, all shall be thine.

The term "get thee hence Satan" is instrumental. The term ends the temptations of Christ. In Matthew it is the last temptation.

Matthew 4:10 Then saith Jesus unto him, Get thee hence, Satan: for it is written, Thou shalt worship the Lord thy God, and him only shalt thou serve.

Luke indicates that Matthew has the correct order. Jesus orders Satan to go and is now finished with the temptations.

Luke 4:8 And Jesus answered and said unto him, Get thee behind me, Satan: for it is written, Thou shalt worship the Lord thy God, and him only shalt thou serve.

This is written in Deuteronomy:
Deuteronomy 6:13 Thou shalt fear the LORD thy God, and serve him, and shalt swear by his name.

Luke writing to a Gentile audience does not stress the King that all of Israel was looking for as Matthew did. Generally, Gentiles do not have the same Jewish understanding. Matthew and Luke dealt first with Satan tempting Jesus's physical weakness. Matthew now deals twice with Jesus Christ's human testing and then offers Christ for His last temptation what God allowed Satan to have for a season, all the kingdoms of the world.

Luke uses the word "and" for this last test of Christ indicating no specific order but that this temptation did happen. Matthew describes the worship of Satan last, but Luke describes the casting down from the pinnacle of the temple last.

Luke 4:9 And he brought him to Jerusalem, and set him on a pinnacle of the temple, and said unto him, If thou be the Son of God, cast thyself down from hence:
Luke 4:10 For it is written, He shall give his angels charge over thee, to keep thee:
Luke 4:11 And in *their* hands they shall bear thee up, lest at any time thou dash thy foot against a stone.
Luke 4:12 And Jesus answering said unto him, It is said, Thou shalt not tempt the Lord thy God.

Jesus once again uses scripture to defeat Satan:
Deuteronomy 6:16 Ye shall not tempt the LORD your God, as ye tempted *him* in Massah.

Luke 4:13 And when the devil had ended all the temptation, he departed from him for a season.

Satan may depart from you for a season. He will return. Because until his time is up, he is the great tempter and will always come back to cast doubt on the words of God.

Only in Luke's Gospel

Jesus needs to get back up to Nazareth which is in the northern Galilee area. This is approximately a four-day journey by foot. Walking briskly, you might be able to do it in less time.

Luke 4:14 And Jesus returned in the power of the Spirit into Galilee: and there went out a fame of him through all the region round about.
Luke 4:15 And he taught in their synagogues, being glorified of all.

Jesus is going to make Himself known by His use of the Words of God. He is about to astonish the Jewish priests and elders in His hometown of Nazareth. Nazareth is due west of the Sea of Galilee and is in the Galilean district. Many who live there have a Galilean dialect and accent.

Luke 4:16 And he came to Nazareth, where he had been brought up: and, as his custom was, he went into the synagogue on the sabbath day, and stood up for to read.
Luke 4:17 And there was delivered unto him the book of the prophet Esaias. And when he had opened the book, he found the place where it was written,

Jesus stands up in the synagogue, the place of worship and the place of Scripture study in the town of Nazareth where Mary

and Joseph were well known. He picks a point in Isaiah and begins to read from that prophet. Remember they did not have chapter and verse divisions at this time. You would really have to know your scripture to find the location of what He is about to quote.

Luke 4:18 The Spirit of the Lord *is* upon me, because he hath anointed me to preach the gospel to the poor; he hath sent me to heal the brokenhearted, to preach deliverance to the captives, and recovering of sight to the blind, to set at liberty them that are bruised,
Luke 4:19 To preach the acceptable year of the Lord.

Jesus stops His reading here. Why? This reading starts a chapter in our bible in the book of Isaiah chapter 61:
Isaiah 61:1 The Spirit of the Lord GOD *is* upon me; because the LORD hath anointed me to preach good tidings unto the meek; he hath sent me to bind up the brokenhearted, to proclaim liberty to the captives, and the opening of the prison to *them that are* bound;
Isaiah 61:2 To proclaim the acceptable year of the LORD, and the day of vengeance of our God; to comfort all that mourn;
Jesus stops reading in the middle of a sentence. He does not even complete the sentence. He ends His reading of this scripture, stopping at the spot that will give new insight as to the two advents of the Messiah. At this point, He closes the Scriptures:

Luke 4:20 And he closed the book, and he gave *it* again to the minister, and sat down. And the eyes of all them that were in the synagogue were fastened on him.

You could have heard a pin drop as everyone was fixated on Jesus. And He was crystal clear what He had just read. It was all about Himself. How the "Spirit of the Lord God" (once again indicating the Trinity all together) being upon Him, that is upon Jesus. Jesus had come to proclaim the acceptable year of the LORD, which was here and now!

Luke 4:21 And he began to say unto them, This day is this scripture fulfilled in your ears.

And Jesus stops in the middle of a sentence? He does not say that the day of vengeance had come. He knew He would present Himself as the King of kings that all Israel was to be looking for. But the "day of vengeance of our God" would be far off yet from this moment in time. The day of vengeance of our Lord is still yet to come. Right now, we are living by God's mercy in a day acceptable. Today, a person can come to Christ freely. However, if you do not come to Jesus in this lifetime, judgement is coming! Are you living for Jesus in the current acceptable years of the LORD???

Isaiah 49:7 Thus saith the LORD, the Redeemer of Israel, *and* his Holy One, to him whom man despiseth, to him whom the nation abhorreth, to a servant of rulers, Kings shall see and arise, princes also shall worship, because of the LORD that is faithful, *and* the Holy One of Israel, and he shall choose thee.

Isaiah 49:8 Thus saith the LORD, In an acceptable time have I heard thee, and in a day of salvation have I helped thee: and I will preserve thee, and give thee for a covenant of the people, to establish the earth, to cause to inherit the desolate heritages;

And in the New Testament:

2Corinthians 6:2 (For he saith, I have heard thee in a time accepted, and in the day of salvation have I succoured thee: behold, now *is* the accepted time; behold, now *is* the day of salvation.)

Everyone in the synagogue of Nazareth bare witness that Jesus was merely only a man. One who was born among them. The son of Joseph. How wrong they were!

Luke 4:22 And all bare him witness, and wondered at the gracious words which proceeded out of his mouth. And they said, Is not this Joseph's son?

Jesus immediately points to what would happen at the cross. He points out the words that would be hurled at Him by all those

on Golgotha. This occurring at the time when He would be on the cross, paying the price for the sins of the whole world.

Luke 4:23 And he said unto them, Ye will surely say unto me this proverb, Physician, heal thyself: whatsoever we have heard done in Capernaum, do also here in thy country.

Looking forward, the synoptic Gospels at the crucifixion all say the same about this physician healing Himself:
Matthew says:
Matthew 27:42 He saved others; himself he cannot save. If he be the King of Israel, let him now come down from the cross, and we will believe him.
Mark says:
Mark 15:30 Save thyself, and come down from the cross.
Mark 15:31 Likewise also the chief priests mocking said among themselves with the scribes, He saved others; himself he cannot save.
Luke also says:
Luke 23:35 And the people stood beholding. And the rulers also with them derided *him,* saying, He saved others; let him save himself, if he be Christ, the chosen of God.

Jesus worked many miracles in His life. All those from the Synagogue in Nazareth heard of many miracles done in Capernaum by the Sea of Galilee. With the number of healings Jesus did He was called a Physician. They wanted to be entertained with some of the same miracles of healing. John, later says if everything was mentioned that Jesus did, it would fill up all the books in the world:
John 21:25 And there are also many other things which Jesus did, the which, if they should be written every one, I suppose that even the world itself could not contain the books that should be written. Amen.

With Jesus stopping in the heart of Isaiah 61:2, in the middle of the sentence and not talking about the day of

vengeance indicates a pause between these two events. The day of vengeance is not mentioned during Christ's public ministry at this first advent. This pause or gap has lasted, as history declares, for about two thousand years as we draw closer to the two-thousandth anniversary of the crucifixion of Christ. The day of vengeance will be that day when the Lord returns in power and great glory:

> Jeremiah 46:10 For this *is* the day of the Lord GOD of hosts, a day of vengeance, that he may avenge him of his adversaries: and the sword shall devour, and it shall be satiate and made drunk with their blood: for the Lord GOD of hosts hath a sacrifice in the north country by the river Euphrates.

And in the New Testament:

> Acts 2:20 The sun shall be turned into darkness, and the moon into blood, before that great and notable day of the Lord come:

Jesus now gives two examples of what the people really think of a prophet. That He would not be accepted by His own people.

Luke 4:24 And he said, Verily I say unto you, No prophet is accepted in his own country.

Luke 4:25 But I tell you of a truth, many widows were in Israel in the days of Elias, when the heaven was shut up three years and six months, when great famine was throughout all the land;

Luke 4:26 But unto none of them was Elias sent, save unto Sarepta, *a city* of Sidon, unto a woman *that was* a widow.

(1 Kings 17:9)

Luke 4:27 And many lepers were in Israel in the time of Eliseus the prophet; and none of them was cleansed, saving Naaman the Syrian.

(2 Kings 5:1-14)

This reply by Jesus was not what the people in the synagogue wanted to hear:

Luke 4:28 And all they in the synagogue, when they heard these things, were filled with wrath,

Luke 4:29 And rose up, and thrust him out of the city, and led him unto the brow of the hill whereon their city was built, that they might cast him down headlong.

Luke 4:30 But he passing through the midst of them went his way,

Jesus was able to escape this mob looking to kill Him. Jesus now goes to Capernaum which is only a day's walk from Nazareth. But again, He is said to be working and teaching on the Sabbath. Notice how God will show us that the Sabbath has changed with Christ's first coming. From a day of rest to a day when Jesus did much of His work to convince all that He was the promised Messiah.

Luke 4:31 And came down to Capernaum, a city of Galilee, and taught them on the sabbath days.

Luke 4:32 And they were astonished at his doctrine: for his word was with power.

The Devil can take over a man's body. The Catholic Church would have an exorcism of some sort at this time. However, a demon will recognize Jesus Christ. He has seen Him in the spirit world. This shows us that there is a battle raging in the spirit world that we cannot see. And Jesus is greater than all. He is greater both here on earth and in the spirit world:

Luke 4:33 And in the synagogue there was a man, which had a spirit of an unclean devil, and cried out with a loud voice,

Luke 4:34 Saying, Let *us* alone; what have we to do with thee, *thou* Jesus of Nazareth? art thou come to destroy us? I know thee who thou art; the Holy One of God.

All devils, all demons, all unclean spirits know and believe that Jesus has all power:
James 2:19 Thou believest that there is one God; thou doest well: the devils also believe, and tremble.
Jesus can and will rebuke any demon. Because they know Him and fear Him. Jesus will now rebuke this devil:

Luke 4:35 And Jesus rebuked him, saying, Hold thy peace, and come out of him. And when the devil had thrown him in the midst, he came out of him, and hurt him not.

Luke 4:36 And they were all amazed, and spake among themselves, saying, What a word *is* this! for with authority and power he commandeth the unclean spirits, and they come out.

I have oft-times said that my Jesus was no mamby pamby type of a leader. He never backs down. Here, He proves it! Notice the quick obedience to the Lord by the devil.

Synoptic in Matthew, Mark, and Luke's Gospel

Here is a synoptic account of Jesus going out with His fame preceding Him. It happens to be with Peter's wife's mother.

Luke 4:37 And the fame of him went out into every place of the country round about.

Luke 4:38 And he arose out of the synagogue, and entered into Simon's house. And Simon's wife's mother was taken with a great fever; and they besought him for her.

Luke 4:39 And he stood over her, and rebuked the fever; and it left her: and immediately she arose and ministered unto them.

Matthew has this account.
> Matthew 8:14 And when Jesus was come into Peter's house, he saw his wife's mother laid, and sick of a fever.
> Matthew 8:15 And he touched her hand, and the fever left her: and she arose, and ministered unto them.

Mark says it like this:
> Mark 1:30 But Simon's wife's mother lay sick of a fever, and anon they tell him of her.
> Mark 1:31 And he came and took her by the hand, and lifted her up; and immediately the fever left her, and she ministered unto them.

Is this strange for Simon (Peter) to have a wife? If Simon was the first pope, how can he have a wife? Unless the rules have changed! A pope is not allowed to be married, or are they? You know, celibacy!

Luke 4:40 Now when the sun was setting, all they that had any sick with divers diseases brought them unto him; and he laid his hands on every one of them, and healed them.
Luke 4:41 And devils also came out of many, crying out, and saying, Thou art Christ the Son of God. And he rebuking *them* suffered them not to speak: for they knew that he was Christ.

The devils who were coming out of so many knew that this Jesus was the Christ, the Messiah, the Anointed one. But he did not want them to reveal this truth. Instead, He went to a secluded place:

Luke 4:42 And when it was day, he departed and went into a desert place: and the people sought him, and came unto him, and stayed him, that he should not depart from them.
Luke 4:43 And he said unto them, I must preach the kingdom of God to other cities also: for therefore am I sent.
Luke 4:44 And he preached in the synagogues of Galilee.

Jesus said what He would do from this point on. That is, He would preach the "kingdom of God." Luke tells us later that you must have the Kingdom of God within you.
> Luke 17:20 And when he was demanded of the Pharisees, when the kingdom of God should come, he answered them and said, The kingdom of God cometh not with observation:
> Luke 17:21 Neither shall they say, Lo here! or, lo there! for, behold, the kingdom of God is within you.

This is different than the "kingdom of heaven." Matthew speaks of the kingdom of heaven 32 times. Nowhere else is the kingdom of heaven mentioned in scripture but in Matthew alone.

To conclude this chapter, the question is stated by Jesus Christ. "I must preach the kingdom of God to other cities also: for therefore am I sent." This chapter is all about Jesus beginning to preach. Have you heard His preaching? The Bible says you must hear the Words of God, to believe the Words of God. There is no other way to become righteous. Even Abraham had to do this.

Romans 4:2 For if Abraham were justified by works, he hath *whereof* to glory; but not before God.

Romans 4:3 For what saith the scripture? Abraham believed God, and it was counted unto him for righteousness.

LUKE CHAPTER 5

Highlights:

Chapter five shows Jesus Christ selecting His closest followers. Jesus heals a leper and a paraplegic. Jesus presents His first public parable.

Main Participants:

Jesus Christ v.1,
Simon later called Peter v.3,
James v.10,
John v.10,
Zebedee v.10,
man with leprosy v.12,
Pharisee's v.17,
Doctors v.17,
The man with the palsy v.18,
Scribes v.21,
Levi (Matthew) v.27,

In Brief:

Jesus seeks out His followers and begins with Simon called Peter. Then James and John, the sons of "Thunder." Along the way He heals those who are sick and transported to Him declaring to the religious leaders of the day, (V.31); "They that are whole need not a physician; but they that are sick." Finally, Jesus speaks His first parable.

Only in Luke's Gospel

Luke 5:1 And it came to pass, that, as the people pressed upon him to hear the word of God, he stood by the lake of Gennesaret,

The Sea of Galilee has many different names. Depending on where you come from this beautiful body of water is 700 ft. below sea level and drains via the Jordan River into the Dead Sea which is 1,300 ft. below sea level. Different names for the Sea of Galilee include the lake of Gennesaret as seen here, and the Sea of Tiberias as seen in the Gospel of John:

John 6:1 After these things Jesus went over the sea of Galilee, which is *the sea of* Tiberias.

And in the Old Testament called the sea of Chinnereth or today called Lake Kinneret by some:

Numbers 34:11 And the coast shall go down from Shepham to Riblah, on the east side of Ain; and the border shall descend, and shall reach unto the side of the sea of Chinnereth eastward:

Only in Luke's Gospel is the detailed view of how Simon first encountered Jesus.

Luke 5:2 And saw two ships standing by the lake: but the fishermen were gone out of them, and were washing *their* nets.

Jesus goes into the ship that belongs to Simon. He gives him a firsthand account whereby Simon would listen but not be ready to obey Jesus. Simon truly becomes a believer in being a fisherman. However, Jesus will turn him into a fisher of men instead of fish.

Luke 5:3 And he entered into one of the ships, which was Simon's, and prayed him that he would thrust out a little from the land. And he sat down, and taught the people out of the ship.

Luke 5:4 Now when he had left speaking, he said unto Simon, Launch out into the deep, and let down your nets for a draught.

The Sea of Galilee has many fishermen fishing for their livelihood. Simon, who later is called Peter, runs a boat that had no luck this night or day of fishing. He is frustrated, tired, hungry and ready for some rest. But Jesus has another idea. Will Simon seek to follow what Jesus said? Follow this Jesus who has been watched and talked about and seen working all kinds of miracles of healing?

Luke 5:5 And Simon answering said unto him, Master, we have toiled all the night, and have taken nothing: nevertheless at thy word I will let down the net.

Simon takes the challenge and heads out again. This is a real entrepreneur. He is more focused on his work than on his physical needs.

Luke 5:6 And when they had this done, they inclosed a great multitude of fishes: and their net brake.
Luke 5:7 And they beckoned unto *their* partners, which were in the other ship, that they should come and help them. And they came, and filled both the ships, so that they began to sink.

Luke is very descriptive about Simon's work. Describing the going out on the ship again and the net being cast and it being so full it broke. Simon Peter seeing what Jesus did with the fish knew he was in special company. Simon knew the sinful life of men at sea. And he would learn that Jesus, who was someone special, was interested in him even with his sinful life style.

Luke 5:8 When Simon Peter saw *it,* he fell down at Jesus' knees, saying, Depart from me; for I am a sinful man, O Lord.
Luke 5:9 For he was astonished, and all that were with him, at the draught of the fishes which they had taken:

Synoptic In Matthew, Mark, and Luke's Gospel

Here is a synoptic case that relates to the first three gospels as synoptic or saying the same thing. Luke describes the call of Peter this way.

Luke 5:10 And so *was* also James, and John, the sons of Zebedee, which were partners with Simon. And Jesus said unto Simon, Fear not; from henceforth thou shalt catch men.

Matthew is not as descriptive as Luke is in the previous verse. Speaking to Simon and Andrew, his brother, while they worked at netting the fish, He calls them both. Jesus changes their occupation to fishers of men.

Matthew 4:18 And Jesus, walking by the sea of Galilee, saw two brethren, Simon called Peter, and Andrew his brother, casting a net into the sea: for they were fishers.
Matthew 4:19 And he saith unto them, Follow me, and I will make you fishers of men. Matthew 4:20 And they straightway left *their* nets, and followed him.

Mark is even less descriptive of the call of Simon and Andrew to become fishers of men:

Mark 1:16 Now as he walked by the sea of Galilee, he saw Simon and Andrew his brother casting a net into the sea: for they were fishers.
Mark 1:17 And Jesus said unto them, Come ye after me, and I will make you to become fishers of men.

These three gospels are in harmony and complete agreement as to the chronology of this event. Luke and the others have stated in their own words therefore there is no collaboration either. The idea of no collaboration is displayed again by how James and John are called. Luke describes how James and John were partners with Simon and Andrew. They were eyewitnesses to his miracle and probably participated in the reaping of the fish.

Luke 5:10 speaks about James and John however, Matthew and Mark describe James and John, that upon seeing this miracle, having no problem leaving their nets and following Jesus. All Jesus had to do was walk by their dock area where their father had them mending nets and Jesus calls out to them.

Matthew has more detail about this than Luke:

Matthew 4:21 And going on from thence, he saw other two brethren, James *the son* of Zebedee, and John his brother, in a ship with Zebedee their father, mending their nets; and he called them.

Matthew 4:22 And they immediately left the ship and their father, and followed him.

Mark concurs:

Mark 1:19 And when he had gone a little further thence, he saw James the *son* of Zebedee, and John his brother, who also were in the ship mending their nets.

Mark 1:20 And straightway he called them: and they left their father Zebedee in the ship with the hired servants, and went after him.

Luke 5:11 And when they had brought their ships to land, they forsook all, and followed him.

Jesus Christ's selection of disciples, or apostles as they would come to be known, has begun. To have men come forward and voluntarily step up to be called disciples now begins. Notice Luke says they forsook all including family. You and I are also called to be disciples. To forsake all and follow Him:

Luke 14:33 So likewise, whosoever he be of you that forsaketh not all that he hath, he cannot be my disciple.

Matthew breaks this down even further:

Matthew 10:37 He that loveth father or mother more than me is not worthy of me: and he that loveth son or daughter more than me is not worthy of me.

Matthew 10:38 And he that taketh not his cross, and followeth after me, is not worthy of me.

Matthew 10:39 He that findeth his life shall lose it: and he that loseth his life for my sake shall find it.

Also, in the synoptic Gospels of Matthew, Mark, and Luke the story of the leper is told.

Luke 5:12 And it came to pass, when he was in a certain city, behold a man full of leprosy: who seeing Jesus fell on *his* face, and besought him, saying, Lord, if thou wilt, thou canst make me clean.
Luke 5:13 And he put forth *his* hand, and touched him, saying, I will: be thou clean. And immediately the leprosy departed from him.

Matthew's Gospel says:
Matthew 8:2 And, behold, there came a leper and worshipped him, saying, Lord, if thou wilt, thou canst make me clean.
Matthew 8:3 And Jesus put forth *his* hand, and touched him, saying, I will; be thou clean. And immediately his leprosy was cleansed.
Matthew 8:4 And Jesus saith unto him, See thou tell no man; but go thy way, shew thyself to the priest, and offer the gift that Moses commanded, for a testimony unto them.

Mark says:
Mark 1:40 And there came a leper to him, beseeching him, and kneeling down to him, and saying unto him, If thou wilt, thou canst make me clean.
Mark 1:41 And Jesus, moved with compassion, put forth *his* hand, and touched him, and saith unto him, I will; be thou clean.
Mark 1:42 And as soon as he had spoken, immediately the leprosy departed from him, and he was cleansed.

Jesus wanted no man to come to Him for entertainment. Whether healing a sick person or performing any other miracle, He was not to be taken lightly. Jesus told this leper to go and tell no one. Jesus also tells the leper to keep the commandments of the ceremonial law because they were still under the Law of Moses:

Luke 5:14 And he charged him to tell no man: but go, and shew thyself to the priest, and offer for thy cleansing, according as Moses commanded, for a testimony unto them.

Luke 5:15 But so much the more went there a fame abroad of him: and great multitudes came together to hear, and to be healed by him of their infirmities.

Jesus would get weary and would want to get alone and spend time with His Father. He would want to talk with the Father, that is pray. This we should do also!

Luke 5:16 And he withdrew himself into the wilderness, and prayed.
Luke 5:17 And it came to pass on a certain day, as he was teaching, that there were Pharisees and doctors of the law sitting by, which were come out of every town of Galilee, and Judaea, and Jerusalem: and the power of the Lord was *present* to heal them.
Luke 5:18 And, behold, men brought in a bed a man which was taken with a palsy: and they sought *means* to bring him in, and to lay *him* before him.

Again, in the synoptic gospels, Jesus will perform a miracle. But this miracle will point the finger directly at Jesus being God! Only God can say your sins are forgiven. But Jesus heals the sick of the palsy also. But just as important, Jesus sees the faith of the four who lowered this man down by breaking open the roof and lowering the sick man down. Jesus proceeds to forgive the sins of the man who was sick. Don't think that your aid and assistance to help anyone seeking Christ goes unnoticed. No one comes to Jesus Christ without God first seeing the faith and the prayers of the helper Christian!

Luke 5:19 And when they could not find by what *way* they might bring him in because of the multitude, they went upon the housetop, and let him down through the tiling with *his* couch into the midst before Jesus.
Luke 5:20 And when he saw their faith, he said unto him, Man, thy sins are forgiven thee.

This is in all three synoptic gospels including Luke above.

In Matthew:

Matthew 9:2 And, behold, they brought to him a man sick of the palsy, lying on a bed: and Jesus seeing their faith said unto the sick of the palsy; Son, be of good cheer; thy sins be forgiven thee.

And in Mark:

Mark 2:3 And they come unto him, bringing one sick of the palsy, which was borne of four.

Mark 2:4 And when they could not come nigh unto him for the press, they uncovered the roof where he was: and when they had broken *it* up, they let down the bed wherein the sick of the palsy lay.

Mark 2:5 When Jesus saw their faith, he said unto the sick of the palsy, Son, thy sins be forgiven thee.

Jesus speaks of the four men who helped lower the man down, when He saw

"THEIR FAITH".

Whose faith? The faith of the four men who tore open the roof and lowered the sick man down. When we pray for a lost loved one, God wants to see it in us. He wants to see our faith in getting that lost one to Jesus!

Luke 5:21 And the scribes and the Pharisees began to reason, saying, Who is this which speaketh blasphemies? Who can forgive sins, but God alone?

The Pharisees knew what Jesus was saying. He was presenting Himself as God. How come certain cults and other beliefs don't see this? The Pharisees did. They knew that Jesus was representing Himself as God! Given this choice, I would rather have my sins forgiven than to be healed of a sickness. Jesus answers their questionable thoughts with a question.

Luke 5:22 But when Jesus perceived their thoughts, he answering said unto them, What reason ye in your hearts?

Luke 5:23 Whether is easier, to say, Thy sins be forgiven thee; or to say, Rise up and walk?

Jesus answers the question from the Pharisees. Many times, Jesus answers his distractor's question with a question. However, at this time, the healing of the man with palsy, Jesus just shows the power that He truly has.

Luke 5:24 But that ye may know that the Son of man hath power upon earth to forgive sins, (he said unto the sick of the palsy,) I say unto thee, Arise, and take up thy couch, and go into thine house.

Satan mimics Christ and is capable to display this power to heal that will be greatly emphasized in the last days. However, it is an entirely different thing to forgive sins. Only God can forgive sins.

Isaiah 43:25 I, *even* I, *am* he that blotteth out thy transgressions for mine own sake, and will not remember thy sins.

And David acknowledges God's divine power to forgive.

Psalms 32:5 I acknowledged my sin unto thee, and mine iniquity have I not hid. I said, I will confess my transgressions unto the LORD; and thou forgavest the iniquity of my sin. Selah.

The man who was sick of the palsy is made to stand up by God and is healed straightway.

Luke 5:25 And immediately he rose up before them, and took up that whereon he lay, and departed to his own house, glorifying God.
Luke 5:26 And they were all amazed, and they glorified God, and were filled with fear, saying, We have seen strange things to day.

We have seen strange things today. Jesus has performed what only God can do! Now there is the call of Matthew, who is better known as Levi. Luke uses the name Levi not the name Matthew.

Luke 5:27 And after these things he went forth, and saw a publican, named Levi, sitting at the receipt of custom: and he said unto him, Follow me.

Luke 5:28 And he left all, rose up, and followed him.
Luke 5:29 And Levi made him a great feast in his own house: and there was a great company of publicans and of others that sat down with them.

It is interesting that Matthew is only referred to as Matthew in Matthew when Jesus finds him.

Matthew 9:9 And as Jesus passed forth from thence, he saw a man, named Matthew, sitting at the receipt of custom: and he saith unto him, Follow me. And he arose, and followed him.

Matthew then narrows down the fact that his name is Matthew and no longer Levi by calling himself Matthew the publican in the list of the twelve apostles.

Matthew 10:3 Philip, and Bartholomew; Thomas, and Matthew the publican; James *the son* of Alphaeus, and Lebbaeus, whose surname was Thaddaeus;

Mark calls him Levi:

Mark 2:14 And as he passed by, he saw Levi the *son* of Alphaeus sitting at the receipt of custom, and said unto him, Follow me. And he arose and followed him.

The scribes and Pharisees knew that Levi was a publican. But when the twelve Apostles are listed, he now has the new name of Matthew.

Luke 5:30 But their scribes and Pharisees murmured against his disciples, saying, Why do ye eat and drink with publicans and sinners?
Luke 5:31 And Jesus answering said unto them, They that are whole need not a physician; but they that are sick.
Luke 5:32 I came not to call the righteous, but sinners to repentance.

Jesus explains why He came. He came to call everyone, that is a sinner, first to repentance. He came to forgive these sins as seen earlier. The scribes and Pharisees who do not accept this now try to trap Jesus.

Luke 5:33 And they said unto him, Why do the disciples of John fast often, and make prayers, and likewise *the disciples* of the Pharisees; but thine eat and drink?

Luke 5:34 And he said unto them, Can ye make the children of the bridechamber fast, while the bridegroom is with them?

Luke 5:35 But the days will come, when the bridegroom shall be taken away from them, and then shall they fast in those days.

Jesus will give a commonsense explanation with a parable. This will be the first of many parables. It is the parable of new wine into new bottles.

Luke 5:36 And he spake also a parable unto them; No man putteth a piece of a new garment upon an old; if otherwise, then both the new maketh a rent, and the piece that was *taken* out of the new agreeth not with the old.

Jesus for the first time uses the word parable. The word parable is a transliterated word from the Greek to English. The word parable means to compare a story with a story and the truth would then be revealed in what is being told. Jesus is about to make this new comparison. He is about to compare the old dispensation of living by the law with the new dispensation of living by grace. He indicates that you cannot add this new age to the old age of law. This new age, that of grace, which He is about to unleash on mankind, cannot be put into old bottles. Even at the smallest repair of an old garment it is the weakest at that point and will tear.

Luke 5:37 And no man putteth new wine into old bottles; else the new wine will burst the bottles, and be spilled, and the bottles shall perish.

Before a person is born again, they are a natural man (Old Bottles) filled with a sin nature derived from Adam and Eve (Old Wine). When a person is born again old things pass away and all things have become new.

2Corinthians 5:17 Therefore if any man *be* in Christ, *he is* a new creature: old things are passed away; behold, all things are become new.

Their identity is now the new man in Christ (New Bottle) filled with the Holy Spirit (New Wine).

Luke 5:38 But new wine must be put into new bottles; and both are preserved.

Luke 5:39 No man also having drunk old *wine* straightway desireth new: for he saith, The old is better.

If left to the old bottles or old clothing, the old man doesn't desire the new life in God because he thinks the old is better. The new man must reach out and receive God, that is the new wine. God then declares he is in Christ Jesus the new bottle because as Christ has been saying, this new age or "the kingdom of God" is at hand. Mark said it best:

Mark 1:15 And saying, The time is fulfilled, and the kingdom of God is at hand: repent ye, and believe the gospel.

At the end of chapter five Jesus begins to speak in parables. He will continue this to explain His way to heaven. In the book of Romans, The Romans Road is given to help with understanding God's simple plan of salvation. To be lost in sin, realize it, repent of it, and by faith receive Jesus Christ as your Lord! God has seen that left to ourselves, all men will sin:

Romans 3:23 For all have sinned, and come short of the glory of God;

God has also pointed out the result of that sin is death or eternal separation from God:

Romans 6:23 For the wages of sin *is* death; but the gift of God *is* eternal life through Jesus Christ our Lord.

God has also made a pathway for man to climb aboard and start the new life with the Holy Spirit within you. That is new wine.

Romans 5:8 But God commendeth his love toward us, in that, while we were yet sinners, Christ died for us.

The lost have a different view of the riches of God through His goodness and despise the things of God so they will not repent.

Romans 2:4 Or despisest thou the riches of his goodness and forbearance and longsuffering; not knowing that the goodness of God leadeth thee to repentance?

Once you have repented of your old way of thinking, that is thinking you can attain heaven on your own and that you can take care of your own sin problem, all you need to do is by faith ask Jesus to save you:

Romans 10:9 That if thou shalt confess with thy mouth the Lord Jesus, and shalt believe in thine heart that God hath raised him from the dead, thou shalt be saved. Romans 10:10 For with the heart man believeth unto righteousness; and with the mouth confession is made unto salvation.

LUKE CHAPTER 6

Highlights:

Chapter six describes Jesus Christ calling out of the Pharisees. Jesus Christ calling out the twelve Apostles. Jesus Christ's sermon of the beatitudes in the plain.

Main Participants:

Jesus Christ, v.1,
His disciples v.1,
the Pharisees v.2,
man with the withered right hand v.6,
Apostles v.13,
Peter v.14,
Andrew v.14,
James v.14,
John v.14,
Philip v.14,
Bartholomew v.14,
Matthew v.15,
Thomas v.15,
James the son of Alphaeus v.15,
Simon called Zelotes v.15,
Judas the brother of James v.16,
Judas Iscariot v.16,
Great Multitude v.17,

In Brief:

Just itching to show the Pharisees their sinful condition, Jesus goes right to work picking other's corn and that on the Sabbath day. He heals on the sabbath and tells all that the Lord is Lord of the Sabbath also. He points out who is blessed and who has woe. The Lord teaches about love of God and mercy also. For a second time some of the beatitudes are quoted but this time it is a sermon on the "plain." Not the "Sermon on the Mount" quoted by Matthew.

Synoptic in Matthew, Mark, and Luke's Gospel

Luke 6:1 And it came to pass on the second sabbath after the first, that he went through the corn fields; and his disciples plucked the ears of corn, and did eat, rubbing *them* in *their* hands.

Matthew gives this account:

Matthew 12:1 At that time Jesus went on the sabbath day through the corn; and his disciples were an hungred, and began to pluck the ears of corn, and to eat.

Matthew 12:2 But when the Pharisees saw *it,* they said unto him, Behold, thy disciples do that which is not lawful to do upon the sabbath day.

Mark says:

Mark 2:23 And it came to pass, that he went through the corn fields on the sabbath day; and his disciples began, as they went, to pluck the ears of corn.

Mark 2:24 And the Pharisees said unto him, Behold, why do they on the sabbath day that which is not lawful?

This synoptic look at the Sabbath day is very important. Jesus is about to clarify one of the ten commandments: commandment number four.

Exodus 20:8 Remember the sabbath day, to keep it holy.

Exodus 20:9 Six days shalt thou labour, and do all thy work:
Exodus 20:10 But the seventh day *is* the sabbath of the LORD thy God: *in it* thou shalt not do any work, thou, nor thy son, nor thy daughter, thy manservant, nor thy maidservant, nor thy cattle, nor thy stranger that *is* within thy gates:
Exodus 20:11 For *in* six days the LORD made heaven and earth, the sea, and all that in them *is,* and rested the seventh day: wherefore the LORD blessed the sabbath day, and hallowed it.

Nowhere in this commandment does it say that the Sabbath is the day of worship. Nowhere in the Old Testament does it say that the last day of the week, known as the Sabbath, is the day of worship. It only says that it is a day of rest. Every day should be a day of worship! God made the Sabbath for man so that man could have a day of rest. Jesus will do all he can to show by example that religious leaders missed the reason that the Sabbath was instituted.

Verse one speaks of corn, however, it is not corn as we know corn today. The corn we eat was discovered here in America from the native people of this land. But the kernels of grains such as wheat or barley or whatever could be grown in this field is what they were eating.

Luke 6:2 And certain of the Pharisees said unto them, Why do ye that which is not lawful to do on the sabbath days?

Some say that Jesus has sinned here. He stole grain out of a farmer's field! The Pharisees accused Jesus of this. They wanted to point out the sin of Jesus taking another man's grain saying it was unlawful in addition to doing it on the Sabbath. However, Jesus did not steal this grain. The Old Testament law of gleaning in the field was still applicable.

Levitcus 23:22 And when ye reap the harvest of your land, thou shalt not make clean riddance of the corners of thy field when thou reapest, neither shalt thou gather any gleaning of thy harvest: thou shalt leave them unto the poor, and to the stranger: I *am* the LORD your God.

The Pharisees where more concerned with Jesus breaking their man-made laws. So, Jesus responded to them:

Luke 6:3 And Jesus answering them said, Have ye not read so much as this, what David did, when himself was an hungred, and they which were with him;

Luke 6:4 How he went into the house of God, and did take and eat the shewbread, and gave also to them that were with him; which it is not lawful to eat but for the priests alone?

Jesus used David their beloved king as an example that when a man needs to eat even the priest should assist at that time.

1Samuel 21:6 So the priest gave him hallowed *bread:* for there was no bread there but the shewbread, that was taken from before the LORD, to put hot bread in the day when it was taken away.

There are plenty of passages that clearly allow a man to eat from his neighbors field. When you are hungry God allows you to eat of the plentiful that He has provided:

Deuteronomy 23:24 When thou comest into thy neighbour's vineyard, then thou mayest eat grapes thy fill at thine own pleasure; but thou shalt not put *any* in thy vessel.

Deuteronomy 23:25 When thou comest into the standing corn of thy neighbour, then thou mayest pluck the ears with thine hand; but thou shalt not move a sickle unto thy neighbour's standing corn.

And then Jesus told them about God's view of the Sabbath.

Luke 6:5 And he said unto them, That the Son of man is Lord also of the sabbath.

Matthew says very simply:

Matthew 12:8 For the Son of man is Lord even of the sabbath day.

Mark adds a great statement about the sabbath:

Mark 2:27 And he said unto them, The sabbath was made for man, and not man for the sabbath:

Mark 2:28 Therefore the Son of man is Lord also of the sabbath.

Jesus has performed His works of miracles primarily on the Sabbath day. He began His public ministry on the Sabbath by reading from Isaiah in chapter 4:16. He then began to teach when the crowds were gathered on the Sabbath as Luke 4:31 explained. In the beginning of this chapter Luke tells us that Jesus was on his second Sabbath. Some have speculated that this must be the second Sabbath after the first day of unleavened Bread Sabbath. This could not have been the case as Jesus was in Galilee and not Judea where the temple is. This could be the second Sabbath that He is in Capernaum.

Mark 1:21 And they went into Capernaum; and straightway on the sabbath day he entered into the synagogue, and taught.

Because of Mark it is known that there was a synagogue in Capernaum and that He was teaching in it.

Luke 6:6 And it came to pass also on another sabbath, that he entered into the synagogue and taught: and there was a man whose right hand was withered.

Luke 6:7 And the scribes and Pharisees watched him, whether he would heal on the sabbath day; that they might find an accusation against him.

Jesus sets a trap for the Pharisees knowing they will fall into it with their own words. He will now set the scribes and Pharisees in their place.

Luke 6:8 But he knew their thoughts, and said to the man which had the withered hand, Rise up, and stand forth in the midst. And he arose and stood forth.

Luke 6:9 Then said Jesus unto them, I will ask you one thing; Is it lawful on the sabbath days to do good, or to do evil? to save life, or to destroy it?

To this current day the Jewish religious leaders have not changed much. Two thousand years later they still have a terrible view of "Is it lawful on the Sabbath days to do good, or to do evil?" In Los Angeles in 1992, the L.A. Times reported the following story:

FROM TIMES STAFF AND WIRE REPORTS
APRIL 26, 1992 12 AM PT

Tenants let three apartments in the predominantly ultra-Orthodox Tel Aviv suburb of Bnei Brak burn while they asked a rabbi whether a call to the fire department on the Sabbath would violate Jewish tenets. Observant Jews are forbidden to use telephones on the Sabbath because to do so would involve breaking an electric current, which is considered a form of work.

Getting back to Luke, Jesus probably has a just cause or some righteous indignation within Him at this point. Mark says He becomes angry:

Mark 3:5 And when he had looked round about on them with anger, being grieved for the hardness of their hearts, he saith unto the man, Stretch forth thine hand. And he stretched *it* out: and his hand was restored whole as the other.

Sidebar: The KJV has the Sermon on the Mount recorded correctly. Other versions do not. Jesus spoke of this kind of anger during this sermon. The KJV along with the NKJV are the only versions to record a very important statement in Matthew. The term, "without a cause" is included here in Matthew 5:22. This phrase is not included in any other version.

Matthew 5:21 Ye have heard that it was said by them of old time, Thou shalt not kill; and whosoever shall kill shall be in danger of the judgment:

Matthew 5:22 But I say unto you, That whosoever is angry with his brother without a cause shall be in danger of the judgment: and whosoever shall say to his brother, Raca, shall be in danger of the council: but whosoever shall say, Thou fool, shall be in danger of hell fire.

New versions have Jesus, who is angry as explained in Mark above, in danger of the judgement!

We need to take a lesson here from Jesus. He could have healed this man on any day of the week. But Jesus wanted to confront the Pharisees with their sin. They had forced the Jewish people to live by their man-made laws that God never intended to have such a stifling effect on the people. Jesus called them out right in the middle of their sin and because of their sin. This is something to follow. It is better to preach against abortion to those committing the abortion than to those who are already against it. It is better to preach against sodomy to those who are living this lifestyle than to those who already stand against it. Jesus took His healing right to where the sin problem was.

Luke 6:10 And looking round about upon them all, he said unto the man, Stretch forth thy hand. And he did so: and his hand was restored whole as the other.

Luke 6:11 And they were filled with madness; and communed one with another what they might do to Jesus.

The religious leaders were filled with madness. Look at the world today. When someone takes a public stand against abortion the world goes nuts with madness. Speak out against GLBTQ+ and see how they are filled with madness. The Pharisees start to conspire and figure out how to deal with this "man" who is performing these miracles on the Sabbath.

Luke 6:12 And it came to pass in those days, that he went out into a mountain to pray, and continued all night in prayer to God.

Jesus would pray much seeking to be off alone with the Father. This night He spends the entire night in prayer as the next day He will select His Apostles.

Luke 6:13 And when it was day, he called *unto him* his disciples: and of them he chose twelve, whom also he named apostles;

Luke 6:14 Simon, (whom he also named Peter,) and Andrew his brother, James and John, Philip and Bartholomew,
Luke 6:15 Matthew and Thomas, James the *son* of Alphaeus, and Simon called Zelotes,
Luke 6:16 And Judas *the brother* of James, and Judas Iscariot, which also was the traitor.

This is the first time the word Apostle is used. It is used also in Mark and Matthew but at later times in His public ministry. The word "Apostle" is not in the Gospel of John.

Only in Luke's Gospel

Now we come to the beatitudes. There is a difference here between Matthew and Luke. Matthew says Jesus went up into a mountain and His disciples followed Him:

Matthew 5:1 And seeing the multitudes, he went up into a mountain: and when he was set, his disciples came unto him:

However, Luke says that they stood in the plain. Jesus was still performing miracles of healing here in the plain. There is no such talk of this taking place in Matthew. The timing is not the same either. Matthew has Jesus naming His Apostles well after the sermon while Luke has named them before he recorded the beatitudes.

Luke 6:17 And he came down with them, and stood in the plain, and the company of his disciples, and a great multitude of people out of all Judaea and Jerusalem, and from the sea coast of Tyre and Sidon, which came to hear him, and to be healed of their diseases;
Luke 6:18 And they that were vexed with unclean spirits: and they were healed.
Luke 6:19 And the whole multitude sought to touch him: for there went virtue out of him, and healed *them* all.

Luke now presents the beatitudes. They are different than Matthew and in a different order. Also, there are many blessings and words excluded. The only way to look at this is that there are two different times when Jesus presents His beatitudes.

Luke 6:20 And he lifted up his eyes on his disciples, and said, Blessed *be ye* poor: for yours is the kingdom of God.

Luke 6:21 Blessed *are ye* that hunger now: for ye shall be filled. Blessed *are ye* that weep now: for ye shall laugh.

Luke 6:22 Blessed are ye, when men shall hate you, and when they shall separate you *from their company,* and shall reproach *you,* and cast out your name as evil, for the Son of man's sake.

Luke 6:23 Rejoice ye in that day, and leap for joy: for, behold, your reward *is* great in heaven: for in the like manner did their fathers unto the prophets.

At this point Matthew and Luke are entirely different. Luke will not speak of the light being hidden under a bushel for two more chapters while Matthew goes into this right after His beatitudes.

Matthew 5:14 Ye are the light of the world. A city that is set on an hill cannot be hid.

Matthew 5:15 Neither do men light a candle, and put it under a bushel, but on a candlestick; and it giveth light unto all that are in the house.

Matthew 5:16 Let your light so shine before men, that they may see your good works, and glorify your Father which is in heaven.

Another difference at this time is how Luke, being the Gospel that declares Jesus as the Son of Man, deals with the problems that beset a man.

Luke 6:24 But woe unto you that are rich! for ye have received your consolation.

Luke 6:25 Woe unto you that are full! for ye shall hunger. Woe unto you that laugh now! for ye shall mourn and weep.

Luke 6:26 Woe unto you, when all men shall speak well of you! for so did their fathers to the false prophets.

Luke describes four events that a man would say these are good things that are happening to me. Plenty of money, and food, and entertainment and recognition by others. However, God knows that these things can corrupt a person if they are your goal in life.

Luke 6:27 But I say unto you which hear, Love your enemies, do good to them which hate you,

Luke 6:28 Bless them that curse you, and pray for them which despitefully use you.

Luke 6:29 And unto him that smiteth thee on the *one* cheek offer also the other; and him that taketh away thy cloke forbid not *to take thy* coat also.

Luke and Matthew speak of the same result when someone offends you.

Matthew 5:38 Ye have heard that it hath been said, An eye for an eye, and a tooth for a tooth:

Matthew 5:39 But I say unto you, That ye resist not evil: but whosoever shall smite thee on thy right cheek, turn to him the other also.

Turning the other cheek is the exact opposite of an eye for an eye spoken of in the Old Testament. An eye for an eye was enacted by God, primarily for God to deal with anyone who hurts a baby while it is still in the womb.

Exodus 21:22 If men strive, and hurt a woman with child, so that her fruit depart *from her,* and yet no mischief follow: he shall be surely punished, according as the woman's husband will lay upon him; and he shall pay as the judges *determine.*

Exodus 21:23 And if *any* mischief follow, then thou shalt give life for life,

Exodus 21:24 Eye for eye, tooth for tooth, hand for hand, foot for foot,

Exodus 21:25 Burning for burning, wound for wound, stripe for stripe.

Luke 6:30 Give to every man that asketh of thee; and of him that taketh away thy goods ask *them* not again.

Only in Matthew and Luke's Gospel

The Golden rule now comes from Jesus. But most people do not quote it correctly from the Bible. Matthew says:

Matthew 7:12 Therefore all things whatsoever ye would that men should do to you, do ye even so to them: for this is the law and the prophets.

This is correctly spoken if you are under the law of the Old Testament. The Golden rule is also presented by Luke:

Luke 6:31 And as ye would that men should do to you, do ye also to them likewise.

Jesus is clearly stating that under the law you must obey this command. But the saved are not under the law but under the grace of God. And now Jesus will explain how a man can carry out this command because he "wants" to do this not because he "has" to.

Luke 6:32 For if ye love them which love you, what thank have ye? for sinners also love those that love them.

Luke 6:33 And if ye do good to them which do good to you, what thank have ye? for sinners also do even the same.

Luke 6:34 And if ye lend *to them* of whom ye hope to receive, what thank have ye? for sinners also lend to sinners, to receive as much again.

Here is the difference between the Old Testament law and Jesus Christ's New Testament of grace, indicated by loving your neighbor. The saved are told to even love our enemies. How did the Old Testament instruct to deal with the enemies of God under the law? God would have His people destroy them. This is a very strange teaching for the Pharisees to understand. It comes from this man, Jesus Christ, sent by God.

Luke 6:35 But love ye your enemies, and do good, and lend, hoping for nothing again; and your reward shall be great, and ye shall be the children of the Highest: for he is kind unto the unthankful and *to* the evil.

Luke 6:36 Be ye therefore merciful, as your Father also is merciful.

Often this next verse is quoted so horribly wrong. Matthew is where it is most familiar:

Matthew 7:1 Judge not, that ye be not judged.

But God commands us to judge righteously. He explains later in Matthew that we are to judge and that is to not be a hypocrite when judging.

Matthew 7:5 Thou hypocrite, first cast out the beam out of thine own eye; and then shalt thou see clearly to cast out the mote out of thy brother's eye.

Luke begins to say exactly what Matthew has said at a different place and a different time:

Luke 6:37a Judge not, and ye shall not be judged:

Only in Luke's Gospel

Luke 6:37b condemn not, and ye shall not be condemned: forgive, and ye shall be forgiven:

However, Luke adds several lines to what Matthew said about Judging in Matthew chapter 7. Luke is the only Gospel to expand on the Golden Rule. Another proof that these were two separate occasions and that there was no collusion between Matthew and Luke. Matthew gives the Sermon on the Mount and Luke the Sermon in the Plain.

Luke 6:38 Give, and it shall be given unto you; good measure, pressed down, and shaken together, and running over, shall men give into your bosom. For with the same measure that ye mete withal it shall be measured to you again.

These are all ways to measure in business. God says to measure accurately and press out the water and shake until dry and fill till it runs over.

Luke will now give a second parable. The word "parable" is a transliterated word. That means the word parable was brought from the Greek language into the English language as the same word. The Greek word is "*Parabole*" and means comparing a similar thing with another of the same likeness but not the same image.

Luke 6:39 And he spake a parable unto them, Can the blind lead the blind? shall they not both fall into the ditch?
Luke 6:40 The disciple is not above his master: but every one that is perfect shall be as his master.

Perfect here has a different meaning than perfect as we know it. It does not mean without error. Here perfect means complete or restored correctly and completely. Therefore, we are "perfect" or complete in Christ when we are living like the Master, that is to love even our enemies.

The parable has ended, and Jesus is now back to teaching more about this Christ endorsed life that is about to be unleashed on the world. This is very similar to the Matthew account, but this is at a different time and location and is a second presentation of this rule that a saved man should live by. Again, Jesus is not on the mountaintop, but He is in the plain. However, He is using the same descriptive terms about hypocrisy.

Luke 6:41 And why beholdest thou the mote that is in thy brother's eye, but perceivest not the beam that is in thine own eye?

Matthew was quick to point out that you are not to be a hypocrite. Luke points out even more clearly that the object of the law is not "judging." The object of the law is to not be a hypocrite!

Luke 6:42 Either how canst thou say to thy brother, Brother, let me pull out the mote that is in thine eye, when thou thyself beholdest not the beam that is in thine own eye? Thou hypocrite, cast out first the beam out of thine own eye, and then shalt thou see clearly to pull out the mote that is in thy brother's eye.

What happens when this new lifestyle of "Christ following" is lived out of love and not out of being told to do this? You can't help but bring forth good fruit.

Luke 6:43 For a good tree bringeth not forth corrupt fruit; neither doth a corrupt tree bring forth good fruit.
Luke 6:44 For every tree is known by his own fruit. For of thorns men do not gather figs, nor of a bramble bush gather they grapes.
Luke 6:45 A good man out of the good treasure of his heart bringeth forth that which is good; and an evil man out of the evil treasure of his heart bringeth forth that which is evil: for of the abundance of the heart his mouth speaketh.

Repentance and having your heart right with God is required for salvation. This will bring you to call upon the Lord. Just saying the sinner's prayer by itself will not save you. Here we are told that the mouth speaks, once the heart is won. That what Jesus Christ says to do we must want to do. We cannot say Jesus is Lord and then not follow His teachings. The steps for Salvation are now given. You need to come and hear and do!

Luke 6:46 And why call ye me, Lord, Lord, and do not the things which I say?
Luke 6:47 Whosoever cometh to me, and heareth my sayings, and doeth them, I will shew you to whom he is like:

Jesus Christ is the rock that we must build upon. Jesus uses an illustration that everyone understands. Anyone who has seen or built or occupies a house knows how important the foundation is. And the foundation itself must be on something very solid. There is nothing more solid than the rock. Rock is as steadfast as the earth can be. A foundation upon a rock is the best. We have the Bible to back that up:

1Corinthians 3:10 According to the grace of God which is given unto me, as a wise masterbuilder, I have laid the foundation, and another buildeth thereon. But let every man take heed how he buildeth thereupon.

1Corinthians 3:11 For other foundation can no man lay than that is laid, which is Jesus Christ.

Luke 6:48 He is like a man which built an house, and digged deep, and laid the foundation on a rock: and when the flood arose, the stream beat vehemently upon that house, and could not shake it: for it was founded upon a rock.

Jesus, the chief cornerstone will give us the foundation that we are to build on. It is the Word of God as presented by the apostles and prophets:

Ephesians 2:19 Now therefore ye are no more strangers and foreigners, but fellowcitizens with the saints, and of the household of God;

Ephesians 2:20 And are built upon the foundation of the apostles and prophets, Jesus Christ himself being the chief corner *stone;*

Jesus also gives warning that you can hear the message of salvation and not take that step by faith and receive it:

Luke 6:49 But he that heareth, and doeth not, is like a man that without a foundation built an house upon the earth; against which the stream did beat vehemently, and immediately it fell; and the ruin of that house was great.

In conclusion, God calls our body a house.

2 Corinthians 5:1 For we know that if our earthly house of *this* tabernacle were dissolved, we have a building of God, an house not made with hands, eternal in the heavens.

2 Corinthians 5:2 For in this we groan, earnestly desiring to be clothed upon with our house which is from heaven:

What is your house built UPON? Is it built upon the foundation of Jesus Christ?

1 Corinthians 3:11 For other foundation can no man lay than that is laid, which is Jesus Christ.

What is your house built WITH? Is it gold, silver, precious stones? Or is your house built with wood, hay, stubble!

1Corinthians 3:12 Now if any man build upon this foundation gold, silver, precious stones, wood, hay, stubble;

One day your house will be subjected to FIRE! What will burn up? What will you have for Christ that the fire purified!

1Corinthians 3:13 Every man's work shall be made manifest: for the day shall declare it, because it shall be revealed by fire; and the fire shall try every man's work of what sort it is.

LUKE CHAPTER 7

Highlights:

Chapter seven describes Jesus Christ and His healing abilities. Jesus being confirmed by John the Baptist. Finally, His true story of the faith of a sinner.

Main Participants:

Jesus Christ, v.1,
a centurion's servant v.2,
Elders of the Jews v.3,
The Centurion's friends v.6,
Widow of Nain v.12,
Young man of Nain raised from the dead v. 14,
Disciples of John v. 18,
John the Baptist v.19,
Pharisees and Lawyers v.30,
Simon the Pharisee v.36,
Sinful woman who washed Jesus's feet with her tears v.37.

In Brief:

Jesus recognizes great faith as quality faith. He heals the centurion's servant. He also heals a dead man in the city of Nain. John the Baptist sends two men as witnesses to question Jesus. Jesus answers John's questions and then preaches about the *kingdom of God*. **Finally, a woman with an Alabaster box of ointment anoints the feet of Jesus.**

Only in Matthew and Luke's Gospel

Luke 7:1 Now when he had ended all his sayings in the audience of the people, he entered into Capernaum.

Luke 7:2 And a certain centurion's servant, who was dear unto him, was sick, and ready to die.

Luke 7:3 And when he heard of Jesus, he sent unto him the elders of the Jews, beseeching him that he would come and heal his servant.

Luke 7:4 And when they came to Jesus, they besought him instantly, saying, That he was worthy for whom he should do this:

Luke 7:5 For he loveth our nation, and he hath built us a synagogue.

Luke 7:6 Then Jesus went with them. And when he was now not far from the house, the centurion sent friends to him, saying unto him, Lord, trouble not thyself: for I am not worthy that thou shouldest enter under my roof:

Luke 7:7 Wherefore neither thought I myself worthy to come unto thee: but say in a word, and my servant shall be healed.

Luke 7:8 For I also am a man set under authority, having under me soldiers, and I say unto one, Go, and he goeth; and to another, Come, and he cometh; and to my servant, Do this, and he doeth *it.*

Luke 7:9 When Jesus heard these things, he marvelled at him, and turned him about, and said unto the people that followed him, I say unto you, I have not found so great faith, no, not in Israel.

Luke 7:10 And they that were sent, returning to the house, found the servant whole that had been sick.

Matthew and Luke have said the same narrative up to this point but now Matthew will add some different instruction from God. Only Matthew will speak of the kingdom of heaven.

Matthew 8:10 When Jesus heard *it,* he marvelled, and said to them that followed, Verily I say unto you, I have not found so great faith, no, not in Israel.

Matthew 8:11 And I say unto you, That many shall come from the east and west, and shall sit down with Abraham, and Isaac, and Jacob, in the kingdom of heaven.

Matthew 8:12 But the children of the kingdom shall be cast out into outer darkness: there shall be weeping and gnashing of teeth.

Matthew 8:13 And Jesus said unto the centurion, Go thy way; and as thou hast believed, so be it done unto thee. And his servant was healed in the selfsame hour.

Matthew has added this because he is the author of the *kingdom of heaven*. Matthew is the Gospel to the Jews and because of this he speaks of Jewish things. The *kingdom of heaven* speaks of Jesus's own people, the children of the house of Israel. Here in Matthew chapter 8, there is some insight as to what will take place in the *kingdom of heaven*. Abraham, Isaac, and Jacob will be there. Matthew tells that those without the right quality of faith, the faith that leads to belief, who think they were physically born into this family will not make it. Without Christ as their Messiah, they are cast out into outer darkness. The *kingdom of heaven* is different than the *kingdom of God*. The *kingdom of heaven* is a place that man seeks to go. This place can only be achieved God's way by believing God and His plan of salvation. This is through His Son, The Lord Jesus Christ. Any other way that man dreams up becomes a violent battle that takes place in the heart when man rejects God's way.

Matthew 11:12 And from the days of John the Baptist until now the kingdom of heaven suffereth violence, and the violent take it by force.

Those who want to make it into the *kingdom of heaven* because they earned it will be cast out. Those who have refused to follow God's plan will find nothing but weeping and gnashing of teeth. Why? Abraham knew why!

Romans 4:1 What shall we say then that Abraham our father, as pertaining to the flesh, hath found?

Romans 4:2 For if Abraham were justified by works, he hath *whereof* to glory; but not before God.

Romans 4:3 For what saith the scripture? Abraham believed God, and it was counted unto him for righteousness.

The *kingdom of heaven* is the place that man seeks to go to be with Abraham, Isaac and Jacob. These three knew to believe God and wait upon the revealing of the promise of His Son. Luke points this out in his letter called "the Acts of the Apostles".

Acts 3:13 The God of Abraham, and of Isaac, and of Jacob, the God of our fathers, hath glorified his Son Jesus; whom ye delivered up, and denied him in the presence of Pilate, when he was determined to let *him* go.

Acts 3:14 But ye denied the Holy One and the Just, and desired a murderer to be granted unto you;

The phrase *kingdom of heaven* appears only in the Gospel of Matthew. It appears 32 times in Matthew only. The phrase the kingdom of God **is in all the Gospels. It speaks of what must take place in a man's heart. The kingdom of God must take place within you!**

Luke 17:20 And when he was demanded of the Pharisees, when the kingdom of God should come, he answered them and said, The kingdom of God cometh not with observation:

Luke 17:21 Neither shall they say, Lo here! or, lo there! for, behold, the kingdom of God is within you.

Only in Luke's Gospel

Luke 7:11 And it came to pass the day after, that he went into a city called Nain; and many of his disciples went with him, and much people.

The city of Nain was a small village off the beaten path, in fact there was only one road in and out of this city. Nain was on the slope of the hill of Moreh which is between Mt Tabor and Mt

Gilboa and identified today with the Jezreel Valley in the Plain of Esdraelon. Earlier in the scriptures, Gideon was camped near this city on the side of the hill of Moreh when he was told by God that he had too many men to attack the Midianites.

Judges 7:1 Then Jerubbaal, who *is* Gideon, and all the people that *were* with him, rose up early, and pitched beside the well of Harod: so that the host of the Midianites were on the north side of them, by the hill of Moreh, in the valley.

Judges 7:2 And the LORD said unto Gideon, The people that *are* with thee *are* too many for me to give the Midianites into their hands, lest Israel vaunt themselves against me, saying, Mine own hand hath saved me.

Luke 7:12 Now when he came nigh to the gate of the city, behold, there was a dead man carried out, the only son of his mother, and she was a widow: and much people of the city was with her.

Matthew Henry, a commentator from many years ago, describes the scene:

> *"That he was really dead was universally agreed. There could be no collusion in the case; for Christ was entering into the town, and had not seen him till now that he met him upon the bier. He was carried out of the city; for the Jews' burying-places were without their cities, and at some distance from them."*

Luke 7:13 And when the Lord saw her, he had compassion on her, and said unto her, Weep not.

Luke 7:14 And he came and touched the bier: and they that bare *him* stood still. And he said, Young man, I say unto thee, Arise.

Luke 7:15 And he that was dead sat up, and began to speak. And he delivered him to his mother.

Luke 7:16 And there came a fear on all: and they glorified God, saying, That a great prophet is risen up among us; and, That God hath visited his people.

Luke 7:17 And this rumour of him went forth throughout all Judaea, and throughout all the region round about.

Only in Matthew and Luke's Gospel

John the Baptist had his disciples. They were very loyal to him. But John the Baptist knew that Jesus was special. He knew it when he baptized Jesus in the Jordan River. But just how special was this Jesus?

Luke 7:18 And the disciples of John shewed him of all these things.
Luke 7:19 And John calling *unto him* two of his disciples sent *them* to Jesus, saying, Art thou he that should come? or look we for another?
Luke 7:20 When the men were come unto him, they said, John Baptist hath sent us unto thee, saying, Art thou he that should come? or look we for another?
Luke 7:21 And in that same hour he cured many of *their* infirmities and plagues, and of evil spirits; and unto many *that were* blind he gave sight.

Jesus did not hold back. He continued with His miracles of healing and destroying evil spirits. This is given to show us just how prevalent evil spirits are in the world. Driving out evil spirits required as much from Jesus as the work of healing that Jesus did. He healed and He cast out evil spirits. He instructed the followers of John to go back and describe these many miracles He was doing.

Luke 7:22 Then Jesus answering said unto them, Go your way, and tell John what things ye have seen and heard; how that the blind see, the lame walk, the lepers are cleansed, the deaf hear, the dead are raised, to the poor the Gospel is preached.
Luke 7:23 And blessed is *he,* whosoever shall not be offended in me.

Matthew records the same about John Baptist:

Matthew 11:4 Jesus answered and said unto them, Go and shew John again those things which ye do hear and see:

Matthew 11:5 The blind receive their sight, and the lame walk, the lepers are cleansed, and the deaf hear, the dead are raised up, and the poor have the Gospel preached to them.

Matthew 11:6 And blessed is *he,* whosoever shall not be offended in me.

Jesus now explains how important John the Baptist is in the requirement of fulfilling scripture:

Luke 7:24 And when the messengers of John were departed, he began to speak unto the people concerning John, What went ye out into the wilderness for to see? A reed shaken with the wind?

Luke 7:25 But what went ye out for to see? A man clothed in soft raiment? Behold, they which are gorgeously apparelled, and live delicately, are in kings' courts.

Luke 7:26 But what went ye out for to see? A prophet? Yea, I say unto you, and much more than a prophet.

Luke 7:27 This is *he,* of whom it is written, Behold, I send my messenger before thy face, which shall prepare thy way before thee.

Jesus says that a certain prophecy has been fulfilled that was written in the prophets. Which Prophet? It is the prediction in Malachi chapter three:

Malachi 3:1 Behold, I will send my messenger, and he shall prepare the way before me: and the Lord, whom ye seek, shall suddenly come to his temple, even the messenger of the covenant, whom ye delight in: behold, he shall come, saith the LORD of hosts.

Jesus says that no one born is greater than John the Baptist. He makes a comparison of those born of women, which are born of water to be born physically on earth, compared to those who have also been born of the spirit that is to seek the kingdom of God and receive it. Jesus says that a born-again believer in the Lord Jesus Christ is greater than John the Baptist. John was killed before the Holy Ghost was gifted to man on the day of Pentecost. If you are

a born-again believer, you have the gift of the Holy Ghost and you are greater than John the Baptist.

Luke 7:28 For I say unto you, Among those that are born of women there is not a greater prophet than John the Baptist: but he that is least in the kingdom of God is greater than he.
Luke 7:29 And all the people that heard *him,* and the publicans, justified God, being baptized with the baptism of John.

Some of the religious leaders felt as if they were too good to be baptized by John. They thought they were above the common man. They rejected to show humility and knew not the first step in being saved is the baptizing unto repentance. The Pharisees would not do this.

Luke 7:30 But the Pharisees and lawyers rejected the counsel of God against themselves, being not baptized of him.

Jesus makes a comparison of the lost self-righteous individuals and compares them to those who will not listen to Him nor follow Him.

Luke 7:31 And the Lord said, Whereunto then shall I liken the men of this generation? and to what are they like?
Luke 7:32 They are like unto children sitting in the marketplace, and calling one to another, and saying, We have piped unto you, and ye have not danced; we have mourned to you, and ye have not wept.

These lost Pharisees and lawyers accuse John the Baptist of having a demon. Devil here is the Greek word "daimonion".

Luke 7:33 For John the Baptist came neither eating bread nor drinking wine; and ye say, He hath a devil.
Luke 7:34 The Son of man is come eating and drinking; and ye say, Behold a gluttonous man, and a winebibber, a friend of publicans and sinners!
Luke 7:35 But wisdom is justified of all her children.

Paul breaks down the wisdom spoken of here. It is God's wisdom that only a child of God can speak of. Only them which are called and thank God it is for both the Jew and the Gentile.

1Corinthians 1:20 Where *is* the wise? where *is* the scribe? where *is* the disputer of this world? hath not God made foolish the wisdom of this world?

1Corinthians 1:21 For after that in the wisdom of God the world by wisdom knew not God, it pleased God by the foolishness of preaching to save them that believe.

1Corinthians 1:22 For the Jews require a sign, and the Greeks seek after wisdom:

1Corinthians 1:23 But we preach Christ crucified, unto the Jews a stumblingblock, and unto the Greeks foolishness;

1Corinthians 1:24 But unto them which are called, both Jews and Greeks, Christ the power of God, and the wisdom of God.

Only in Luke's Gospel

Unique to Luke's Gospel is this story of the woman with an alabaster box. It is unique as Luke points out that she washes the "feet" of Jesus. Later in Matthew and in Mark it speaks of a woman that anoints Jesus' head. In both situations the woman remains unknown.

Luke 7:36 And one of the Pharisees desired him that he would eat with him. And he went into the Pharisee's house, and sat down to meat.

Luke 7:37 And, behold, a woman in the city, which was a sinner, when she knew that *Jesus* sat at meat in the Pharisee's house, brought an alabaster box of ointment,

There has been much speculation as to who this woman with an alabaster box of ointment is. Many think it is Mary, the sister of Martha. Some think it is Mary Magdalene. However, God has chosen to keep her discrete.

Luke 7:38 And stood at his feet behind *him* weeping, and began to wash his feet with tears, and did wipe *them* with the hairs of her head, and kissed his feet, and anointed *them* with the ointment.

There are two times that a woman comes and pours ointment from an alabaster box upon Jesus. Here the woman washes the feet of Jesus. Later, in Bethany, just two days before the Passover meal and crucifixion of Jesus, Matthew and Mark speak of having his head anointed by another unknown woman with an alabaster box. Perhaps the same woman? Probably not as the locations are very far apart.

Matthew 26:6 Now when Jesus was in Bethany, in the house of Simon the leper,

Matthew 26:7 There came unto him a woman having an alabaster box of very precious ointment, and poured it on his head, as he sat *at meat.*

Matthew 26:8 But when his disciples saw *it,* they had indignation, saying, To what purpose *is* this waste?

Matthew 26:9 For this ointment might have been sold for much, and given to the poor.

Matthew 26:10 When Jesus understood *it,* he said unto them, Why trouble ye the woman? for she hath wrought a good work upon me.

In Matthew and Mark, at this later time, Jesus is in Bethany, near Jerusalem. Many think this woman in Matthew was Mary the sister of Martha. But that is an assumption. However, here in Luke, He is in the north near Galilee by Nain. This is not Mary Magdalene either, for Jesus does not meet her until a short time later in Luke's Gospel.

Luke 7:39 Now when the Pharisee which had bidden him saw *it,* he spake within himself, saying, This man, if he were a prophet, would have known who and what manner of woman *this is* that toucheth him: for she is a sinner.

This description points to a woman like Mary Magdalene as a sinner, a woman of the night, but it was not Mary Magdalene. Jesus has something to say to the accusers:

Luke 7:40 And Jesus answering said unto him, Simon, I have somewhat to say unto thee. And he saith, Master, say on.

Jesus will now unveil a truth to the Pharisee named Simon. This is not a parable as Jesus does not describe it as one.

Luke 7:41 There was a certain creditor which had two debtors: the one owed five hundred pence, and the other fifty.
Luke 7:42 And when they had nothing to pay, he frankly forgave them both. Tell me therefore, which of them will love him most?
Luke 7:43 Simon answered and said, I suppose that *he,* to whom he forgave most. And he said unto him, Thou hast rightly judged.

Judgement is not forgiveness. It is true that when Jesus does the forgiving, it matters not how many or how deep the sin is. What matters is what you are doing now that Christ has forgiven you? This Pharisee named Simon did little for Jesus but, as it says above, he invited Him to dinner to accuse Him. Now the woman bows at His feet and acknowledges Jesus.

Luke 7:44 And he turned to the woman, and said unto Simon, Seest thou this woman? I entered into thine house, thou gavest me no water for my feet: but she hath washed my feet with tears, and wiped *them* with the hairs of her head.

What had Simon done for Jesus? Jesus is quick to point out nothing! But this woman continually kisses the feet of Jesus.

Luke 7:45 Thou gavest me no kiss: but this woman since the time I came in hath not ceased to kiss my feet.
Luke 7:46 My head with oil thou didst not anoint: but this woman hath anointed my feet with ointment.

This is different than the woman that anointed Jesus' head which Matthew and Mark describe. That took place later at the time of Passover. Jesus does what only God can do. He forgave all her sins.

Luke 7:47 Wherefore I say unto thee, Her sins, which are many, are forgiven; for she loved much: but to whom little is forgiven, *the same* loveth little.

This woman knew she had a sin problem. She repented of that sin when she saw the Master. She knelt before him in submission and Jesus forgave her because of her belief in Him:

Luke 7:48 And he said unto her, Thy sins are forgiven.

The Pharisees realize what has just taken place. No man can forgive sins but God only.

Luke 7:49 And they that sat at meat with him began to say within themselves, Who is this that forgiveth sins also?

Here is the proof. What saved this woman that her sins could be forgiven? What saves any of us and allows Jesus to forgive our sins? It is by faith and faith alone.

Luke 7:50 And he said to the woman, Thy faith hath saved thee; go in peace.

As this chapter concludes, Jesus sums it up best in Ephesians. It is He that makes us alive (quickened) while we are yet in our sin.

Ephesians 2:1 And you *hath he quickened,* who were dead in trespasses and sins; Ephesians 2:2 Wherein in time past ye walked according to the course of this world, according to the prince of the power of the air, the spirit that now worketh in the children of disobedience:

Ephesians 2:3 Among whom also we all had our conversation in times past in the lusts of our flesh, fulfilling the desires of the flesh and of the mind; and were by nature the children of wrath, even as others.

Isn't this a great thing! "But God" who is rich, "But God" who loves us, "But God" who quickens us, that is makes us alive again.

Ephesians 2:4 But God, who is rich in mercy, for his great love wherewith he loved us,

Ephesians 2:5 Even when we were dead in sins, hath quickened us together with Christ, (by grace ye are saved;)

Ephesians 2:6 And hath raised *us* up together, and made *us* sit together in heavenly *places* in Christ Jesus:

Ephesians 2:7 That in the ages to come he might shew the exceeding riches of his grace in *his* kindness toward us through Christ Jesus.

Ephesians 2:8 For by grace are ye saved through faith; and that not of yourselves: *it is* the gift of God:

Ephesians 2:9 Not of works, lest any man should boast.

Ephesians 2:10 For we are his workmanship, created in Christ Jesus unto good works, which God hath before ordained that we should walk in them.

Again "But God" as Paul says in Romans:

Romans 5:8 But God commendeth his love toward us, in that, while we were yet sinners, Christ died for us.

LUKE CHAPTER 8

Highlights:

Chapter eight describes Jesus Christ relationship with sinners. His power over nature. His power over demons. His healing powers, and His power to raise from death.

Main Participants:

Jesus Christ v.1,
The Twelve v.1,
Mary Magdalene v.2,
Joanna v.3,
Chuza.3,
Susanna v.3,
Much People v.4,
Jesus's mother v.19,
Jesus's brothers v.19,
The man of Gadarene v.27,
Jairus v.41,
Woman with an issue of blood v.43,
One from the synagogue's house v.49,
Peter, James, John v.51,
The father (Jairus) and mother of the deceased maid v.51,
The risen maid v.54.

In Brief:

Jesus Christ's first encounter with Mary Magdalene and two other women who began to follow Him. Jesus speaks the parable of the Sower. Then the Parable of the candle raised on a candlestick. He stills the waves on the Sea of Galilee and casts demons named Legion with many other demons out of the man from Gadarenes. A woman with an issue of blood healed and Jairus's daughter raised from the dead.

Only in Luke's Gospel

Luke 8:1 And it came to pass afterward, that he went throughout every city and village, preaching and shewing the glad tidings of the kingdom of God: and the twelve *were* with him,

Jesus is preaching the glad tidings of the Kingdom of God which remember is within you. Jesus must be preaching that you need to ask God to come into your heart. Remember at this time there was no death burial and resurrection of Christ. However, you were still saved in the same manner. Like Paul says of Abraham:

Romans 4:1 What shall we say then that Abraham our father, as pertaining to the flesh, hath found?

Romans 4:2 For if Abraham were justified by works, he hath *whereof* to glory; but not before God.

Romans 4:3 For what saith the scripture? Abraham believed God, and it was counted unto him for righteousness.

Unique to Luke, Jesus calls out Mary of Magdala. This is the first mention of Mary Magdalene. Magdala is a small city on the coast of the Sea of Galilee about 3 miles north of Tiberias. Magdala was a small fishing village which meant everyone probably knew Mary and her shenanigans. Jesus heals her of demon possessions,

plural. He probably healed Joanna and Susanna of demon possession also since verse 2 and verse 3 should be read together.

Luke 8:2 And certain women, which had been healed of evil spirits and infirmities, Mary called Magdalene, out of whom went seven devils,
Luke 8:3 And Joanna the wife of Chuza Herod's steward, and Susanna, and many others, which ministered unto him of their substance.

Synoptic in Matthew, Mark, and Luke's Gospel

Luke 8:4 And when much people were gathered together, and were come to him out of every city, he spake by a parable:

Now we begin to hear the many parables that will be spoken by Jesus in the heart of His ministry as recorded by Luke. Matthew says there will be many things spoken in parables. This is a parable that Jesus may have used many times. Matthew and Mark could be writing about a different time in Christ's ministry. But the Parable, though spoken at different times is the same in all three accounts.
Matthew 13:3 And he spake many things unto them in parables, saying, Behold, a sower went forth to sow;
Mark says it in his own way:
Mark 4:2 And he taught them many things by parables, and said unto them in his doctrine,
Mark 4:3 Hearken; Behold, there went out a sower to sow:

Here is God's plan to witness, that is spread the Words of God. This is why it is synoptic in three of the four gospels. To tell everyone about the Gospel. Some will hear. When they do hear there is the power of multiplication, not addition. Multiplication to the tune of a hundred times.

Luke 8:5 A sower went out to sow his seed: and as he sowed, some fell by the way side; and it was trodden down, and the fowls of the air devoured it.

Luke 8:6 And some fell upon a rock; and as soon as it was sprung up, it withered away, because it lacked moisture.

Luke 8:7 And some fell among thorns; and the thorns sprang up with it, and choked it.

Luke 8:8 And other fell on good ground, and sprang up, and bare fruit an hundredfold. And when he had said these things, he cried, He that hath ears to hear, let him hear.

Jesus says that you must hear His method of witnessing. This becomes God's method for man to understand Christianity and what it is based upon. You must hear God's plan of salvation from the Bible and believe it. Quoting and reciting scripture is the greatest thing a man can do.

Romans 10:17 So then faith *cometh* by hearing, and hearing by the word of God.

And again, in Galatians it says:

Galatians 3:1 O foolish Galatians, who hath bewitched you, that ye should not obey the truth, before whose eyes Jesus Christ hath been evidently set forth, crucified among you?

Galatians 3:2 This only would I learn of you, Received ye the Spirit by the works of the law, or by the hearing of faith?

Jesus now explains this parable. Remember the definition of this transliterated word, *parable,* is to compare a story with another likeness, a truth. Jesus will again reaffirm His message based on hearing and understanding the mysteries of the kingdom of God which is in you.

Luke 8:9 And his disciples asked him, saying, What might this parable be?

Luke 8:10 And he said, Unto you it is given to know the mysteries of the kingdom of God: but to others in parables; that seeing they might not see, and hearing they might not understand.

Jesus says that these parables are being spoken to fulfill the prophetic word. However, without the Holy Spirit to reveal this, hearing this parable a lost person will not be able to understand this parable.

Isaiah is where this prophecy comes from according to Matthew:

> Matthew 13:13 Therefore speak I to them in parables: because they seeing see not; and hearing they hear not, neither do they understand.
>
> Matthew 13:14 And in them is fulfilled the prophecy of Esaias, which saith, By hearing ye shall hear, and shall not understand; and seeing ye shall see, and shall not perceive:

This comes from Isaiah 6:9:

> Isaiah 6:9 And he said, Go, and tell this people, Hear ye indeed, but understand not; and see ye indeed, but perceive not.

The similar likeness and truth of the parable is now described:

Luke 8:11 Now the parable is this: The seed is the word of God.

Luke 8:12 Those by the way side are they that hear; then cometh the devil, and taketh away the word out of their hearts, lest they should believe and be saved.

Today when the word is preached to little ones at Vacation Bible School or camp, or older ones at work or in church, the devil always comes and takes away what he can. He takes away any desire to know what has been said about Jesus. Let's compare this to the sport of baseball and those who follow the sport. There are those who want nothing to do with baseball, those by the wayside, unbelievers. That is those by the wayside.

Luke 8:13 They on the rock *are they,* which, when they hear, receive the word with joy; and these have no root, which for a while believe, and in time of temptation fall away.

Then there are those who have heard of Jesus. Seed that falls on the rock. These are ones who have heard of this game called baseball. They occasionally go to a game but are uninterested in the game, not a real believer.

Luke 8:14 And that which fell among thorns are they, which, when they have heard, go forth, and are choked with cares and riches and pleasures of *this* life, and bring no fruit to perfection.

Then there are those who are fans (fanatics) of the game and go often to the game and cheer and scream for a while, who discuss the game but on Monday morning it is forgotten. Work and money and cares of this world overtake their thoughts and attention.

Luke 8:15 But that on the good ground are they, which in an honest and good heart, having heard the word, keep *it,* and bring forth fruit with patience.

Here is where Christ wants His followers. Believers! Good ground! These are those who believe in the game of baseball. They bring the scoring book to every game. They know the players' names and numbers. They know their batting average and number of strikeouts. They are called "believers" in the game of baseball. This is where a believer belongs. With this last group receiving the Word of God! To understand this parable, Jesus will shed light on the work that needs to be done. All saved people must spread this word from God which has the Power of God unto salvation.

Romans 1:16 For I am not ashamed of the gospel of Christ: for it is the power of God unto salvation to every one that believeth; to the Jew first, and also to the Greek

The Gospel must be declared! What Christ did for us must be spoken. Jesus is the light of the world, and the light must shine:

Only in Luke's Gospel

This passage in Luke sounds like the passage in Matthew 5:15-16 and Mark 4:21-23. However, the words are different, and the timing is totally different. Luke never mentions a bushel as Matthew and Mark do and both are at a different location at the sermon on the mount. Luke is nowhere near that area of Galilee.

Luke 8:16 No man, when he hath lighted a candle, covereth it with a vessel, or putteth *it* under a bed; but setteth *it* on a candlestick, that they which enter in may see the light.
Luke 8:17 For nothing is secret, that shall not be made manifest; neither *any thing* hid, that shall not be known and come abroad.

A scary passage indeed for someone who will not have the kingdom of God within them. All those who truly are not saved will have even less in eternity.

Luke 8:18 Take heed therefore how ye hear: for whosoever hath, to him shall be given; and whosoever hath not, from him shall be taken even that which he seemeth to have.

This lines up with what happens directly after the rapture. When all the saved are taken off the earth. But then those which are not truly born again from God will have even the truth taken away from them:

2Thesalonians 2:10 And with all deceivableness of unrighteousness in them that perish; because they received not the love of the truth, that they might be saved.
2Thesalonians 2:11 And for this cause God shall send them strong delusion, that they should believe a lie:
2Thesalonians 2:12 That they all might be damned who believed not the truth, but had pleasure in unrighteousness.

Throughout his public ministry, Jesus was understood differently by His family:

Synoptic in Matthew, Mark, and Luke's Gospel

Though this is listed in the three gospels and called synoptic there is reason to believe that Jesus spoke this on more than one occasion. Matthew has some different statements, and he could have quoted Jesus saying this later in His public ministry. Mark says something at two different times about Christ's family looking for Him.

Luke 8:19 Then came to him *his* mother and his brethren, and could not come at him for the press.
Luke 8:20 And it was told him *by certain* which said, Thy mother and thy brethren stand without, desiring to see thee.

Mark mentions several times that those who knew Him thought Jesus to be crazy, that is mad or besides Himself:
Mark 3:21 And when his friends heard *of it,* they went out to lay hold on him: for they said, He is beside himself.
Again ten verses later in Mark:
Mark 3:31 There came then his brethren and his mother, and, standing without, sent unto him, calling him.

Luke 8:21 And he answered and said unto them, My mother and my brethren are these which hear the word of God, and do it.

To "hear" the word of God and "do" it! This is what to look for if someone says they are saved and a part of the family of God. Someone who can testify that they heard the words of salvation and who are now living for Jesus.

Luke 8:22 Now it came to pass on a certain day, that he went into a ship with his disciples: and he said unto them, Let us go over unto the other side of the lake. And they launched forth.
Luke 8:23 But as they sailed he fell asleep: and there came down a storm of wind on the lake; and they were filled *with water,* and were in jeopardy.

Luke 8:24 And they came to him, and awoke him, saying, Master, master, we perish. Then he arose, and rebuked the wind and the raging of the water: and they ceased, and there was a calm.

Luke 8:25 And he said unto them, Where is your faith? And they being afraid wondered, saying one to another, What manner of man is this! for he commandeth even the winds and water, and they obey him.

Jesus was many times on the Sea of Galilee also known as Lake Tiberias. There could have been several occasions when the disciples feared because of the tempest. However, Jesus shows His power over the things of nature. I'll take Jesus over mother nature anyday!

Matthew has a little different account of this. Matthew, Mark and Luke could all be talking about the same crossing as it appears they were. Matthew says they arrived at a different location called the country of the Gergesenes which is different than Gadarene.

Matthew 8:28 And when he was come to the other side into the country of the Gergesenes, there met him two possessed with devils, coming out of the tombs, exceeding fierce, so that no man might pass by that way.

This is because on the eastern side of the Sea of Galilee is a village called Gergasa which today called Kersa or Kursi and Gadara which was the name of the region where this village was located. These were not Israelites on this side of the Sea of Galilee as indicated by the swine being kept.

Luke 8:26 And they arrived at the country of the Gadarenes, which is over against Galilee.

Matthew also describes two men coming out of the tombs where Mark and Luke describe only one. Mark and Luke speak of only one called Legion for he obviously was the spokesperson. Matthew, who said two were there, never mentions the name Legion.

Luke 8:27 And when he went forth to land, there met him out of the city a certain man, which had devils long time, and ware no clothes, neither abode in *any* house, but in the tombs.

Luke 8:28 When he saw Jesus, he cried out, and fell down before him, and with a loud voice said, What have I to do with thee, Jesus, *thou* Son of God most high? I beseech thee, torment me not.

Luke 8:29 (For he had commanded the unclean spirit to come out of the man. For oftentimes it had caught him: and he was kept bound with chains and in fetters; and he brake the bands, and was driven of the devil into the wilderness.)

Luke 8:30 And Jesus asked him, saying, What is thy name? And he said, Legion: because many devils were entered into him.

Luke 8:31 And they besought him that he would not command them to go out into the deep.

Luke 8:32 And there was there an herd of many swine feeding on the mountain: and they besought him that he would suffer them to enter into them. And he suffered them.

Luke 8:33 Then went the devils out of the man, and entered into the swine: and the herd ran violently down a steep place into the lake, and were choked.

The word *suffer* in verse 32 means to allow or accept or tolerate in addition to suffering from pain. It is an English word that may also be used to allow someone to do something. Today, it's primarily used to describe a person where pain has set in. Here it is used as a word that means to allow or to tolerate the legion of demons to enter into the swine. Mark says there was about two thousand of the swine that jumped into the lake.

Mark 5:12 And all the devils besought him, saying, Send us into the swine, that we may enter into them.

Mark 5:13 And forthwith Jesus gave them leave. And the unclean spirits went out, and entered into the swine: and the herd ran violently down a steep place into the sea, (they were about two thousand;) and were choked in the sea.

The town's people were very scared. They did not know how to take this work of Jesus. They knew the man with the Legion

was demon possessed. Now they see this man under control and acting civilized.

Luke 8:34 When they that fed *them* saw what was done, they fled, and went and told *it* in the city and in the country.
Luke 8:35 Then they went out to see what was done; and came to Jesus, and found the man, out of whom the devils were departed, sitting at the feet of Jesus, clothed, and in his right mind: and they were afraid.
Luke 8:36 They also which saw *it* told them by what means he that was possessed of the devils was healed.
Luke 8:37 Then the whole multitude of the country of the Gadarenes round about besought him to depart from them; for they were taken with great fear: and he went up into the ship, and returned back again.

This man from the tomb of the Gadarenes knew who he was dealing with. He wanted to stay with Jesus. Jesus declared directly to the man that "God" had loosed the devils. This reveals again that Jesus is God as declared by the demons earlier in verse 28.

Luke 8:38 Now the man out of whom the devils were departed besought him that he might be with him: but Jesus sent him away, saying,
Luke 8:39 Return to thine own house, and shew how great things God hath done unto thee. And he went his way, and published throughout the whole city how great things Jesus had done unto him.

It was God who had done great things! Jesus said to go and show what great things "God" has done? I thought Jesus did these great things. The man went away and said what great things Jesus had done. This can only mean that Jesus right here declares that He is God! Mark says the healed man was to say, "how great things the Lord hath done for thee", making Jesus Christ both God and Lord.

Mark 5:19 Howbeit Jesus suffered him not, but saith unto him, Go home to thy friends, and tell them how great things the Lord hath done for thee, and hath had compassion on thee.

133

Luke 8:40 And it came to pass, that, when Jesus was returned, the people *gladly* received him: for they were all waiting for him.

Synoptic in Matthew, Mark, and Luke's Gospel

Again, Jesus will bring someone back from the dead. This time it is Jairus' daughter. This can be found in Matthew and Mark also.

Luke 8:41 And, behold, there came a man named Jairus, and he was a ruler of the synagogue: and he fell down at Jesus' feet, and besought him that he would come into his house:
Luke 8:42 For he had one only daughter, about twelve years of age, and she lay a dying. But as he went the people thronged him.

However, before Jesus gets to Jairus' house He has an encounter with another woman:

Luke 8:43 And a woman having an issue of blood twelve years, which had spent all her living upon physicians, neither could be healed of any,
Luke 8:44 Came behind *him,* and touched the border of his garment: and immediately her issue of blood stanched.

All she did was touch the clothes Jesus was wearing. Immediately the blood issue she was having stopped.

Luke 8:45 And Jesus said, Who touched me? When all denied, Peter and they that were with him said, Master, the multitude throng thee and press *thee,* and sayest thou, Who touched me?

Now Jesus being God knew all along who had touched Him. Matthew leaves no doubt that Jesus knew this woman:
Matthew 9:20 And, behold, a woman, which was diseased with an issue of blood twelve years, came behind *him,* and touched the hem of his garment:

A PERFECT UNDERSTANDING
LUKE CHAPTER 8

Matthew 9:21 For she said within herself, If I may but touch his garment, I shall be whole.

Matthew 9:22 But Jesus turned him about, and when he saw her, he said, Daughter, be of good comfort; thy faith hath made thee whole. And the woman was made whole from that hour.

But Jesus says something here that is not recorded in Matthew. In Mark and Luke Jesus says somebody touched me! Jesus knew who had touched Him for He is God and God is omniscient; that is all knowing. Jesus will prove once again that He is God by His omniscience. However, He wanted His disciples to observe this and so He draws attention to the woman. He also wants to show the faith of this unnamed woman by having her own up to what she has done, that is putting her faith and trust in just touching any part of the Savior. Jesus will use any instrument in the world to bring someone to a saving knowledge of Him. But God will always require you to reach out to Him by faith as this woman did.

Luke 8:46 And Jesus said, Somebody hath touched me: for I perceive that virtue is gone out of me.

Mark has recorded it this way.

Mark 5:30 And Jesus, immediately knowing in himself that virtue had gone out of him, turned him about in the press, and said, Who touched my clothes?

She was unclean according to Jewish law and according to what the scriptures say.

Luke 8:47 And when the woman saw that she was not hid, she came trembling, and falling down before him, she declared unto him before all the people for what cause she had touched him, and how she was healed immediately.

Luke 8:48 And he said unto her, Daughter, be of good comfort: thy faith hath made thee whole; go in peace.

This woman who knew she was unclean will be comforted by Jesus. He comforts her by calling her "Daughter" just as Jesus

called the man who was sick of the palsy "Son". To the Jew these terms are heartwarming and endearing.

Back to Jairus now and Jesus overhears that the daughter is dead.

Luke 8:49 While he yet spake, there cometh one from the ruler of the synagogue's *house,* saying to him, Thy daughter is dead; trouble not the Master.
Luke 8:50 But when Jesus heard *it,* he answered him, saying, Fear not: believe only, and she shall be made whole.

Jesus again puts His reputation on the line and takes His inner core of the three disciples and says the daughter sleeps.

Luke 8:51 And when he came into the house, he suffered no man to go in, save Peter, and James, and John, and the father and the mother of the maiden.
Luke 8:52 And all wept, and bewailed her: but he said, Weep not; she is not dead, but sleepeth.

The world laughs at Jesus and most of His words. The world says, "I would rather laugh with the sinners than cry with the saints." The world thinks it knows better.

Luke 8:53 And they laughed him to scorn, knowing that she was dead.

But when Jesus is about to deal with the soul of a person, He puts everything aside and focuses on that soul only.

Luke 8:54 And he put them all out, and took her by the hand, and called, saying, Maid, arise.
Luke 8:55 And her spirit came again, and she arose straightway: and he commanded to give her meat.
Luke 8:56 And her parents were astonished: but he charged them that they should tell no man what was done.

All would soon know that the daughter was healed. Yet perhaps Jesus did not want anyone to know "how" He healed the

twelve-year-old daughter. Perhaps Jesus knew that the people would hold Him up as king and this was not His time to be king. Perhaps Jesus wanted to work on the minds of those who laughed Him to scorn and make them humble. Paul has said this about the mind of Jesus:

Philippians 2:5 Let this mind be in you, which was also in Christ Jesus:

Philippians 2:6 Who, being in the form of God, thought it not robbery to be equal with God:

Philippians 2:7 But made himself of no reputation, and took upon him the form of a servant, and was made in the likeness of men:

Philippians 2:8 And being found in fashion as a man, he humbled himself, and became obedient unto death, even the death of the cross.

Philippians 2:9 Wherefore God also hath highly exalted him, and given him a name which is above every name:

Philippians 2:10 That at the name of Jesus every knee should bow, of *things* in heaven, and *things* in earth, and *things* under the earth;

Philippians 2:11 And *that* every tongue should confess that Jesus Christ *is* Lord, to the glory of God the Father.

In any event Jesus was fully in control during Luke's time and two thousand years later, He is still fully in control. To understand what Jesus is accomplishing at this time you need a complete understanding of Him based on all the Gospels. All the Gospels are now pointing to Jesus Christ's compassion for the lost and the hurting. Miracle upon miracle being worked for the convincing of man that this is truly God come down in the flesh.

Have you trusted Jesus Christ as your Lord? It is a simple thing to do. And yet souls come hard to Jesus. But just like Jairus's daughter, Jesus will put all else aside to deal with your heart as He does with all who will be saved.

LUKE CHAPTER 9

Highlights:

Chapter Nine describes Jesus Christ's relationship with His disciples. Jesus foretells of His death, burial, and resurrection. His Transfiguration takes place. His final departure from Galilee.

Main Participants:

Jesus Christ v.1,
the twelve disciples v.1,
Herod v.7,
The people v.11,
Peter v.20,
John and James v.28,
Father of possessed child v.38,
The possessed child v.42,
Certain man who would follow Jesus v.57,
another man who wanted to follow but delayed to bid farewell v.61.

In Brief:

Jesus asks the disciples who they think Jesus is. He gives the twelve disciples power and authority over all devils. He sends the twelve to preach the kingdom of God. Herod hears of this and desires to see Jesus. Jesus will not see Herod at this time. Jesus feeds the five thousand. Jesus hears the confession of Peter as to whom he thinks Jesus is. Jesus foretells His death, and no one

A PERFECT UNDERSTANDING
FRED A. KUYPERS

understands this. He transfigures Himself into His glorified body with His inner three core friends watching. He rebukes the disciples for their unbelief and challenges the disciples with testing to prove that they really did set Christ first in their lives.

Only in Mark and Luke's Gospel

Luke 9:1 Then he called his twelve disciples together, and gave them power and authority over all devils, and to cure diseases.

He gave them power over all devils. This is a firm indication that there are many devils and perhaps different kinds of devils. This was a miracle that Jesus had been performing and most times people had no idea how to accept this. They were afraid in many instances.

Curing diseases was something Jesus was also doing. The people could understand this. Most times they looked at it as entertainment. And now the apostles were given the power to do this also.

Luke had listed the twelve back in chapter 6 and Matthew lists the twelve also in His Gospel:
Matthew 10:2 Now the names of the twelve apostles are these; The first, Simon, who is called Peter, and Andrew his brother; James *the son* of Zebedee, and John his brother;
Matthew 10:3 Philip, and Bartholomew; Thomas, and Matthew the publican; James *the son* of Alphaeus, and Lebbaeus, whose surname was Thaddaeus;
Matthew 10:4 Simon the Canaanite, and Judas Iscariot, who also betrayed him.
The apostles were to preach the "kingdom of God". At this time, verse six below, says that they were to preach the gospel. What gospel? The "kingdom of God" is the only "gospel" at this time!

140

Luke 9:2 And he sent them to preach the kingdom of God, and to heal the sick.

Did the apostles have special gifts to heal the sick? Where they able to do things that were chosen especially for them? There is some scripture to back this up:

2Corinthians 12:11 I am become a fool in glorying; ye have compelled me: for I ought to have been commended of you: for in nothing am I behind the very chiefest apostles, though I be nothing.

2Corinthians 12:12 Truly the signs of an apostle were wrought among you in all patience, in signs, and wonders, and mighty deeds.

Paul certainly indicated this. He included himself as the apostle born out of due time.

1Corinthians 15:7 After that, he was seen of James; then of all the apostles.

1Corinthians 15:8 And last of all he was seen of me also, as of one born out of due time.

The apostles were given instruction to totally depend on God for their sustenance.

Luke 9:3 And he said unto them, Take nothing for *your* journey, neither staves, nor scrip, neither bread, neither money; neither have two coats apiece.

Luke 9:4 And whatsoever house ye enter into, there abide, and thence depart.

Luke 9:5 And whosoever will not receive you, when ye go out of that city, shake off the very dust from your feet for a testimony against them.

The synoptic gospels all say the same here. God does not repeat this in all three of the synoptic gospels just for repetitions sake. He is emphasizing that many have rejected the Gospel already in their heart and we are to move on with our witnessing.

Luke 9:6 And they departed, and went through the towns, preaching the gospel, and healing every where.

Is repentance a part of the gospel? Many think repentance is a work. However, God makes repentance a part of the Gospel right here! Right now! Mark makes this clear. What were the apostles supposed to preach according to Luke in the above verse? The gospel! But Mark says they preached repentance. Repentance must be a part of the gospel.

Mark 6:11 And whosoever shall not receive you, nor hear you, when ye depart thence, shake off the dust under your feet for a testimony against them. Verily I say unto you, It shall be more tolerable for Sodom and Gomorrha in the day of judgment, than for that city.

Mark 6:12 And they went out, and preached that men should repent.

Mark 6:13 And they cast out many devils, and anointed with oil many that were sick, and healed *them.*

Men were to repent! Luke says preach the gospel. Mark says preach repentance. Keep in mind at this time the death burial and resurrection of Christ was unknown and unheard of. The Gospel currently is to repent as Mark points out and to follow that up with a belief in the kingdom of God. A belief that God will do the healing, casting out etc. and the saving! Remember the "kingdom of God" is within you. You must have Christ within.

Herod is now worried about another instigator. At this point, Luke writes and reveals that John the Baptist has already been beheaded. And Herod can't figure out what is happening and why the crowds are following Jesus.

Luke 9:7 Now Herod the tetrarch heard of all that was done by him: and he was perplexed, because that it was said of some, that John was risen from the dead;

Luke 9:8 And of some, that Elias had appeared; and of others, that one of the old prophets was risen again.

Luke 9:9 And Herod said, John have I beheaded: but who is this, of whom I hear such things? And he desired to see him.

Matthew chapter 14 and Mark chapter 6 both expound on the story of the death of John the Baptist and how it occurred, but Luke does not. Harod has such a desire to see Jesus, however, it will not happen at this time. Jesus, knowing it was not His time to be offered up will not allow Herod at this time to interrogate Him.

Luke 9:10 And the apostles, when they were returned, told him all that they had done. And he took them, and went aside privately into a desert place belonging to the city called Bethsaida.

Bethsaida is due north of the Sea of Galilee. Philip, Peter, and Andrew were born there.

John 1:44 Now Philip was of Bethsaida, the city of Andrew and Peter.

Bethsaida is also known as a city where Christ worked many signs and wonders; and this city was given a warning by Jesus which will be heard in the next chapter of Luke and was also quoted in Matthew:

Matthew 11:21 Woe unto thee, Chorazin! woe unto thee, Bethsaida! for if the mighty works, which were done in you, had been done in Tyre and Sidon, they would have repented long ago in sackcloth and ashes.

Here also we see the importance of repentance as Jesus points out. Gentile cities could repent and come to believe in the saving Knowledge of Christ. We know now that the Gospel did go out to Gentile cities and today, it is commanded to preach this to all who will hear.

Luke 9:11 And the people, when they knew *it,* followed him: and he received them, and spake unto them of the kingdom of God, and healed them that had need of healing.

Jesus preached the "kingdom of God". This was the Gospel message that was revealed at this time. The kingdom of God was

not tangible. **The kingdom of God was nothing that could be handled or worked on. Jesus said the kingdom of God is not by observation:**

Luke 17:20 And when he was demanded of the Pharisees, when the kingdom of God should come, he answered them and said, The kingdom of God cometh not with observation:

Luke 17:21 Neither shall they say, Lo here! or, lo there! for, behold, the kingdom of God is within you.

The death burial and resurrection of Christ had not taken place yet. And when Jesus would begin to reveal this fact that He would have to go to the cross and die, His closest apostles did not understand. Mark reveals this very clearly:

Mark 9:31 For he taught his disciples, and said unto them, The Son of man is delivered into the hands of men, and they shall kill him; and after that he is killed, he shall rise the third day.

Mark 9:32 But they understood not that saying, and were afraid to ask him.

The Gospel has never changed. What we are to believe about God is that He will provide the way of salvation. Prior to the cross the need was to believe that God would provide a way. After the cross the need is that God HAS provided the way! The most important part for a man to do is believe this. If a man stops at repentance without believing he will die without Christ and go to hell. This is before the cross and after the cross.

Synoptic in Matthew, Mark, Luke, and John's Gospel

In all four gospels there is the feeding of five thousand. All five thousand are fed and again the number twelve comes into play as Jesus Christ has come full circle by providing for five thousand and having twelve baskets left over.

Luke 9:12 And when the day began to wear away, then came the twelve, and said unto him, Send the multitude away, that they may go into the towns and country round about, and lodge, and get victuals: for we are here in a desert place.

Luke 9:13 But he said unto them, Give ye them to eat. And they said, We have no more but five loaves and two fishes; except we should go and buy meat for all this people.

Luke 9:14 For they were about five thousand men. And he said to his disciples, Make them sit down by fifties in a company.

Luke 9:15 And they did so, and made them all sit down.

Luke 9:16 Then he took the five loaves and the two fishes, and looking up to heaven, he blessed them, and brake, and gave to the disciples to set before the multitude.

Luke 9:17 And they did eat, and were all filled: and there was taken up of fragments that remained to them twelve baskets.

Later Matthew and Mark will explain the feeding of four thousand. Luke will write nothing about the four thousand.

Synoptic in Matthew, Mark, and Luke's Gospel

Luke 9:18 And it came to pass, as he was alone praying, his disciples were with him: and he asked them, saying, Whom say the people that I am?

Luke 9:19 They answering said, John the Baptist; but some *say,* Elias; and others *say,* that one of the old prophets is risen again.

Matthew lists some of the prophets that men were saying came back as this Jesus:
Matthew 16:14 And they said, Some *say that thou art* John the Baptist: some, Elias; and others, Jeremias, or one of the prophets.
Mark is very clear about this:
Mark 8:27 And Jesus went out, and his disciples, into the towns of Caesarea Philippi: and by the way he asked his disciples, saying unto them, Whom do men say that I am?

Mark 8:28 And they answered, John the Baptist: but some *say,* Elias; and others, One of the prophets.

Mark 8:29 And he saith unto them, But whom say ye that I am? And Peter answereth and saith unto him, Thou art the Christ.

The three gospels reveal that many people had a wrong view of Jesus Christ. So, Jesus put it to His disciples straightforward:

Luke 9:20 He said unto them, But whom say ye that I am? Peter answering said, The Christ of God.

Peter's answer was correct. Jesus commends Peter very much in Matthew which is the only Gospel to speak of this blessing:

Matthew 16:17 And Jesus answered and said unto him, Blessed art thou, Simon Barjona: for flesh and blood hath not revealed *it* unto thee, but my Father which is in heaven.

Peter's response reveals that the kingdom of God is within him. Jesus says that the Father revealed this unto him. Nothing on the outside that man could see. No good work, no continuing prayer, no ascetic or self-inflicted punishment revealed the answer to Peter. But the kingdom of God which must be within you.

Matthew and Mark are the only gospels that speak of Peter's great outburst that the death, burial, and resurrection should not happen!

Peter stop!

This must take place for my sins! The death, burial, and resurrection are why Jesus came. Jesus rebuked Satan by speaking directly to Peter who was being controlled by Satan at this moment:

Matthew 16:20 Then charged he his disciples that they should tell no man that he was Jesus the Christ.

Matthew 16:21 From that time forth began Jesus to shew unto his disciples, how that he must go unto Jerusalem, and suffer many things of the elders and chief priests and scribes, and be killed, and be raised again the third day.

Matthew 16:22 Then Peter took him, and began to rebuke him, saying, Be it far from thee, Lord: this shall not be unto thee.

Notice that Mark describes the death and burial to be more than three days by saying "after three days" He shall rise again.

Mark 8:31 And he began to teach them, that the Son of man must suffer many things, and be rejected of the elders, and *of* the chief priests, and scribes, and be killed, and after three days rise again. Mark 8:32 And he spake that saying openly. And Peter took him, and began to rebuke him.

In the Gospels of Matthew and Mark, Jesus condemns Satan, Luke mentions it not.

Matthew:

Matthew 16:23 But he turned, and said unto Peter, Get thee behind me, Satan: thou art an offence unto me: for thou savourest not the things that be of God, but those that be of men.

Mark:

Mark 8:33 But when he had turned about and looked on his disciples, he rebuked Peter, saying, Get thee behind me, Satan: for thou savourest not the things that be of God, but the things that be of men.

However, Luke mentions nothing about Peter and Satan as Matthew and Mark say that Peter was possessed by Satan himself. Luke was silent about what took place with Peter and Satan. Perhaps because Luke gives a firsthand account and was not an eyewitness to this event.

Luke 9:21 And he straitly charged them, and commanded *them* to tell no man that thing;

Why would Jesus immediately charge the disciples to tell no man that He was the Christ? Because the time was not at hand for the "Christ" to become the suffering "Messiah" who was predicted by so many of the prophets in the Old Testament. However, shortly after the death burial and resurrection of Jesus Christ it would be known. Later, Luke will bring this up when he writes his account of the Acts of the Apostles.

Acts 8:30 And Philip ran thither to *him,* and heard him read the prophet Esaias, and said, Understandest thou what thou readest?

Acts 8:31 And he said, How can I, except some man should guide me? And he desired Philip that he would come up and sit with him.

Acts 8:32 The place of the scripture which he read was this, He was led as a sheep to the slaughter; and like a lamb dumb before his shearer, so opened he not his mouth:

Acts 8:33 In his humiliation his judgment was taken away: and who shall declare his generation? for his life is taken from the earth.

Luke explains this passage from Isaiah to an unsaved person, namely the Ethiopian eunuch, what Jesus Christ went through.

Isaiah 53:7 He was oppressed, and he was afflicted, yet he opened not his mouth: he is brought as a lamb to the slaughter, and as a sheep before her shearers is dumb, so he openeth not his mouth.

Isaiah 53:8 He was taken from prison and from judgment: and who shall declare his generation? for he was cut off out of the land of the living: for the transgression of my people was he stricken.

Luke will now describe the Gospel that will take place upon Christ's death burial and resurrection: and the start of the "church" that Jesus spoke of in Matthew.

Matthew 16:18 And I say also unto thee, That thou art Peter, and upon this rock I will build my church; and the gates of hell shall not prevail against it.

Matthew 16:19 And I will give unto thee the keys of the kingdom of heaven: and whatsoever thou shalt bind on earth shall be bound in heaven: and whatsoever thou shalt loose on earth shall be loosed in heaven.

Luke 9:22 Saying, The Son of man must suffer many things, and be rejected of the elders and chief priests and scribes, and be slain, and be raised the third day.

This start of the "church" that Jesus addressed to Peter being the statement that Jesus is the Christ, that is the Anointed one, the Promised one is also in Mark.

Mark 8:29 And he saith unto them, But whom say ye that I am? And Peter answereth and saith unto him, Thou art the Christ.

Mark concurs that Jesus said to tell no one that He is the anointed one, the Christ.

Mark 8:30 And he charged them that they should tell no man of him.

Mark writes that they were taught about the sufferings of Christ. And that He would be killed. And that after three days He would rise again.

Mark 8:31 And he began to teach them, that the Son of man must suffer many things, and be rejected of the elders, and *of* the chief priests, and scribes, and be killed, and after three days rise again.

At this point Jesus speaks of what it means to be a follower of Christ. He knew that the disciples could not comprehend what He was about to tell them. Peter shows that Christ's mission on earth is totally misunderstood, by Peter and the disciples with this rebuke:

Mark 8:32 And he spake that saying openly. And Peter took him, and began to rebuke him.

Jesus was compelled as described in Matthew and Mark to call out the one who was more against the death burial and resurrection than anyone else, Satan himself. It must be understood that Satan did all he could to stop the cross for he knew what would be accomplished there!

Matthew 16:22 Then Peter took him, and began to rebuke him, saying, Be it far from thee, Lord: this shall not be unto thee.

Matthew 16:23 But he turned, and said unto Peter, Get thee behind me, Satan: thou art an offence unto me: for thou savourest not the things that be of God, but those that be of men.

Jesus gives us understanding on how to recognize someone who is truly surrendered and has bowed the knee to Christ:

Luke 9:23 And he said to *them* all, If any *man* will come after me, let him deny himself, and take up his cross daily, and follow me.

Luke 9:24 For whosoever will save his life shall lose it: but whosoever will lose his life for my sake, the same shall save it.

Luke 9:25 For what is a man advantaged, if he gain the whole world, and lose himself, or be cast away?

You cannot witness for Jesus if you are ashamed of Him.

Luke 9:26 For whosoever shall be ashamed of me and of my words, of him shall the Son of man be ashamed, when he shall come in his own glory, and *in his* Father's, and of the holy angels.

Mark speaks the same of being ashamed:
> Mark 8:38 Whosoever therefore shall be ashamed of me and of my words in this adulterous and sinful generation; of him also shall the Son of man be ashamed, when he cometh in the glory of his Father with the holy angels.

Every Christian will bend the knee as Isaiah says:
> Isaiah 45:22 Look unto me, and be ye saved, all the ends of the earth: for I *am* God, and *there is* none else.
> Isaiah 45:23 I have sworn by myself, the word is gone out of my mouth *in* righteousness, and shall not return, That unto me every knee shall bow, every tongue shall swear.
> Isaiah 45:24 Surely, shall *one* say, in the LORD have I righteousness and strength: *even* to him shall *men* come; and all that are incensed against him shall be ashamed.

And every Christian will want to say:
> Romans 1:16 For I am not ashamed of the gospel of Christ: for it is the power of God unto salvation to every one that believeth; to the Jew first, and also to the Greek.

Synoptic in Matthew, Mark, and Luke's Gospel

Jesus makes a strange statement at this point. He shouts so that some in ear shot of Him would hear and would not die without seeing the kingdom of God. Something was about to happen that

would present someone or something that was already a part of the kingdom of God. Some would receive this.

Luke 9:27 But I tell you of a truth, there be some standing here, which shall not taste of death, till they see the kingdom of God.

Just eight days later, the transfiguration of Christ to Peter, James and John is about to take place. These three are about to see Jesus Christ in His kingdom glory.

Luke 9:28 And it came to pass about an eight days after these sayings, he took Peter and John and James, and went up into a mountain to pray.
Luke 9:29 And as he prayed, the fashion of his countenance was altered, and his raiment *was* white *and* glistering.
Luke 9:30 And, behold, there talked with him two men, which were Moses and Elias:

Matthew and Mark say six days later. This only tells us that Jesus, day by day was continually letting His disciples know that an event of great magnitude was about to take place. The three were about to have a glimpse of the kingdom of God.
Matthew:
> Matthew 17:1 And after six days Jesus taketh Peter, James, and John his brother, and bringeth them up into an high mountain apart,

Mark:
> Mark 9:2 And after six days Jesus taketh *with him* Peter, and James, and John, and leadeth them up into an high mountain apart by themselves: and he was transfigured before them.

Jesus Christ appears with two witnesses from the Old Testament. How did the three disciples recognize Moses and Elias? How could they know that it was these two men whom everyone knew went on to be in the kingdom of God? Moses and Elias speak of the death burial and resurrection of Jesus Christ which was about to take place in Jerusalem. The three were sound

asleep when this information was given. Shortly Jesus will repeat His planned crucifixion, and they would "perceive it not."

Luke 9:31 Who appeared in glory, and spake of his decease which he should accomplish at Jerusalem.

Luke is the only writer who tells us Moses and Elias spoke to the three who in reality were heavy with sleep. Heavy with sleep?? What's wrong with this picture!

Luke 9:32 But Peter and they that were with him were heavy with sleep: and when they were awake, they saw his glory, and the two men that stood with him.

But the three awoke and saw the glory of the kingdom of God with the two men standing beside Jesus. Peter, being always the boisterous one spoke up.

Luke 9:33 And it came to pass, as they departed from him, Peter said unto Jesus, Master, it is good for us to be here: and let us make three tabernacles; one for thee, and one for Moses, and one for Elias: not knowing what he said.

Peter again bursts out and certainly not thinking it through wants to worship Moses and Elias. When the time comes to look for direction in anything in life we should always turn to God's "voice" from heaven. That is, God's words that have already been spoken; the Holy Bible.

Luke 9:34 While he thus spake, there came a cloud, and overshadowed them: and they feared as they entered into the cloud.
Luke 9:35 And there came a voice out of the cloud, saying, This is my beloved Son: hear him.

Once the voice of God ended Moses and Elias were gone. The cloud was gone. The glorious white apparel was gone. The glorious, transfigured Christ was back to looking like a normal man.

Luke 9:36 And when the voice was past, Jesus was found alone. And they kept *it* close, and told no man in those days any of those things which they had seen.

The three literally blew it and missed the explanation of the death burial and resurrection of Jesus. They missed the Gospel by so much that Mark tells us Jesus spoke on the way down from the mountain and the three knew not the meaning of the gospel.

Mark 9:9 And as they came down from the mountain, he charged them that they should tell no man what things they had seen, till the Son of man were risen from the dead.

Mark 9:10 And they kept that saying with themselves, questioning one with another what the rising from the dead should mean.

They questioned one with another. They had no idea what Jesus was talking about. This is after having spent the entire night on the mountain having Jesus all to themselves as Luke says. Matthew takes this event to an even deeper level. Aside from Jesus explaining the death, burial, and resurrection, He reveals another Old Testament prophecy that has been fulfilled:

Matthew 17:9 And as they came down from the mountain, Jesus charged them, saying, Tell the vision to no man, until the Son of man be risen again from the dead.

Matthew 17:10 And his disciples asked him, saying, Why then say the scribes that Elias must first come?

Matthew 17:11 And Jesus answered and said unto them, Elias truly shall first come, and restore all things.

Matthew 17:12 But I say unto you, That Elias is come already, and they knew him not, but have done unto him whatsoever they listed. Likewise shall also the Son of man suffer of them.

Matthew 17:13 Then the disciples understood that he spake unto them of John the Baptist.

Elijah must truly first come! Jesus now reveals another mystery to these three. The Old Testament has a specific prophecy in Malachi about Elijah declaring:

Malachi 4:5 Behold, I will send you Elijah the prophet before the coming of the great and dreadful day of the LORD:

Once this prophecy is revealed to the three by Jesus, it is now revealed and well known throughout the bible comprehending world. The secret of Elijah coming first has been revealed:

Deuteronomy 29:29 The secret *things belong* unto the LORD our God: but those *things which are* revealed *belong* unto us and to our children for ever, that *we* may do all the words of this law.

Peter had understanding. He was no dummy. God is so wise and good to His children. He will always honor His words as He does here with these three giving them the truth that Elijah came, and it was John the Baptist. This they understood.

Can you imagine this night that the three spent with Jesus? All alone with the Master. What a night this should have been! Matthew and Mark say nothing about this night, but Luke makes it known that Peter James and John spent the night with Jesus after seeing Moses and Elijah, the two witnesses at the transfiguration.

Luke 9:37 And it came to pass, that on the next day, when they were come down from the hill, much people met him.

Jesus is again in demand to work miracles and healing:

Luke 9:38 And, behold, a man of the company cried out, saying, Master, I beseech thee, look upon my son: for he is mine only child.
Luke 9:39 And, lo, a spirit taketh him, and he suddenly crieth out; and it teareth him that he foameth again, and bruising him hardly departeth from him.
Luke 9:40 And I besought thy disciples to cast him out; and they could not.

The disciples were powerless as before.

Luke 9:41 And Jesus answering said, O faithless and perverse generation, how long shall I be with you, and suffer you? Bring thy son hither.
Luke 9:42 And as he was yet a coming, the devil threw him down, and tare *him.* And Jesus rebuked the unclean spirit, and healed the child, and delivered him again to his father.

The disciples could not do what only Jesus could do. Why? Because of their unbelief! Matthew gives us the reason of the powerless disciples:

Matthew 17:19 Then came the disciples to Jesus apart, and said, Why could not we cast him out?

Several times Jesus uses a mustard seed as a metaphor. This is one of the times in Matthew a mustard seed is used. Metaphors are good. They get us thinking!

Matthew 17:20 And Jesus said unto them, Because of your unbelief: for verily I say unto you, If ye have faith as a grain of mustard seed, ye shall say unto this mountain, Remove hence to yonder place; and it shall remove; and nothing shall be impossible unto you.

This is true today. No one can cast out demons or heal the sick or cause miracles to happen except by faith in and by using the name of Jesus Christ. The apostles knew it even after the gift of the Holy Ghost was given:

Acts 3:6 Then Peter said, Silver and gold have I none; but such as I have give I thee: In the name of Jesus Christ of Nazareth rise up and walk.

We also are amazed at the mighty power of God. Jesus is called God right here:

Luke 9:43 And they were all amazed at the mighty power of God. But while they wondered every one at all things which Jesus did, he said unto his disciples,

Luke 9:44 Let these sayings sink down into your ears: for the Son of man shall be delivered into the hands of men.

Once again Jesus will now tell the disciples of why He came to this earth. He calls Himself here the Son of Man. The Son of man appears 198 times in the bible. 108 times in the Old Testament. Moses once, and Job, David and the four major prophets with Ezekiel saying it the most. None of the minor prophets use the phrase at all. In the New Testament, after the Gospels it is used

twice in Revelation and once in Acts and Hebrews. But it is a well-known description of the one who is coming in the name of God:

Luke 9:45 But they understood not this saying, and it was hid from them, that they perceived it not: and they feared to ask him of that saying.
Luke 9:46 Then there arose a reasoning among them, which of them should be greatest.

Again, the disciples could not grasp how Jesus was describing His death. The disciples were just regular guys. They thought and acted just like today when a group of guys get together. Who's the best at Basketball? Who's the best at Jeopardy? I can eat more hot dogs than you can! The notion that the apostles were created better than any other Christian by God is wrong. Once the gift of the Holy Spirit was given the reader will never hear this kind of argument come out of an Apostle. What you will hear is the argument for all to be saved by grace by the name of the Lord Jesus Christ. So Jesus sets the disciples in their place. They would not even answer the Lord they felt so childish. (Mark 9: 33-37)

Luke 9:47 And Jesus, perceiving the thought of their heart, took a child, and set him by him,
Luke 9:48 And said unto them, Whosoever shall receive this child in my name receiveth me: and whosoever shall receive me receiveth him that sent me: for he that is least among you all, the same shall be great.

It is said that there is nothing more innocent and truer than the faith of a child. When a child is ready to follow the leading of mom or dad and simply believe what he has been told it is ultra-important at that time that the truth is presented to him. Mom and dad, always speak the truth of the Gospel to that little one. Matthew 18:1-6 says God will be watching. Those who offend one of His little ones who believe in Christ, it is better for them to have a millstone around his neck and drown. (Mark 9:42 also has the message of the millstone.)

Only in Mark and Luke's Gospel

Luke 9:49 And John answered and said, Master, we saw one casting out devils in thy name; and we forbad him, because he followeth not with us.
Luke 9:50 And Jesus said unto him, Forbid *him* not: for he that is not against us is for us.

Mark says the same about what Christ said but the words are slightly different.
> Mark 9:38 And John answered him, saying, Master, we saw one casting out devils in thy name, and he followeth not us: and we forbad him, because he followeth not us.
> Mark 9:39 But Jesus said, Forbid him not: for there is no man which shall do a miracle in my name, that can lightly speak evil of me.
> Mark 9:40 For he that is not against us is on our part.

Baptists never think like this at all?? It is easy to think that we have a corner on the gospel. Can there be saved Catholics? Of course! However, those who follow a faith that lowers Christ in favor of anyone or anything else means they are against us.

Only in Luke's Gospel

The last trip in Christ's three-year public ministry is about to take place. He is to go from Galilee to Judea. The offering of His body up to God will take place with this last trip to Jerusalem.

Luke 9:51 And it came to pass, when the time was come that he should be received up, he stedfastly set his face to go to Jerusalem,
Luke 9:52 And sent messengers before his face: and they went, and entered into a village of the Samaritans, to make ready for him.
Luke 9:53 And they did not receive him, because his face was as though he would go to Jerusalem.

The rift between a Jew and a Samaritan was especially strong. Racism was rampant at the time of Christ. And the Jews would usually have nothing to do with a Samaritan. However, the journey south to Judea from Galilee took the disciples right through the heart of Samaria. And as much as they hated it they would have to ask the Samaritans for victuals. Look at how immature the disciples were with this power of God they thought they had!

Luke 9:54 And when his disciples James and John saw *this,* they said, Lord, wilt thou that we command fire to come down from heaven, and consume them, even as Elias did?

It is so good that we have a God who will rebuke His child. The important thing here is to know whether you are a child of God or not.

Luke 9:55 But he turned, and rebuked them, and said, Ye know not what manner of spirit ye are of.
Luke 9:56 For the Son of man is not come to destroy men's lives, but to save *them.* And they went to another village.

Only in Matthew and Luke's Gospel

How far are you as a child of God willing to go to follow the Lord Jesus Christ? Here is Christ's response to that question.

Luke 9:57 And it came to pass, that, as they went in the way, a certain *man* said unto him, Lord, I will follow thee whithersoever thou goest.
Luke 9:58 And Jesus said unto him, Foxes have holes, and birds of the air *have* nests; but the Son of man hath not where to lay *his* head.
Luke 9:59 And he said unto another, Follow me. But he said, Lord, suffer me first to go and bury my father.
Luke 9:60 Jesus said unto him, Let the dead bury their dead: but go thou and preach the kingdom of God.

Luke 9:61 And another also said, Lord, I will follow thee; but let me first go bid them farewell, which are at home at my house.
Luke 9:62 And Jesus said unto him, No man, having put his hand to the plough, and looking back, is fit for the kingdom of God.

As a child of God, your statement that you are about to enter a life of following Christ, there should be nothing that you can put before Him. When Jesus says come and follow me, family and possessions and relationships are now secondary to Him. It is time! Put your hand to the plow! Don't look back. We need to be fit for the kingdom of God!

LUKE CHAPTER 10

Highlights:

Chapter ten describes Jesus Christ sending His disciples into the cities. Jesus talks about the good Samaritan. Jesus meets Mary and Martha.

Main Participants:

Jesus Christ v.1,
The seventy v.1,
A certain lawyer v.25,
Martha v.38,
Mary, Martha's sister v.39.

In Brief:

Jesus Christ gives the twelve disciples power and authority over all devils. He sends the twelve to preach the kingdom of God. The famous Good Samaritan passage is preached, and the lawyer is given clear instruction on who his neighbor is. Jesus meets Martha and Mary who are sisters to Lazarus and shows a huge difference between the two.

Only in Matthew and Luke's Gospel

These instructions are given to those who are willing to following Christ.

Luke 10:1 After these things the Lord appointed other seventy also, and sent them two and two before his face into every city and place, whither he himself would come.

Going out two by two, that is to every place in every city is a principal way of reaching the lost for Christ. Remember that we also are sent. Not to stay home. The great commission to everyone is to "go" and teach all things about Christ in Matthew.

Matthew 28:19 Go ye therefore, and teach all nations, baptizing them in the name of the Father, and of the Son, and of the Holy Ghost:

Matthew 28:20 Teaching them to observe all things whatsoever I have commanded you: and, lo, I am with you alway, *even* unto the end of the world. Amen.

Luke 10:2 Therefore said he unto them, The harvest truly *is* great, but the labourers *are* few: pray ye therefore the Lord of the harvest, that he would send forth labourers into his harvest.

Luke 10:3 Go your ways: behold, I send you forth as lambs among wolves.

Following Christ as lambs among wolves is not very appealing. It is scary. It makes most people say, "I'm not going to do that."

Luke 10:4 Carry neither purse, nor scrip, nor shoes: and salute no man by the way.

Purse would be for money. Carry no money, no gold no silver no credit cards. Scrip would be for food. Carry no items to support the body that is food, water, etc. And no extra sandals just those on your feet.

Luke 10:5 And into whatsoever house ye enter, first say, Peace *be* to this house.

Luke 10:6 And if the son of peace be there, your peace shall rest upon it: if not, it shall turn to you again.

Luke 10:7 And in the same house remain, eating and drinking such things as they give: for the labourer is worthy of his hire. Go not from house to house.

Luke 10:8 And into whatsoever city ye enter, and they receive you, eat such things as are set before you:

It is God's obligation to provide meals and clothing to all. God promises this to His followers. Missionaries that follow Christ in this way are taught to eat the food of the land they are witnessing to. A change in diet is sometimes a hard thing to do. But Christ tells us here to eat and enjoy. (Whether you like it or not!)

Luke 10:9 And heal the sick that are therein, and say unto them, The kingdom of God is come nigh unto you.

Luke 10:10 But into whatsoever city ye enter, and they receive you not, go your ways out into the streets of the same, and say,

Luke 10:11 Even the very dust of your city, which cleaveth on us, we do wipe off against you: notwithstanding be ye sure of this, that the kingdom of God is come nigh unto you.

Many people reject the words of Christ and refuse to follow Him. They have made their choice. They have denied Christ so much that God says rid yourself of them even the dust in their house. Matthew says the same but elaborates more:

Matthew 10:11 And into whatsoever city or town ye shall enter, enquire who in it is worthy; and there abide till ye go thence.

Matthew 10:12 And when ye come into an house, salute it.

Matthew 10:13 And if the house be worthy, let your peace come upon it: but if it be not worthy, let your peace return to you.

Matthew 10:14 And whosoever shall not receive you, nor hear your words, when ye depart out of that house or city, shake off the dust of your feet.

Matthew 10:15 Verily I say unto you, It shall be more tolerable for the land of Sodom and Gomorrha in the day of judgment, than for that city.

Matthew 10:16 Behold, I send you forth as sheep in the midst of wolves: be ye therefore wise as serpents, and harmless as doves.

Wolves are out there. They will attack anyone who is living a life for Christ. This is happening, especially in this last church age, the age of Laodicea. Christ has warned us about these evil days approaching. He says that He is outside of the church itself trying to get in! Being prayed up and dependent on Christ is needed to help in these last days.

Revelation 3:19 As many as I love, I rebuke and chasten: be zealous therefore, and repent.

Revelation 3:20 Behold, I stand at the door, and knock: if any man hear my voice, and open the door, I will come in to him, and will sup with him, and he with me.

Revelation 3:21 To him that overcometh will I grant to sit with me in my throne, even as I also overcame, and am set down with my Father in his throne.

Revelation 3:22 He that hath an ear, let him hear what the Spirit saith unto the churches.

Luke 10:12 But I say unto you, that it shall be more tolerable in that day for Sodom, than for that city.

Luke 10:13 Woe unto thee, Chorazin! woe unto thee, Bethsaida! for if the mighty works had been done in Tyre and Sidon, which have been done in you, they had a great while ago repented, sitting in sackcloth and ashes.

Things were not that tolerable for Sodom back in Lot's Day. However, it will be even less tolerable for these four cities in Israel. They were cities that needed the Gospel preached to them. Christ gave the disciples the authority to go to these cities and spread the good news of the kingdom of God which needed to be accepted and now be within you. God pronounces a "Woe" at this point. Not Good!

Luke 10:14 But it shall be more tolerable for Tyre and Sidon at the judgment, than for you. Luke 10:15 And thou, Capernaum, which art exalted to heaven, shalt be thrust down to hell.

Luke 10:16 He that heareth you heareth me; and he that despiseth you despiseth me; and he that despiseth me despiseth him that sent me.

Luke 10:17 And the seventy returned again with joy, saying, Lord, even the devils are subject unto us through thy name.

Luke 10:18 And he said unto them, I beheld Satan as lightning fall from heaven.

Luke 10:19 Behold, I give unto you power to tread on serpents and scorpions, and over all the power of the enemy: and nothing shall by any means hurt you.

Luke 10:20 Notwithstanding in this rejoice not, that the spirits are subject unto you; but rather rejoice, because your names are written in heaven.

That is, written in the Lamb's book of life. There are names that are not written in this book in heaven. During the tribulation period those not written in the book of life will be exposed. They will be easy to spot. Because they remained on this earth after the saints are caught up, raptured.

Revelation 13:8 And all that dwell upon the earth shall worship him, whose names are not written in the book of life of the Lamb slain from the foundation of the world.

The Lamb's book of life is the discerning factor as to who dwells on this earth and who does not, when the beast is revealed who was and is not, and yet is.

Revelation 17:8 The beast that thou sawest was, and is not; and shall ascend out of the bottomless pit, and go into perdition: and they that dwell on the earth shall wonder, whose names were not written in the book of life from the foundation of the world, when they behold the beast that was, and is not, and yet is.

Jesus will do what everyone can do; that is pray. Luke is constantly pointing out how to pray, like Christ.

Luke 10:21 In that hour Jesus rejoiced in spirit, and said, I thank thee, O Father, Lord of heaven and earth, that thou hast hid these things from the wise and prudent, and hast revealed them unto babes: even so, Father; for so it seemed good in thy sight.
Luke 10:22 All things are delivered to me of my Father: and no man knoweth who the Son is, but the Father; and who the Father is, but the Son, and *he* to whom the Son will reveal *him.*

It is at this point that Luke and Matthew go in different directions. Luke is about to unveil one of the most discussed portions of scripture that is out there.

Only in Luke's Gospel

Luke 10:23 And he turned him unto *his* disciples, and said privately, Blessed *are* the eyes which see the things that ye see:
Luke 10:24 For I tell you, that many prophets and kings have desired to see those things which ye see, and have not seen *them;* and to hear those things which ye hear, and have not heard *them.*

Luke begins a series of stories and parables that are unmatched. For the next ten chapters Luke will quote Jesus continually. At this point, Luke describes the lesson of the Good Samaritan. This true story is only in the Gospel of Luke. This is not a parable. Jesus says it is certain. It truly happened. The command to love your neighbor as yourself is brought into focus.

However, the question is much deeper than what meets the eye. This Lawyer is trying to justify himself as righteous. He wants to do something to inherit eternal life. This is the question about to be asked of Jesus.

Luke 10:25 And, behold, a certain lawyer stood up, and tempted him, saying, Master, what shall I do to inherit eternal life?

Jesus knows this lawyer's heart and puts a very simple question to him:

Luke 10:26 He said unto him, What is written in the law? how readest thou?

This is done so that this lawyer will be without excuse. He will not be able to say I did not understand. He gives his personal interpretation of the law and how to live by it.

Luke 10:27 And he answering said, Thou shalt love the Lord thy God with all thy heart, and with all thy soul, and with all thy strength, and with all thy mind; and thy neighbour as thyself.

Jesus says that the answer the lawyer gives is correct! The golden rule has been taught to many as "Love your neighbor as yourself." But it is rare that the first part of the golden rule is included. To "love the Lord thy God with all thy heart, and with all thy soul, and with all thy strength, and with all thy mind" is the first part of the golden rule. Without getting the first part right, the second part is useless.

Luke 10:28 And he said unto him, Thou hast answered right: this do, and thou shalt live.

Jesus backs this up when He declares that the Law of Moses is basically reduced to two commands. And that the first command is the greatest commandment. Once the first commandment is understood and mastered, the second one falls into place.

Matthew 22:36 Master, which *is* the great commandment in the law?

Matthew 22:37 Jesus said unto him, Thou shalt love the Lord thy God with all thy heart, and with all thy soul, and with all thy mind.

Matthew 22:38 This is the first and great commandment.

Matthew 22:39 And the second *is* like unto it, Thou shalt love thy neighbour as thyself.

Matthew 22:40 On these two commandments hang all the law and the prophets.

God has established that this is the way that you can earn your self-righteousness. Throughout the Bible God has pointed out this way and that no man can attain this level of perfectness. This lawyer wanted more than anything else to justify himself by his good deeds But he begins to act like a lawyer asking foolish questions.

Luke 10:29 But he, willing to justify himself, said unto Jesus, And who is my neighbour?

Jesus gives the perfect answer to this question. The following instruction on who is your neighbor is as good as it gets. Your neighbor is not always someone you know. But it almost always is someone in need. In this case medical attention was required. But it could be something other than medical. It could be material needs. But to be a "Good Samaritan" you must do and continue to do what Jesus explains below and even more for the one in need.

Luke 10:30 And Jesus answering said, A certain *man* went down from Jerusalem to Jericho, and fell among thieves, which stripped him of his raiment, and wounded *him,* and departed, leaving *him* half dead.
Luke 10:31 And by chance there came down a certain priest that way: and when he saw him, he passed by on the other side.
Luke 10:32 And likewise a Levite, when he was at the place, came and looked *on him,* and passed by on the other side.
Luke 10:33 But a certain Samaritan, as he journeyed, came where he was: and when he saw him, he had compassion *on him,*
Luke 10:34 And went to *him,* and bound up his wounds, pouring in oil and wine, and set him on his own beast, and brought him to an inn, and took care of him.
Luke 10:35 And on the morrow when he departed, he took out two pence, and gave *them* to the host, and said unto him, Take care of him; and whatsoever thou spendest more, when I come again, I will repay thee.

Who has gone to this extreme measure of doing these things for a person that was formerly unknown to them? Jesus said this and even more needed to be done if you want to attain the position of a righteous person! And you must do this for every person that becomes your neighbor or comes near to you. Don't be like this lawyer seeking to justify yourself. You cannot do it! Jesus says this is what it takes to earn the reputation of being good.

Luke 10:36 Which now of these three, thinkest thou, was neighbour unto him that fell among the thieves?
Luke 10:37 And he said, He that shewed mercy on him. Then said Jesus unto him, Go, and do thou likewise.

The simplest example on how to understand who a neighbor is, is presented by Jesus. Lawyers are not looked on as very desirable people to know. Sometimes their ethics are below even the lowest of professions. But Jesus told this account and gave exact instruction to the lawyer. Go, and do thou likewise is a command for all to follow.

Now there is the first introduction to some lifelong friends of Jesus. Jesus will spend time with Martha and Mary. These two are sisters to Lazarus who will become a very close friend to Jesus. Luke chapter 10 is the first glimpse of Martha and Mary. The two sisters are seen in very contrasting roles. The only other place they are mentioned is in John chapters 11 and 12 when Jesus raises their brother, Lazarus, from the dead.

Luke 10:38 Now it came to pass, as they went, that he entered into a certain village: and a certain woman named Martha received him into her house.
Luke 10:39 And she had a sister called Mary, which also sat at Jesus' feet, and heard his word.
Luke 10:40 But Martha was cumbered about much serving, and came to him, and said, Lord, dost thou not care that my sister hath left me to serve alone? bid her therefore that she help me. Luke 10:41 And

Jesus answered and said unto her, Martha, Martha, thou art careful and troubled about many things:

Luke 10:42 But one thing is needful: and Mary hath chosen that good part, which shall not be taken away from her.

When the Master showed up at Martha and Mary's house, He said it was needful to be like Mary. Have you, like Mary, sat at the feet of Jesus? This is what was most important to Mary. However, Martha was a person who constantly looked after the cares and needs of others. Both Luke and John explain that Martha was a servant to everyone she could help. Later in the book of John after Christ raised her brother Lazarus, Mary will anoint the feet of Jesus. Some say she went too far with the expensive ointment, but Jesus would not say that!

John 12:1 Then Jesus six days before the passover came to Bethany, where Lazarus was which had been dead, whom he raised from the dead.

John 12:2 There they made him a supper; and Martha served: but Lazarus was one of them that sat at the table with him.

John 12:3 Then took Mary a pound of ointment of spikenard, very costly, and anointed the feet of Jesus, and wiped his feet with her hair: and the house was filled with the odour of the ointment.

It is easy to become encumbered with the cares of this world. Martha was doing a good thing in serving tables. Serving is a great thing, which is the Greek word, "diakonos" or deacon meaning to serve,

Acts 6:2 Then the twelve called the multitude of the disciples unto them, and said, It is not reason that we should leave the word of God, and serve tables.

But just as the Apostles described a need for servants or waiters, it is just as important for all of us like Mary to sit at the feet of Jesus who is the "Word of God." There is a time to work and a time to sit at the Master's feet. Jesus declared that to love

the Lord thy God with all your heart, soul, mind, strength is to be the first and greatest commandment just as the lawyer described. Mark agrees:

> Mark 12:30 And thou shalt love the Lord thy God with all thy heart, and with all thy soul, and with all thy mind, and with all thy strength: this *is* the first commandment.

LUKE CHAPTER 11

Highlights:

Chapter eleven has Jesus Christ giving instruction on how to pray. Jesus gives signs of His next coming to earth. Jesus pronounces "Woes."

Main Participants:

Jesus Christ v.1,
One of His Disciples v.1,
The dumb one who spoke v.14,
A certain woman v.27,
People gathered v.29,
A certain Pharisee v.37,
A certain lawyer v.45,
Scribes and Pharisees v.53.

In Brief:

Jesus Christ gives a second example after Matthew's account on how to pray. He speaks of the divided house and kingdom. Jesus answers the blasphemous Pharisees. Pronouncing the "Woes" upon the Pharisees. Jesus including the lawyers in with the Pharisees. Scribes and Pharisees trying to trap Jesus in His own words.

Only in Luke's Gospel

Luke 11:1 And it came to pass, that, as he was praying in a certain place, when he ceased, one of his disciples said unto him, Lord, teach us to pray, as John also taught his disciples.

A well-known commentator from the past is Matthew Henry. He was an English Presbyterian minister who lived until 1714 and died at the age of 51. He is well read by many looking for some comments on the Bible. Over two hundred years ago, Matthew Henry's introduction to this chapter reads as follows:

> *"Prayer is one of the great laws of natural religion. That man is a brute, is a monster, that never prays, that never gives glory to his Maker, nor feels his favour, nor owns his dependence upon him. One great design therefore of Christianity is to assist us in prayer, to enforce the duty upon us, to instruct us in it, and encourage us to expect advantage by it."*

Many use the Lord's Prayer as their only prayer to God and repeat it over and over again. Here is the Lord's Prayer as quoted in Matthew chapter 6:

Matthew 6:9 After this manner therefore pray ye: Our Father which art in heaven, Hallowed be thy name.
Matthew 6:10 Thy kingdom come. Thy will be done in earth, as *it is* in heaven.
Matthew 6:11 Give us this day our daily bread.
Matthew 6:12 And forgive us our debts, as we forgive our debtors.
Matthew 6:13 And lead us not into temptation, but deliver us from evil: For thine is the kingdom, and the power, and the glory, for ever. Amen.

Luke's example of how to pray is at a different time and a different place than Matthew's example. In Matthew, Jesus was on the mount where the Beatitudes were presented and thus the

name of the sermon by Jesus in Matthew is known as the "Sermon on the Mount." In both cases, these are entirely instructional ways to pray, not what to pray or what to repeat. There is a certain place where Jesus went to pray, and it is pointed out by Luke. This precedes the instruction of how to pray.

Luke 11:2 And he said unto them, When ye pray, say, Our Father which art in heaven, Hallowed be thy name. Thy kingdom come. Thy will be done, as in heaven, so in earth.
Luke 11:3 Give us day by day our daily bread.
Luke 11:4 And forgive us our sins; for we also forgive every one that is indebted to us. And lead us not into temptation; but deliver us from evil.

Seeing the difference in what Jesus says before and after the prayer in Matthew and in Luke makes it clear that the so called "Lord's prayer" is an example on how to pray and not a specific prayer. It is not to be a prayer done in vain repetition.

One way to evaluate this is to review the way modern translations have omitted so much of this prayer. Notice the difference in how the translators have done this. This prayer in Luke is nowhere near the example of how to pray in Matthew. If God wanted this prayer to be the "Lord's Prayer" I'm sure God could have made all the examples say the exact same thing.

Here is Luke 11 verse 2 in various versions of the Bible:

KJV And he said unto them, When ye pray, say, Our Father which art in heaven, Hallowed be thy name. Thy kingdom come. Thy will be done, as in heaven, so in earth.

NIV He said to them, "When you pray, say: "'Father, hallowed be your name, your kingdom come.

ESV And he said to them, "When you pray, say: "Father, hallowed be your name. Your kingdom come.

NASB And He said to them, "When you pray, say: 'Father, hallowed be Your name. Your kingdom come.

If God wanted this prayer repeated, why are two portions omitted?
(Which art in heaven) and
(Thy will be done, as in heaven, so in earth)

Here is Luke 11 verse 3 in various versions of the Bible:
 KJV Give us day by day our daily bread.
 NIV Give us each day our daily bread.
 ESV Give us each day our daily bread.
 NASB Give us each day our daily bread.

Here is Luke 11 verse 4:
 KJV And forgive us our sins; for we also forgive every one that is indebted to us. And lead us not into temptation; but deliver us from evil.
 NIV Forgive us our sins, for we also forgive everyone who sins against us. And lead us not into temptation.
 ESV and forgive us our sins, for we ourselves forgive everyone who is indebted to us. And lead us not into temptation.
 NASB And forgive us our sins, For we ourselves also forgive everyone who is indebted to us. And do not lead us into temptation.

Again, if God wanted this prayer repeated, why omit the last part?
(but deliver us from evil)

God wants us to pray with importunity. This is a great word!
At this point it is used in scripture.

Luke 11:5 And he said unto them, Which of you shall have a friend, and shall go unto him at midnight, and say unto him, Friend, lend me three loaves;
Luke 11:6 For a friend of mine in his journey is come to me, and I have nothing to set before him?
Luke 11:7 And he from within shall answer and say, Trouble me not: the door is now shut, and my children are with me in bed; I cannot rise and give thee.
Luke 11:8 I say unto you, Though he will not rise and give him, because he is his friend, yet because of his importunity he will rise and give him as many as he needeth.

The result of asking God from the heart is that God will hear you. This friend truly had a need that God would see for one reason the man would not get out of bed. He did not know how serious the man needing three loaves was. Here is a need for three loaves of bread. His friend is saying I'm too busy with my own life and family and it's late and I'm not getting out of bed for you! When a friend comes asking for something at an inopportune time, most will say to that friend "no way I'm in bed already" or they may even say "figure it out yourself"

Here is a word that appears only once in the Bible. "Importunity" in Luke 11 verse 8. Every adult who has children knows exactly what this word means. When a child is persistent in asking for something and that child won't let up. It is exactly what God wants to see from His children who desire something. How do we know that? Because Jesus goes right into asking, and seeking, and knocking, so that God sees your desire and will thus open it unto you.

Luke 11:9 And I say unto you, Ask, and it shall be given you; seek, and ye shall find; knock, and it shall be opened unto you.
Luke 11:10 For every one that asketh receiveth; and he that seeketh findeth; and to him that knocketh it shall be opened.

Jesus begins to express the "need" of the Father to see the "want" in the heart from the one in need.

Luke 11:11 If a son shall ask bread of any of you that is a father, will he give him a stone? or if *he ask* a fish, will he for a fish give him a serpent?
Luke 11:12 Or if he shall ask an egg, will he offer him a scorpion?
Luke 11:13 If ye then, being evil, know how to give good gifts unto your children: how much more shall *your* heavenly Father give the Holy Spirit to them that ask him?

As men are born into this world, both by nature and physical, they are conceived in sin, shaped in iniquity; are evil from their youth, and transgressors from the womb; man is corrupt, and he does abominable things with a desperately wicked heart. Yet they can desire to ask for good gifts for their children? How much greater is God when he gives us the gift of the Holy Spirit. This gift happens at the second birth when our spirit is made new and walks hand in hand with God's Holy Spirit. Amos the prophet said clearly:

Amos 3:3 Can two walk together, except they be agreed?

Luke 11:14 And he was casting out a devil, and it was dumb. And it came to pass, when the devil was gone out, the dumb spake; and the people wondered.

Luke 11:15 But some of them said, He casteth out devils through Beelzebub the chief of the devils.

Beelzebub is another name for Satan. It is of Chaldean origin and believed to mean the "dung god".

Jesus, after He was tempted again, would not give a sign from heaven but would speak the following great passage of a house divided:

Luke 11:16 And others, tempting *him,* sought of him a sign from heaven.

Luke 11:17 But he, knowing their thoughts, said unto them, Every kingdom divided against itself is brought to desolation; and a house *divided* against a house falleth.

Luke 11:18 If Satan also be divided against himself, how shall his kingdom stand? because ye say that I cast out devils through Beelzebub.

Luke 11:19 And if I by Beelzebub cast out devils, by whom do your sons cast *them* out? therefore shall they be your judges.

Luke 11:20 But if I with the finger of God cast out devils, no doubt the kingdom of God is come upon you.

Luke 11:21 When a strong man armed keepeth his palace, his goods are in peace:

Luke 11:22 But when a stronger than he shall come upon him, and overcome him, he taketh from him all his armour wherein he trusted, and divideth his spoils.

Luke 11:23 He that is not with me is against me: and he that gathereth not with me scattereth.

Jesus now describes the awful results of not being "armed" with the armor of God. Remember that the devil is still much stronger than any mortal.

Luke 11:24 When the unclean spirit is gone out of a man, he walketh through dry places, seeking rest; and finding none, he saith, I will return unto my house whence I came out.

Luke 11:25 And when he cometh, he findeth *it* swept and garnished.

Luke 11:26 Then goeth he, and taketh *to him* seven other spirits more wicked than himself; and they enter in, and dwell there: and the last *state* of that man is worse than the first.

Luke 11:27 And it came to pass, as he spake these things, a certain woman of the company lifted up her voice, and said unto him, Blessed *is* the womb that bare thee, and the paps which thou hast sucked.

The womb which bare Jesus has an honor being paid to it. This is an honor now being paid to Mary as the mother of Jesus. Remember that God said all will call her blessed back in chapter one.

> Luke 1:48 For he hath regarded the low estate of his handmaiden: for, behold, from henceforth all generations shall call me blessed.

Knowing the heart of this woman, Jesus sees that she is taking this blessing of Mary in the wrong direction and a bit too far. Many today do exactly such a thing as this. They need to be corrected. Jesus explains this correction of a wrong view of Mary. So, He sets her straight.

Luke 11:28 But he said, Yea rather, blessed *are* they that hear the word of God, and keep it.

Jesus again speaks of how evil man is in his unregenerate state. Man is always seeking after a sign.

Luke 11:29 And when the people were gathered thick together, he began to say, This is an evil generation: they seek a sign; and there shall no sign be given it, but the sign of Jonas the prophet.

Luke 11:30 For as Jonas was a sign unto the Ninevites, so shall also the Son of man be to this generation.

What was the sign of Jonas to Ninevah. That they needed to repent!

Jonah 1:2 Arise, go to Nineveh, that great city, and cry against it; for their wickedness is come up before me.

Jonah did not want to do this. He went to Tarshish instead, the opposite direction from Ninevah. But God turned him around with a great fish story. And Jonah finally turned (that is repented) and went and told Nineveh:

Jonah 3:4 And Jonah began to enter into the city a day's journey, and he cried, and said, Yet forty days, and Nineveh shall be overthrown.

Jesus will explain that the people of Ninevah repented. This first coming of Jesus should have been the sign that all the scholars of the scriptures looked for. But all they wanted were miracles and works that would appeal to the flesh. Looking for these miraculous signs of wealth and health and not looking for Jesus Christ as the all-sufficient Saviour. The people needed to repent. This happened to Ninevah as Jesus would describe here:

Luke 11:31 The queen of the south shall rise up in the judgment with the men of this generation, and condemn them: for she came from the utmost parts of the earth to hear the wisdom of Solomon; and, behold, a greater than Solomon *is* here.

Luke 11:32 The men of Nineve shall rise up in the judgment with this generation, and shall condemn it: for they repented at the preaching of Jonas; and, behold, a greater than Jonas *is* here.

Of course, the sign Jesus wanted the crowd to have was the repentance that had been preached by John the Baptist. The same

repentance Jonah had when he was in the belly of the whale for three full days and three full nights. The same repentance Ninevah had.

Matthew 12:39 But he answered and said unto them, An evil and adulterous generation seeketh after a sign; and there shall no sign be given to it, but the sign of the prophet Jonas:

Matthew 12:40 For as Jonas was three days and three nights in the whale's belly; so shall the Son of man be three days and three nights in the heart of the earth.

There are sensors in the body that take things in. Ears to hear, hands to feel, Nose to smell, but perhaps the most efficient mode of sensory comes with the eyes to see the light.

Luke 11:33 No man, when he hath lighted a candle, putteth *it* in a secret place, neither under a bushel, but on a candlestick, that they which come in may see the light.

Luke 11:34 The light of the body is the eye: therefore when thine eye is single, thy whole body also is full of light; but when *thine eye* is evil, thy body also *is* full of darkness.

Jesus wants to be that light that we take in. He declares this Himself:

John 8:12 Then spake Jesus again unto them, saying, I am the light of the world: he that followeth me shall not walk in darkness, but shall have the light of life.

Luke 11:35 Take heed therefore that the light which is in thee be not darkness.

Luke 11:36 If thy whole body therefore *be* full of light, having no part dark, the whole shall be full of light, as when the bright shining of a candle doth give thee light.

Jesus takes the light to the next level. That is when you are saved and a follower of Jesus Christ you become that light to the world!

Matthew 5:14 Ye are the light of the world. A city that is set on an hill cannot be hid.

A PERFECT UNDERSTANDING
FRED A. KUYPERS

To wash one's hands is very important in today's world. But Jesus shows that it is much more important to be clean by taking things in and cleansing from the inside. This is done by taking in the Word of God, which is the Bible.

Luke 11:37 And as he spake, a certain Pharisee besought him to dine with him: and he went in, and sat down to meat.
Luke 11:38 And when the Pharisee saw *it,* he marvelled that he had not first washed before dinner.
Luke 11:39 And the Lord said unto him, Now do ye Pharisees make clean the outside of the cup and the platter; but your inward part is full of ravening and wickedness.
Luke 11:40 *Ye* fools, did not he that made that which is without make that which is within also?

It is true that one result of being born again is that you become willing to give. Jesus mentions alms here but also speaks of the tithe. Alms are what we give for the needy.

Luke 11:41 But rather give alms of such things as ye have; and, behold, all things are clean unto you.

Jesus describes how you give from the heart, and this is a good thing. However, Jesus describes another form of giving. Those who give and are depending on their giving to earn them a standing with God. Jesus warns against this type of giving. A good clean giving from the heart is what God wants to see.

Luke 11:42 But woe unto you, Pharisees! for ye tithe mint and rue and all manner of herbs, and pass over judgment and the love of God: these ought ye to have done, and not to leave the other undone.

A good clean giving from the heart is what God wants to see. A cheerful giver:
2Co 9:7 Every man according as he purposeth in his heart, *so let him give;* not grudgingly, or of necessity: for God loveth a cheerful giver.

A PERFECT UNDERSTANDING

You could tell that Pharisees were not Baptists. They wanted the front seats and the uppermost seats for notoriety.

Luke 11:43 Woe unto you, Pharisees! for ye love the uppermost seats in the synagogues, and greetings in the markets.
Luke 11:44 Woe unto you, scribes and Pharisees, hypocrites! for ye are as graves which appear not, and the men that walk over *them* are not aware *of them.*

Even the lawyers were thinking that Jesus was singling them out:

Luke 11:45 Then answered one of the lawyers, and said unto him, Master, thus saying thou reproachest us also.

And Jesus was about to do just that to the lawyers!

Luke 11:46 And he said, Woe unto you also, *ye* lawyers! for ye lade men with burdens grievous to be borne, and ye yourselves touch not the burdens with one of your fingers.
Luke 11:47 Woe unto you! for ye build the sepulchres of the prophets, and your fathers killed them.
Luke 11:48 Truly ye bear witness that ye allow the deeds of your fathers: for they indeed killed them, and ye build their sepulchres.

God would warn His people throughout history with prophets and apostles sent to forewarn of the awfulness of hell and the people would not receive them.

Luke 11:49 Therefore also said the wisdom of God, I will send them prophets and apostles, and *some* of them they shall slay and persecute:
Luke 11:50 That the blood of all the prophets, which was shed from the foundation of the world, may be required of this generation;

The life of all the prophets will be required at the hand of every person that God judges. We have the words of every prophet and apostle who ever lived up to today. God will require from us what we learned from these men that God has chosen in the past. From A to Z, we should have heard them all!

Luke 11:51 From the blood of Abel unto the blood of Zacharias, which perished between the altar and the temple: verily I say unto you, It shall be required of this generation.

By controlling the scriptures and the books of learning of the day, lawyers were singled out by Jesus. How many times have lawyers told us it is up to them to interpret the law? No it is up to each one of us to read and determine what God is saying to us.

Luke 11:52 Woe unto you, lawyers! for ye have taken away the key of knowledge: ye entered not in yourselves, and them that were entering in ye hindered.

The religious leaders will continue to try and trap Jesus in His own words.

Luke 11:53 And as he said these things unto them, the scribes and the Pharisees began to urge *him* vehemently, and to provoke him to speak of many things:
Luke 11:54 Laying wait for him, and seeking to catch something out of his mouth, that they might accuse him.

It is of the utmost importance that we read what Jesus had to say. We have His words, and they are in the entire account of the Holy Bible. Have you read them? Are you following them? Do you believe in the death, burial, and resurrection of the Lord Jesus Christ? are you following what God said to do? Do you walk in the truth?

3John 1:3 For I rejoiced greatly, when the brethren came and testified of the truth that is in thee, even as thou walkest in the truth.

3John 1:4 I have no greater joy than to hear that my children walk in truth.

LUKE CHAPTER 12

Highlights:

Chapter twelve has Jesus Christ giving warnings. Jesus speaks in parables about where your heart is. Jesus came to bring division.

Main Participants:

Jesus Christ v.1,
Innumerable Multitude v.1,
His disciples v.1,
one in the company v.13,
Peter and all the people gathered v.41,

In Brief:

Jesus Christ warns His disciples of the sins of the Pharisees. Jesus explains the parable of the rich fool building bigger barns. Jesus warns his disciples of His second coming. Jesus explains to Peter about the wise steward. And that being baptized into the family of God will be divisive even with family.

Only in Luke's Gospel

Luke 12:1 In the mean time, when there were gathered together an innumerable multitude of people, insomuch that they trode one upon another, he began to say unto his disciples first of all, Beware ye of the leaven of the Pharisees, which is hypocrisy.

Luke 12:2 For there is nothing covered, that shall not be revealed; neither hid, that shall not be known.

As chapter twelve opens it is apparent that something was transpiring which was mentioned previously in Luke chapter eleven. This chapter begins "In the mean time." In the meantime, of what? It was a time of entrapment by the religious leaders of the day. They sought to accuse Jesus of heresy and the more they had Him speak, the better chance to entrap Him in His own words. They did not know they were dealing with God Almighty in their midst and that He would entrap them in their own words! So, the Lord, who knows what is transpiring against Him, looks directly at the religious leaders trying to entrap Him and delivers His great speech against gossip and hypocrisy.

Luke 12:3 Therefore whatsoever ye have spoken in darkness shall be heard in the light; and that which ye have spoken in the ear in closets shall be proclaimed upon the housetops.

How true this is! Every secret sin will one day be unveiled. We have God's word on this:

Numbers 32:23 But if ye will not do so, behold, ye have sinned against the LORD: and be sure your sin will find you out.

Jesus begins to point out how our lives are viewed. Viewed both by the world and by the Lord. This world can have the power to take the life of a person while on earth. But the world system has no power in eternal life. All of the power in eternal life belongs to God.

Luke 12:4 And I say unto you my friends, Be not afraid of them that kill the body, and after that have no more that they can do.

Luke 12:5 But I will forewarn you whom ye shall fear: Fear him, which after he hath killed hath power to cast into hell; yea, I say unto you, Fear him.

The word *fear* in this passage is almost exclusively the Greek word "Phobeo" which can mean a fear of reverence or to be in "awe". This is used randomly throughout the New Testament with the Greek word "Phobos" which is alarm, fright or terror. There is one time the word "fear" appears that has an entirely different meaning. The Greek word, "deilia" meaning *timid,* and it has to do with our witnessing:

2Ti 1:7 For God hath not given us the spirit of fear; but of power, and of love, and of a sound mind.

God explains the value of a person compared to the rest of His creation. How much greater man is than the rest of creation. Those who hold up animals as equal to man in importance should understand that God who created the sparrows says man is much more important. This God also created the copper that the farthing, a coin, is made of. He also created us and explains how much more valuable we are than anything else in His creation.

Luke 12:6 Are not five sparrows sold for two farthings, and not one of them is forgotten before God?
Luke 12:7 But even the very hairs of your head are all numbered. Fear not therefore: ye are of more value than many sparrows.

God says to "fear not". The same as the word fear above, phobeo. What God is saying with the negative in front of fear is do not be in AWE that God has made you higher and better and closer to Him than mineral, plant, or animal life; rather we are to proclaim it!

Luke 12:8 Also I say unto you, Whosoever shall confess me before men, him shall the Son of man also confess before the angels of God:
Luke 12:9 But he that denieth me before men shall be denied before the angels of God.

In refute of Calvinism, it is seen how God will honor us if we honor His Son. This is true of all of salvation. If you, then God will.... If you believe the Gospel, then God will save you. If you receive him, God gives you the power to become a son of God. Salvation will not happen unless you believe it. Romans says you have to confess it. If you repent of your sin, God will forgive. If you will do good deeds, God will reward with crowns. If you will confess Jesus before men, God will acknowledge you and not deny you. Even if you say something opposed to Jesus Christ, you can have forgiveness it says:

Luke 12:10 And whosoever shall speak a word against the Son of man, it shall be forgiven him: but unto him that blasphemeth against the Holy Ghost it shall not be forgiven.

Blaspheme is another transliterated word. This means that there was no comparable word to translate into English. So, the translators just used the Greek word itself, "Blasphemeo". It means to rail on, or to speak evil of. It is the Holy Ghost who dwells within the believer. If you speak evil of or rail against the Holy Ghost how can the divided house stand? God already pointed that out in Luke:

Luke 11:17 But he, knowing their thoughts, said unto them, Every kingdom divided against itself is brought to desolation; and a house *divided* against a house falleth.

Even clearer in Mark:

Mark 3:25 And if a house be divided against itself, that house cannot stand.

There are two powers that strive to have the power over a person. One is over the outward man; one is over the inward man. Synagogues and magistrates are both mentioned here.

Luke 12:11 And when they bring you unto the synagogues, and *unto* magistrates, and powers, take ye no thought how or what thing ye shall answer, or what ye shall say:

Luke 12:12 For the Holy Ghost shall teach you in the same hour what ye ought to say.

A PERFECT UNDERSTANDING

The Holy Spirit of Christ has come to the rescue of many a follower by giving them the words to speak in the hour of need. Has He ever been able to help you in a situation where you were speechless? Perhaps when you were witnessing or when someone has tried to entrap you in your Christianity? This is when the Spirit of Jesus Christ will come to the rescue. But this answer was questioned by the group that surrounded the Master. They wanted to apply the help of the Spirit of God in a family civil matter. Jesus is quick to set them in their place:

Luke 12:13 And one of the company said unto him, Master, speak to my brother, that he divide the inheritance with me.
Luke 12:14 And he said unto him, Man, who made me a judge or a divider over you?

Jesus knew the heart of this man and that he was trying to use what Jesus said for his own advantage. Jesus then pointed out the tenth commandment.

Luke 12:15 And he said unto them, Take heed, and beware of covetousness: for a man's life consisteth not in the abundance of the things which he possesseth.

Jesus will now use a parable to describe to this man what he should be aware of; that is to lay up more treasure on earth than what you need, that is being covetous.

Luke 12:16 And he spake a parable unto them, saying, The ground of a certain rich man brought forth plentifully:
Luke 12:17 And he thought within himself, saying, What shall I do, because I have no room where to bestow my fruits?
Luke 12:18 And he said, This will I do: I will pull down my barns, and build greater; and there will I bestow all my fruits and my goods.
Luke 12:19 And I will say to my soul, Soul, thou hast much goods laid up for many years; take thine ease, eat, drink, *and* be merry.

Luke 12:20 But God said unto him, *Thou* fool, this night thy soul shall be required of thee: then whose shall those things be, which thou hast provided?

Luke 12:21 So *is* he that layeth up treasure for himself, and is not rich toward God.

I once saw a bumper sticker that said this.

The one who dies with the most toys wins?

It was a real eye opener. Years later I can still remember this saying. How covetous can one be? Jesus is warning against this philosophy.

Luke 12:22 And he said unto his disciples, Therefore I say unto you, Take no thought for your life, what ye shall eat; neither for the body, what ye shall put on.

Jesus says not to worry. Take no thought. He gives us His assurance that He will take care of us and is all about providing food and clothing for us. God provides twenty-four billion meals a day (3 meals a day for 8 billion people, not counting animals) He provides enough clothing for everyone to be covered by Him when he says "He hath clothed me":

> Isaiah 61:10 I will greatly rejoice in the LORD, my soul shall be joyful in my God; for he hath clothed me with the garments of salvation, he hath covered me with the robe of righteousness, as a bridegroom decketh *himself* with ornaments, and as a bride adorneth *herself* with her jewels.

Luke 12:23 The life is more than meat, and the body *is more* than raiment.

Luke 12:24 Consider the ravens: for they neither sow nor reap; which neither have storehouse nor barn; and God feedeth them: how much more are ye better than the fowls?

Luke 12:25 And which of you with taking thought can add to his stature one cubit?

Luke 12:26 If ye then be not able to do that thing which is least, why take ye thought for the rest?

Matthew has the same message as Luke has here.

Matthew 6:27 Which of you by taking thought can add one cubit unto his stature?

Matthew 6:28 And why take ye thought for raiment? Consider the lilies of the field, how they grow; they toil not, neither do they spin:

However, Matthew describes what Jesus said during Christ's famous *Sermon on the Mount* and now Jesus is giving the same message; traveling through the cities and villages, teaching, and journeying toward Jerusalem (quoted from Luke 13:22).

Luke 12:27 Consider the lilies how they grow: they toil not, they spin not; and yet I say unto you, that Solomon in all his glory was not arrayed like one of these.

Luke 12:28 If then God so clothe the grass, which is to day in the field, and to morrow is cast into the oven; how much more *will he clothe* you, O ye of little faith?

It is wrong to say that what Jesus spoke, He only said once and only on one occasion.

Matthew 6:29 And yet I say unto you, That even Solomon in all his glory was not arrayed like one of these.

Matthew 6:30 Wherefore, if God so clothe the grass of the field, which to day is, and to morrow is cast into the oven, *shall he* not much more *clothe* you, O ye of little faith?

All four gospels say similar accounts but at different times. It is not good witnessing to try and collaborate all four gospels at the same time. Jesus declared many times, the same things, and why He came to die at many different times and in many different places.

Luke 12:29 And seek not ye what ye shall eat, or what ye shall drink, neither be ye of doubtful mind.

Luke 12:30 For all these things do the nations of the world seek after: and your Father knoweth that ye have need of these things.
Luke 12:31 But rather seek ye the kingdom of God; and all these things shall be added unto you.

Once again Jesus speaks to a remnant. Fear not little flock! There are very few who have sought the kingdom of God so that eternal life may be added unto you.

Luke 12:32 Fear not, little flock; for it is your Father's good pleasure to give you the kingdom.
Luke 12:33 Sell that ye have, and give alms; provide yourselves bags which wax not old, a treasure in the heavens that faileth not, where no thief approacheth, neither moth corrupteth.

Sometimes it seems in scripture that Jesus commands us to not have anything. If your heart is set on material things then it would be better that you have nothing at all. But just like Jesus said "If thy right hand offends thee cut it off" does not mean that every follower of Jesus must cut off his right hand so Jesus is not saying the social Gospel is the way to the kingdom of God. These are statements to the heart of a man. God gives good direction in Proverbs

> Proverbs 6:6 Go to the ant, thou sluggard; consider her ways, and be wise:
> Proverbs 6:7 Which having no guide, overseer, or ruler,
> Proverbs 6:8 Provideth her meat in the summer, *and* gathereth her food in the harvest.

Luke 12:34 For where your treasure is, there will your heart be also.

AH! Here is the message Jesus is trying to get across. God says it is always a heart problem.

> Matthew 15:18 But those things which proceed out of the mouth come forth from the heart; and they defile the man.
> Matthew 15:19 For out of the heart proceed evil thoughts, murders, adulteries, fornications, thefts, false witness, blasphemies:

Luke 12:35 Let your loins be girded about, and *your* lights burning;

What does Jesus say to use as a covering for our loins? It is declared in the whole armour of God:

Ephesians 6:13 Wherefore take unto you the whole armour of God, that ye may be able to withstand in the evil day, and having done all, to stand.

Ephesians 6:14 Stand therefore, having your loins girt about with truth, and having on the breastplate of righteousness;

Ephesians 6:15 And your feet shod with the preparation of the gospel of peace;

Ephesians 6:16 Above all, taking the shield of faith, wherewith ye shall be able to quench all the fiery darts of the wicked.

Our loins are to be girted about with truth! Where will we find truth? Only one place and that is the Bible, God's Holy Word.

Luke 12:36 And ye yourselves like unto men that wait for their lord, when he will return from the wedding; that when he cometh and knocketh, they may open unto him immediately.

Luke 12:37 Blessed *are* those servants, whom the lord when he cometh shall find watching: verily I say unto you, that he shall gird himself, and make them to sit down to meat, and will come forth and serve them.

Luke 12:38 And if he shall come in the second watch, or come in the third watch, and find *them* so, blessed are those servants.

Luke 12:39 And this know, that if the goodman of the house had known what hour the thief would come, he would have watched, and not have suffered his house to be broken through.

Here begins Jesus' discussion on what God's timing is all about. God was greatly concerned with the first coming of His Son to this earth. He gave that timing in Daniel with his prophesy of seventy weeks. Sixty-nine of those weeks were about to be fulfilled when Messiah would be cut off. But now we are talking about the throne. We are talking about the reign of Christ. We are talking about God's heartthrob; to see His Son, the Lord Jesus Christ as the King of kings and the Lord of lords. This will happen at

the second coming of Christ. We know when that is. It is directly after the seven years of Jacob's trouble. It is immediately after the seventieth week of Daniel. Immediately after the seven years of tribulation. But what Jesus is saying here is that we do not know when that last week, those final seven years begins. It is now in this age, the age of grace that we are to be ready, always serving and witnessing for Jesus.

Luke 12:40 Be ye therefore ready also: for the Son of man cometh at an hour when ye think not.

Peter wanted to know, is this just for the twelve Apostles or is it a message to everyone?

Luke 12:41 Then Peter said unto him, Lord, speakest thou this parable unto us, or even to all?
Luke 12:42 And the Lord said, Who then is that faithful and wise steward, whom *his* lord shall make ruler over his household, to give *them their* portion of meat in due season?
Luke 12:43 Blessed *is* that servant, whom his lord when he cometh shall find so doing.

The Lord is still in the "when he cometh" stage. Peter was asking if the third and final watch was for him. Is today then the final watch for all? Watching, witnessing, and waiting for the Lord?

Luke 12:44 Of a truth I say unto you, that he will make him ruler over all that he hath.
Luke 12:45 But and if that servant say in his heart, My lord delayeth his coming; and shall begin to beat the menservants and maidens, and to eat and drink, and to be drunken;
Luke 12:46 The lord of that servant will come in a day when he looketh not for *him,* and at an hour when he is not aware, and will cut him in sunder, and will appoint him his portion with the unbelievers.
Luke 12:47 And that servant, which knew his lord's will, and prepared not *himself,* neither did according to his will, shall be beaten with many *stripes.*

Luke 12:48 But he that knew not, and did commit things worthy of stripes, shall be beaten with few *stripes.* For unto whomsoever much is given, of him shall be much required: and to whom men have committed much, of him they will ask the more.

This verse is backed up with a very motivating verse by God in preparing us for the rapture to come. Much is given already to anyone who has heard the Gospel. The much that is required of him is to believe. But souls come very hard to Jesus Christ for salvation. But this is God's requirement. Only BELIEVE! Those who have been witnessed to and are still rejecting Christ; God says much is required of you. And when this age is over God will follow through with His requirement! IF you do not turn to my Son,

"You will believe the lie"

2Thessalonians 2:10 And with all deceivableness of unrighteousness in them that perish; because they received not the love of the truth, that they might be saved.

2Thessalonians 2:11 And for this cause God shall send them strong delusion, that they should believe a lie:

2Thessalonians 2:12 That they all might be damned who believed not the truth, but had pleasure in unrighteousness.

The hatred of God has swelled ever since the days of Cain and Abel. Cain hated God for His choice of Abel. God used water to destroy the world at that time. However now Christ will bring judgement with fire, the bonfire is set:

Luke 12:49 I am come to send fire on the earth; and what will I, if it be already kindled?

Luke 12:50 But I have a baptism to be baptized with; and how am I straitened till it be accomplished!

Luke 12:51 Suppose ye that I am come to give peace on earth? I tell you, Nay; but rather division:

Luke 12:52 For from henceforth there shall be five in one house divided, three against two, and two against three.

God says if you are truly witnessing and following Him, expect division. But one day those who have Believed in the death, burial, and resurrection of our Lord will be united again. This is a great hope that a Christian has.

1Thessalonians 4:13 But I would not have you to be ignorant, brethren, concerning them which are asleep, that ye sorrow not, even as others which have no hope.

1Thessalonians 4:14 For if we believe that Jesus died and rose again, even so them also which sleep in Jesus will God bring with him.

1Thessalonians 4:15 For this we say unto you by the word of the Lord, that we which are alive *and* remain unto the coming of the Lord shall not prevent them which are asleep.

1Thessalonians 4:16 For the Lord himself shall descend from heaven with a shout, with the voice of the archangel, and with the trump of God: and the dead in Christ shall rise first:

1Thessalonians 4:17 Then we which are alive *and* remain shall be caught up together with them in the clouds, to meet the Lord in the air: and so shall we ever be with the Lord.

1Thessalonians 4:18 Wherefore comfort one another with these words.

This promise is only for those who have taken care of their sin problem. God will not have any part of sin in His world. It must be eradicated by His plan through the work of His Son.

Luke 12:51 Suppose ye that I am come to give peace on earth? I tell you, Nay; but rather division:

Luke 12:52 For from henceforth there shall be five in one house divided, three against two, and two against three.

Luke 12:53 The father shall be divided against the son, and the son against the father; the mother against the daughter, and the daughter against the mother; the mother in law against her daughter in law, and the daughter in law against her mother in law.

If this is not happening to you and yours, maybe you are not watching, witnessing, and waiting. God does not describe this account of a family of five in the house for just talk!

Luke 12:54 And he said also to the people, When ye see a cloud rise out of the west, straightway ye say, There cometh a shower; and so it is.

Luke 12:55 And when *ye see* the south wind blow, ye say, There will be heat; and it cometh to pass.

Luke 12:56 *Ye* hypocrites, ye can discern the face of the sky and of the earth; but how is it that ye do not discern this time?

Luke 12:57 Yea, and why even of yourselves judge ye not what is right?

Luke 12:58 When thou goest with thine adversary to the magistrate, *as thou art* in the way, give diligence that thou mayest be delivered from him; lest he hale thee to the judge, and the judge deliver thee to the officer, and the officer cast thee into prison.

Luke 12:59 I tell thee, thou shalt not depart thence, till thou hast paid the very last mite.

Here is God telling us that the closer we get to this event Jesus spoke of just a few short verses above, (the rapture we call it), saying we can know the season of this event. Folks, we are defiantly in the season. My Lord will not delay His coming. It is time to have division!

LUKE CHAPTER 13

Highlights:

Chapter thirteen has Jesus Christ speaking again in parables. Jesus healing on the sabbath. Finally, Jesus cries out over Jerusalem.

Main Participants:

Jesus Christ v.1,
Some that spoke v.1,
Woman with a spirit of infirmity v.11,
Ruler of the Synagogue v.14,
One who asked question if there are few that be saved v.23,
Pharisees v.31,

In Brief:

Jesus Christ warns His disciples to repent of their sins. Jesus says to bear fruit. Jesus heals on the Sabbath. Jesus speaks in parables of mustard seed and leaven and entering at the strait gate as He makes his way to Jerusalem for the last time. As he approaches Jerusalem He laments over the city.

Only in Luke's Gospel

Luke 13:1 There were present at that season some that told him of the Galilaeans, whose blood Pilate had mingled with their sacrifices.

Pilate has been around. He has been on the scene for about 30 years or so. Luke writes more about Pilate than any other writer. We heard of him back in chapter 3:

Luke 3:1 Now in the fifteenth year of the reign of Tiberius Caesar, Pontius Pilate being governor of Judaea, and Herod being tetrarch of Galilee, and his brother Philip tetrarch of Ituraea and of the region of Trachonitis, and Lysanias the tetrarch of Abilene,

Pilate would be known as a cowardly, evil man for ordering the crucifixion of Christ but that is not the only evil thing he ever did. He mingled the blood of Galileans with the blood of the animal sacrifices that Jews were offering to God. How horrible can a man be? Remember that Pilate did not think highly of Jesus either, as He was a Galilean also. He was from Nazareth a city up near the Sea of Galilee. Later, at the crucifixion, Pilate's disdain is seen against the Galileans by his dealings with Herod:

Luke 23:6 When Pilate heard of Galilee, he asked whether the man were a Galilaean.

Luke 23:7 And as soon as he knew that he belonged unto Herod's jurisdiction, he sent him to Herod, who himself also was at Jerusalem at that time.

The idea that Pilate was not a friend of the Galileans and not a friend of Herod in general is acknowledged by the scriptures saying that Herod and Pilate were enemies as Luke will describe later:

Luke 23:11 And Herod with his men of war set him at nought, and mocked *him,* and arrayed him in a gorgeous robe, and sent him again to Pilate.

Luke 23:12 And the same day Pilate and Herod were made friends together: for before they were at enmity between themselves.

Luke 13:2 And Jesus answering said unto them, Suppose ye that these Galilaeans were sinners above all the Galilaeans, because they suffered such things?

Luke 13:3 I tell you, Nay: but, except ye repent, ye shall all likewise perish.

This is such an incredible statement by Jesus. How important is repentance? This is why it is stressed so much at true bible believing churches. That repentance must first come for a person to be saved. However, if repentance is all you have, you will fall short of salvation. Repentance will not save you. You must follow through with the requirement of God to believe. Believe as John 3:16 says. Believe as 1John 5: 11-13 says. Believe as Paul says in Romans 10:9. Believe as Mark says in chapter 16. Believe as Peter says in 1Peter 1:21.

Luke 13:4 Or those eighteen, upon whom the tower in Siloam fell, and slew them, think ye that they were sinners above all men that dwelt in Jerusalem?

Luke 13:5 I tell you, Nay: but, except ye repent, ye shall all likewise perish.

Jesus does not repeat Himself here because He has dementia. He is not forgetful. He is emphasizing the importance of repentance. Repentance is required for belief to become a reality in one's heart.

Some people think they have had their "hell on earth". Through tragedy they believe they will receive eternal reward and the kingdom of God. Even them on who the towers fell! Sounds like a eulogy of today does it not? Jesus clearly says what is required of everyone; those killed by command and those killed by accident all have the same requirement, REPENT! REPENT AND BELIEVE!

Jesus returns to speaking in parables:

Luke 13:6 He spake also this parable; A certain *man* had a fig tree planted in his vineyard; and he came and sought fruit thereon, and found none.

Luke 13:7 Then said he unto the dresser of his vineyard, Behold, these three years I come seeking fruit on this fig tree, and find none: cut it down; why cumbereth it the ground?
Luke 13:8 And he answering said unto him, Lord, let it alone this year also, till I shall dig about it, and dung *it:*
Luke 13:9 And if it bear fruit, *well:* and if not, *then* after that thou shalt cut it down.

A reminder that a parable has a parallel meaning. And since the next passage of scripture moves on to dealing with the Sabbath, Jesus must be using this parable to refer to repentance as discussed above in verse 5. Here in Matthew, John the Baptist, who baptized with the baptism unto repentance, explains this fruit that the husbandman is looking for:

Matthew 3:7 But when he saw many of the Pharisees and Sadducees come to his baptism, he said unto them, O generation of vipers, who hath warned you to flee from the wrath to come?
Matthew 3:8 Bring forth therefore fruits meet for repentance:

Luke 13:10 And he was teaching in one of the synagogues on the sabbath.
Luke 13:11 And, behold, there was a woman which had a spirit of infirmity eighteen years, and was bowed together, and could in no wise lift up *herself.*
Luke 13:12 And when Jesus saw her, he called *her to him,* and said unto her, Woman, thou art loosed from thine infirmity.
Luke 13:13 And he laid *his* hands on her: and immediately she was made straight, and glorified God.
Luke 13:14 And the ruler of the synagogue answered with indignation, because that Jesus had healed on the sabbath day, and said unto the people, There are six days in which men ought to work: in them therefore come and be healed, and not on the sabbath day.

Jesus is once again accused of working His mighty works on the Sabbath. If Jesus doesn't rebuke Sabbath day observance by the ruler at this time, then what is he saying here and now? The Sabbath is never once mentioned as the day of worship in the

Bible. IT IS A DAY OF REST. God explains the need of man to follow God and make one day a day of rest as the commandment says. But Jesus certainly cleared the air about this day when He said in the gospel of Mark:

Mark 2:27 And he said unto them, The sabbath was made for man, and not man for the sabbath:

Mark 2:28 Therefore the Son of man is Lord also of the sabbath.

Jesus calls out the ruler. He set the worship of the Sabbath day straight at this time. When work is needful on the Sabbath, it is OK with God!

Luke 13:15 The Lord then answered him, and said, *Thou* hypocrite, doth not each one of you on the sabbath loose his ox or *his* ass from the stall, and lead *him* away to watering?

Luke 13:16 And ought not this woman, being a daughter of Abraham, whom Satan hath bound, lo, these eighteen years, be loosed from this bond on the sabbath day?

It's amazing today that all who hold the Sabbath as sanctimoniously as this ruler, do not repent and become ashamed of this thinking even as Jesus Christ's adversaries did:

Luke 13:17 And when he had said these things, all his adversaries were ashamed: and all the people rejoiced for all the glorious things that were done by him.

Jesus gives two accounts of how the gospel, known at this time as the kingdom of God will progress. First that it will start out small, but it will expand like a seed producing a mighty tree and be exposed to the world and man and his sin represented by the fowls in its branches.

Luke 13:18 Then said he, Unto what is the kingdom of God like? and whereunto shall I resemble it?

Luke 13:19 It is like a grain of mustard seed, which a man took, and cast into his garden; and it grew, and waxed a great tree; and the fowls of the air lodged in the branches of it.

That sin will always expand to corrupt the whole is evident in this parable. What man touches corrupts. God again shows that His kingdom could be everywhere if sin would not hinder it.

Luke 13:20 And again he said, Whereunto shall I liken the kingdom of God?
Luke 13:21 It is like leaven, which a woman took and hid in three measures of meal, till the whole was leavened.

Today the whole of the church age, that is the saved of today known as the body of Christ is filled with leaven. Leaven is always a symbol of sin. It is described as such.

1Corinthians 5:8 Therefore let us keep the feast, not with old leaven, neither with the leaven of malice and wickedness; but with the unleavened *bread* of sincerity and truth.

This last parable mentions that the kingdom of God will always be exposed to sin and Satan himself. He will go about as a roaring lion to attack those that have the kingdom of God within them. Everyone is ordered to resist this attack from Satan.

1Peter 5:8 Be sober, be vigilant; because your adversary the devil, as a roaring lion, walketh about, seeking whom he may devour:
1Peter 5:9 Whom resist stedfast in the faith, knowing that the same afflictions are accomplished in your brethren that are in the world.

Luke 13:22 And he went through the cities and villages, teaching, and journeying toward Jerusalem.

Many believe that this is the time just before the Feast of Dedication.

John 10:22 And it was at Jerusalem the feast of the dedication, and it was winter.

Today this feast is called Hanukkah. This is during the winter months, so it is cold and wintery. Jesus is focused on getting the message of the "kingdom of God" out to the people. He is traveling to different cities and villages to teach about the kingdom of God

as seen in the verse above. His death, burial and resurrection are still not understood. Jesus describes what it will be like at the end of each age. That includes the church age that is full of leaven.

Luke 13:23 Then said one unto him, Lord, are there few that be saved? And he said unto them,
Luke 13:24 Strive to enter in at the strait gate: for many, I say unto you, will seek to enter in, and shall not be able.

This sounds a lot like Matthew 7:13-14 where Jesus says to enter in at the straight gate, but this is at a different time and a different place. Jesus is now near to Jerusalem and in Matthew he was up on the mount near Galilee where He delivered His sermon on the mount.

Luke 13:25 When once the master of the house is risen up, and hath shut to the door, and ye begin to stand without, and to knock at the door, saying, Lord, Lord, open unto us; and he shall answer and say unto you, I know you not whence ye are:

Jesus makes this sound a lot like in Noah's day. In a few short chapters, chapter 17, Jesus will give the two scenarios of man's heart using Noah's generation and Lot's generation as another. Jesus explains here that today as it was in Noah's day that it is the Master who shuts the door.
Genesis 7:15 And they went in unto Noah into the ark, two and two of all flesh, wherein *is* the breath of life.
Genesis 7:16 And they that went in, went in male and female of all flesh, as God had commanded him: and the LORD shut him in.
Jesus will be an accurate judge at this time and make no mistakes. There will be no excuses as to why in a lifetime you have not accepted God's plan of salvation.

Luke 13:26 Then shall ye begin to say, We have eaten and drunk in thy presence, and thou hast taught in our streets.
Luke 13:27 But he shall say, I tell you, I know you not whence ye are; depart from me, all *ye* workers of iniquity.

Luke 13:28 There shall be weeping and gnashing of teeth, when ye shall see Abraham, and Isaac, and Jacob, and all the prophets, in the kingdom of God, and you *yourselves* thrust out.

Here is a statement that portrays the difference between "Kingdom of God" saints, and "church age" or "age of Grace" saints. Jesus says all the Old Testament prophets are in the "Kingdom of God". However, those saved after Pentecost, that is the church age saints, will be known as the bride of Christ. This is only for those who are saved and receive the gift of the Holy Ghost which began on the day of Pentecost. Those who are sealed unto the day of redemption:

Ephesians 4:30 And grieve not the holy Spirit of God, whereby ye are sealed unto the day of redemption.

This current age of grace will end with the rapture of these saints at the last trump of God.

Luke 13:29 And they shall come from the east, and *from* the west, and from the north, and *from* the south, and shall sit down in the kingdom of God.

Paul explains that even during this "age of law" referred to as the kingdom of God that salvation is open to everyone that has believed God just as Abraham did:

Romans 4:2 For if Abraham were justified by works, he hath *whereof* to glory; but not before God.

Romans 4:3 For what saith the scripture? Abraham believed God, and it was counted unto him for righteousness.

Romans 4:4 Now to him that worketh is the reward not reckoned of grace, but of debt.

Luke 13:30 And, behold, there are last which shall be first, and there are first which shall be last.

Jesus explains that there will be levels or positions in eternal life. But the key is to make it into eternal life before God shuts the door. During this dispensation, that door will be shut at the

rapture. There will not be a single saved person left on earth and this will happen in the twinkling of an eye.

Luke 13:31 The same day there came certain of the Pharisees, saying unto him, Get thee out, and depart hence: for Herod will kill thee.

Herod being tetrarch of Galilee was upset with the number of followers that Jesus had. However, Jesus was not afraid and here explains the importance of why He came to earth.

Luke 13:32 And he said unto them, Go ye, and tell that fox, Behold, I cast out devils, and I do cures to day and to morrow, and the third *day* I shall be perfected.
Luke 13:33 Nevertheless I must walk to day, and to morrow, and the *day* following: for it cannot be that a prophet perish out of Jerusalem.

This is now the last time Jesus will travel to Judea. He will spend the rest of His days alive in the Judean area. As He approaches Jerusalem, the city that is the apple of God's eye, He begins to cry out, not because of the buildings and the city itself. It is the failure of God's people to see the promise of God about to walk into this area. God's son who will soon be put to death by everyone of us.

Luke 13:34 O Jerusalem, Jerusalem, which killest the prophets, and stonest them that are sent unto thee; how often would I have gathered thy children together, as a hen *doth gather* her brood under *her* wings, and ye would not!
Luke 13:35 Behold, your house is left unto you desolate: and verily I say unto you, Ye shall not see me, until *the time* come when ye shall say, Blessed *is* he that cometh in the name of the Lord.

Jesus came to earth to save that which was lost.
Matthew 18:11 For the Son of man is come to save that which was lost.
This chapter is all about what Jesus did and said to convince the people who met Him that what He did and what He said was what God wanted man to hear.

Romans 10:17 So then faith *cometh* by hearing, and hearing by the word of God.

Did Jesus have anything to say to you in this chapter of the Gospel of Luke? Salvation must come by hearing what God has to say. God must say it. We must hear it. Then we need to apply it to our heart by faith.

LUKE CHAPTER 14

Highlights:

Chapter fourteen has Jesus Christ healing on the Sabbath. He continues speaking in many parables. Jesus tests His disciple's faithfulness.

Main Participants:

Jesus Christ v.1,
A Chief Pharisee v.1,
A certain man with the dropsy v.2,
Lawyers and Pharisees v.3,
Great multitudes v.25,

In Brief:

Jesus Christ heals the man who has dropsy on the Sabbath. Jesus speaks against holding the sabbath as a special day to do no work on that day. He speaks in parables with Lawyers and Pharisees not to take the highest seat. Jesus has great multitudes follow Him as He tests their faithfulness to Him. He says three more parables to get His disciples to think of where they stand with God. He that hath ears to hear, let him hear!

Only in Luke's Gospel

Luke 14:1 And it came to pass, as he went into the house of one of the chief Pharisees to eat bread on the sabbath day, that they watched him.

One thing Jesus liked to do when he saw men spouting about their own righteousness was to give them something to watch for. He did everything He could to point out the religious error. To prove this point, more good works are recorded on the Sabbath day by Jesus than any other day of the week. He healed more on the Sabbath than any other day in the scriptures.

Luke 14:2 And, behold, there was a certain man before him which had the dropsy.

Dropsy is a problem known today as edema. Dropsy was a term used to describe the general swelling in the legs and was an indication of congestive heart failure.

Luke 14:3 And Jesus answering spake unto the lawyers and Pharisees, saying, Is it lawful to heal on the sabbath day?

Jesus gets directly in their face with the question about healing on the Sabbath. Jesus was a man among men! He is so articulate that the Pharisees said not a word.

Luke 14:4 And they held their peace. And he took *him,* and healed him, and let him go;

Let him go! The same word in the Greek as in chapter 13 verses 11 and 12 when Jesus healed the woman and said, "loosed from". The Greek word "Apoluo" means to set free and here it is translated as "let him go" which could mean set him free from his affliction. There are many times that God spells out emphatically that Jesus did this work on the Sabbath. And remember that Luke

earlier explained that Jesus came to be known as a physician, a physician that would heal seven days a week.

Luke 4:23 And he said unto them, Ye will surely say unto me this proverb, Physician, heal thyself: whatsoever we have heard done in Capernaum, do also here in thy country.

All four Gospels mentioned healing on the Sabbath:
In Matthew:

Matthew 12:10 And, behold, there was a man which had *his* hand withered. And they asked him, saying, Is it lawful to heal on the sabbath days? that they might accuse him.

In Mark:

Mark 3:2 And they watched him, whether he would heal him on the sabbath day; that they might accuse him.

In Luke:

Luke 13:14 And the ruler of the synagogue answered with indignation, because that Jesus had healed on the sabbath day, and said unto the people, There are six days in which men ought to work: in them therefore come and be healed, and not on the sabbath day.

And in John:

John 9:14 And it was the sabbath day when Jesus made the clay, and opened his eyes.

John 9:15 Then again the Pharisees also asked him how he had received his sight. He said unto them, He put clay upon mine eyes, and I washed, and do see.

John 9:16 Therefore said some of the Pharisees, This man is not of God, because he keepeth not the sabbath day. Others said, How can a man that is a sinner do such miracles? And there was a division among them.

Jesus came to fulfill the law. He points out that the law that was established for the Sabbath have been met and fulfilled by Him. Jesus gives a commonsense answer that is so accurate the Pharisees became speechless:

Luke 14:5 And answered them, saying, Which of you shall have an ass or an ox fallen into a pit, and will not straightway pull him out on the sabbath day?

Luke 14:6 And they could not answer him again to these things.

Again, Jesus speaks again in parables:

Luke 14:7 And he put forth a parable to those which were bidden, when he marked how they chose out the chief rooms; saying unto them,

Luke 14:8 When thou art bidden of any *man* to a wedding, sit not down in the highest room; lest a more honourable man than thou be bidden of him;

Luke 14:9 And he that bade thee and him come and say to thee, Give this man place; and thou begin with shame to take the lowest room.

Luke 14:10 But when thou art bidden, go and sit down in the lowest room; that when he that bade thee cometh, he may say unto thee, Friend, go up higher: then shalt thou have worship in the presence of them that sit at meat with thee.

Luke 14:11 For whosoever exalteth himself shall be abased; and he that humbleth himself shall be exalted.

Here is a good application of an Old Testament scripture.

> Proverbs 15:33 The fear of the LORD *is* the instruction of wisdom; and before honour *is* humility.

Jesus now flips the lesson from the person being invited, to the person doing the invitations. Jesus says to invite those who may not be on the guest list.

Luke 14:12 Then said he also to him that bade him, When thou makest a dinner or a supper, call not thy friends, nor thy brethren, neither thy kinsmen, nor *thy* rich neighbours; lest they also bid thee again, and a recompence be made thee.

Luke 14:13 But when thou makest a feast, call the poor, the maimed, the lame, the blind:

Luke 14:14 And thou shalt be blessed; for they cannot recompense thee: for thou shalt be recompensed at the resurrection of the just.

Notice that there is a recompense at the resurrection of the just. The word "recompense" is the same word Jesus uses to describe how vengeance is to be recompensed by the Lord. In Romans 12:19 the word "repay" is this very same word.

> Romans 12:19 Dearly beloved, avenge not yourselves, but *rather* give place unto wrath: for it is written, Vengeance *is* mine; I will repay, saith the Lord.

The translators tried to express a difference between the same word being used for good or for evil. Recompensed in verse fourteen speaks of rewards being handed out. This is seen at the "Bema Seat" or judgement seat of Christ:

> 2Corinthians 5:10 For we must all appear before the judgment seat of Christ; that every one may receive the things *done* in *his* body, according to that he hath done, whether *it be* good or bad.

Luke 14:15 And when one of them that sat at meat with him heard these things, he said unto him, Blessed *is* he that shall eat bread in the kingdom of God.

The kingdom of God is spoken of as something to be desired. That desire is in the heart of every man. That is why in a few short chapters Jesus will say that the kingdom of God is within a man.

> Luke 17:20 And when he was demanded of the Pharisees, when the kingdom of God should come, he answered them and said, The kingdom of God cometh not with observation:
> Luke 17:21 Neither shall they say, Lo here! or, lo there! for, behold, the kingdom of God is within you.

It is time for a real event to be spoken of and not a parable. This event really happened. Yes, there was a "certain man" the scripture says. It may just be the Lord's method of witnessing that He is talking about.

Luke 14:16 Then said he unto him, A certain man made a great supper, and bade many:

Luke 14:17 And sent his servant at supper time to say to them that were bidden, Come; for all things are now ready.

Luke 14:18 And they all with one *consent* began to make excuse. The first said unto him, I have bought a piece of ground, and I must needs go and see it: I pray thee have me excused.
Luke 14:19 And another said, I have bought five yoke of oxen, and I go to prove them: I pray thee have me excused.
Luke 14:20 And another said, I have married a wife, and therefore I cannot come.

The excuses have been heard from many. "I don't have time to go to Church" or "I am too tired," or "I am working," or "I have tickets to a ball game," or It's the only day I can play golf, baseball, soccer, etc.

Most of us when we become saved, witness to our loved ones and those who are closest to us. With this passage, Jesus instructs not to stop there. Go to the lost wherever they can be found for there are many who have yet to hear the gospel.

Luke 14:21 So that servant came, and shewed his lord these things. Then the master of the house being angry said to his servant, Go out quickly into the streets and lanes of the city, and bring in hither the poor, and the maimed, and the halt, and the blind.
Luke 14:22 And the servant said, Lord, it is done as thou hast commanded, and yet there is room.
Luke 14:23 And the lord said unto the servant, Go out into the highways and hedges, and compel *them* to come in, that my house may be filled.
Luke 14:24 For I say unto you, That none of those men which were bidden shall taste of my supper.

The result of not hearing the call to come to Jesus in this life cannot be overstated. Jesus says none of these men which were bidden, and refused to come, shall taste what God has prepared for those who do come to Him.

Luke 14:25 And there went great multitudes with him: and he turned, and said unto them,

Jesus is once again quick with his style of teaching and with the metaphors and parables as seen in previous statements. He uses terminology that will invoke one to think. Eye and hand cut off:

Matthew 5:29 And if thy right eye offend thee, pluck it out, and cast *it* from thee: for it is profitable for thee that one of thy members should perish, and not *that* thy whole body should be cast into hell.

Matthew 5:30 And if thy right hand offend thee, cut it off, and cast *it* from thee: for it is profitable for thee that one of thy members should perish, and not *that* thy whole body should be cast into hell.

Camel passing through eye of needle:

Matthew 19:24 And again I say unto you, It is easier for a camel to go through the eye of a needle, than for a rich man to enter into the kingdom of God.

Beam in one's eye:

Luke 6:41 And why beholdest thou the mote that is in thy brother's eye, but perceivest not the beam that is in thine own eye?

Luke 14:26 If any *man* come to me, and hate not his father, and mother, and wife, and children, and brethren, and sisters, yea, and his own life also, he cannot be my disciple.

Here He uses the word "hate". This is a word that will not allow anyone to sit on the fence. I see God as hating fence sitters. So much so that He says it makes Him want to puke.

Revelation 3:15 I know thy works, that thou art neither cold nor hot: I would thou wert cold or hot.

Revelation 3:16 So then because thou art lukewarm, and neither cold nor hot, I will spue thee out of my mouth.

Know this for sure that God does not say to hate our family. God says in many other places to love our family:

1Timothy 5:8 But if any provide not for his own, and specially for those of his own house, he hath denied the faith, and is worse than an infidel.

God wants a man to consider carefully his decision to follow Jesus Christ and give up all. No one should think it is an easy thing to surrender all to Jesus Christ. We sing the song "I Surrender All" by J. W. Van DeVenter

All to Jesus I surrender	**All to Him I freely give**
I will ever love and trust Him	**In His presence daily live**
All to Jesus I surrender	**Humbly at His feet I bow**
Worldly pleasures all forsaken	**Take me Jesus take me now.**

Luke 14:27 And whosoever doth not bear his cross, and come after me, cannot be my disciple.

Luke 14:28 For which of you, intending to build a tower, sitteth not down first, and counteth the cost, whether he have *sufficient* to finish *it?*

Luke 14:29 Lest haply, after he hath laid the foundation, and is not able to finish *it,* all that behold *it* begin to mock him,

Luke 14:30 Saying, This man began to build, and was not able to finish.

This example explains starting something and not finishing. WOE to those who hear about Jesus and fail to make the appropriate heart conditions of repentance and believing.

Luke 14:31 Or what king, going to make war against another king, sitteth not down first, and consulteth whether he be able with ten thousand to meet him that cometh against him with twenty thousand?

Luke 14:32 Or else, while the other is yet a great way off, he sendeth an ambassage, and desireth conditions of peace.

Luke 14:33 So likewise, whosoever he be of you that forsaketh not all that he hath, he cannot be my disciple.

Luke 14:34 Salt *is* good: but if the salt have lost his savour, wherewith shall it be seasoned?

Luke 14:35 It is neither fit for the land, nor yet for the dunghill; *but* men cast it out. He that hath ears to hear, let him hear.

The "it" here refers to who or what is salted. A Christian is salt to the lost. He is salt to the world. If a Christian loses his savory, that is his desire to serve Christ and witness, he is no longer fit for the land or anything else in this world. By not witnessing a person is sealing the fate of the lost one. For God has declared that:

> Romans 10:14 How then shall they call on him in whom they have not believed? and how shall they believe in him of whom they have not heard? and how shall they hear without a preacher? Romans 10:15 And how shall they preach, except they be sent? as it is written, How beautiful are the feet of them that preach the gospel of peace, and bring glad tidings of good things!

LUKE CHAPTER 15

Highlights:

Chapter fifteen has Jesus Christ seeking one, by leaving the ninety and nine. He presents the great story of repentance by the prodigal son.

Main Participants:

Jesus Christ v.1,
Publicans v.1
Sinners v.1,
Pharisees v.2,
Scribes v.2,

In Brief:

Jesus Christ eats with sinners. He sets the leaders back on their heels with a parable. He speaks of going after one lost child even if it means leaving ninety-nine behind. His next story is one that has been repeated more than any other in scripture. It is called the prodigal son. But it is really about both sons. Both have a problem. Both are sought after by the father. Both, in spite of the wrong they have done are loved by the father. There is a lot of truth here.

Only in Luke's Gospel

Luke 15:1 Then drew near unto him all the publicans and sinners for to hear him.

Luke 15:2 And the Pharisees and scribes murmured, saying, This man receiveth sinners, and eateth with them.

There is some indication that Luke is recording sayings that Jesus spoke in His last year of public ministries. This can be drawn from the verse below which follows the next two chapters of Jesus speaking parables and true stories:

Luke 17:11 And it came to pass, as he went to Jerusalem, that he passed through the midst of Samaria and Galilee.

Perhaps this destination "As He went to Jerusalem" speaks of His final trip to Jerusalem. However, before He arrives in Jerusalem, He would first walk through Samaria and back to Galilee and all this while He is speaking to His disciples and to Pharisees and others who will listen. This is not always the same crowd because He is in different villages with each speech. All this takes time and days for walking and resting. And so, this chapter begins with Jesus, as He walks through Israel, speaking to four classes of people: publicans and sinners and Pharisees and scribes:

Luke 15:3 And he spake this parable unto them, saying,

Many assume that this parable by Christ is given also in Matthew. In Matthew 18 there is a similar account:

Matthew 18:12 How think ye? if a man have an hundred sheep, and one of them be gone astray, doth he not leave the ninety and nine, and goeth into the mountains, and seeketh that which is gone astray?

Matthew 18:13 And if so be that he find it, verily I say unto you, he rejoiceth more of that *sheep,* than of the ninety and nine which went not astray.

Matthew 18:14 Even so it is not the will of your Father which is in heaven, that one of these little ones should perish.

However, Matthew speaks just four or five days before His final trip to Judea an entirely different time when Jesus would move on to Jerusalem for Passover. And the location is specific as we are told He is at Capernaum when He speaks of this search for the lost sheep.

> Matthew 17:24 And when they were come to Capernaum, they that received tribute *money* came to Peter, and said, Doth not your master pay tribute?

Perhaps in His final year of public ministry, Christ used this parable in several locations.

Luke 15:4 What man of you, having an hundred sheep, if he lose one of them, doth not leave the ninety and nine in the wilderness, and go after that which is lost, until he find it?

One of the great songs of the faith comes from this parable and was originally drafted as a poem. Ira Sankey of D. L. Moody fame was the one who put it to music. It was about a man who was saved and serving the Lord Jesus Christ. He went astray and the Lord left all to search for this single lost sheep, out in the world. Never is it said that this man had lost his salvation. The Lord just continued trying to bring him back. D. L. Moody preached this as many others would also.

Here is the poem that was written by Elizabeth C. Clephane. The poem was said to be written after the death of her brother, George Clephane who died in 1851. She believed he was saved but fell away and had a troubled life in Canada. As the story goes, he fell from his horse one day while intoxicated, struck his head upon a rock and died.

The Ninety and Nine

There were ninety and nine that safely
Lay In the shelter of the fold;
But one was out on the hills away,
Far off from the gates of gold.
Away on the mountains wild and bare;
Away from the tender Shepherd's Care.

"Lord, Thou hast here Thy ninety and nine;
Are they not enough for Thee?"
But the Shepherd made answer:
"This Of mine Has wandered away from Me.
And although the road be rough and
Steep, I go to the desert to find
My sheep."

But none of the ransomed ever knew
How deep were the waters crossed;
Nor how dark was the night the Lord passed through
Ere He found His sheep that was lost.
Out in the desert He heard its cry;
'Twas sick and helpless and ready to die.

Luke 15:5 And when he hath found *it,* he layeth *it* on his shoulders,
rejoicing.

"Lord, whence are those blood-drops all the way,
That mark out the mountain's track?"
"They were shed for one who had gone astray
Ere the Shepherd could bring him back."
"Lord, whence are thy hands so rent and torn?"
"They're pierced tonight by many a thorn."

Luke 15:6 And when he cometh home, he calleth together *his* friends and neighbours, saying unto them, Rejoice with me; for I have found my sheep which was lost.

> And all through the mountains, thunder-riv'n,
> And up from the rocky steep,
> There arose a glad cry to the gate of heav'n,
>
> "Rejoice! I have found My sheep!"
> And the angels echoed around the throne,
> "Rejoice, for the Lord brings back His Own!"

Luke 15:7 I say unto you, that likewise joy shall be in heaven over one sinner that repenteth, more than over ninety and nine just persons, which need no repentance.

Luke describes that this parable is all about repentance. It is amazing how God speaks continuously of repentance. Maybe we should take note of that. The sheep already belong to Jesus. So, this is a statement by Christ that even though a man can go astray, you still belong to Him even though repentance is needed. Once Jesus saves you, you cannot lose your salvation.

Jesus continues with this parable to reinforce His statement that repentance is the key needed to open the heart to belief. Now Jesus speaks of a coin that has been lost but this loss is not eternal it is but for a time and Jesus will not let go until the coin is found again.

Luke 15:8 Either what woman having ten pieces of silver, if she lose one piece, doth not light a candle, and sweep the house, and seek diligently till she find *it?*

The coin already belonged to the woman. The ten are already in the possession of the owner. This is about being already saved but then falling away. A Bible word for this is backsliding. The word backsliding comes from the Old Testament and is used to

describe the nation of Israel that already belonged to God. Due to God's unconditional covenant with Israel, nothing Israel can do will break this covenant. This is true for the believer also. When God says "Thou shalt be saved" you can put it down in writing that you are saved.

But sometimes Israel, like all of us fell away from this love of God. However, Israel remains as God's chosen people. It is just as wonderful to realize that God never falls away from us!

Hosea 14:1 O Israel, return unto the LORD thy God; for thou hast fallen by thine iniquity.

Hosea 14:2 Take with you words, and turn to the LORD: say unto him, Take away all iniquity, and receive *us* graciously: so will we render the calves of our lips.

Hosea 14:3 Asshur shall not save us; we will not ride upon horses: neither will we say any more to the work of our hands, *Ye are* our gods: for in thee the fatherless findeth mercy.

Hosea 14:4 I will heal their backsliding, I will love them freely: for mine anger is turned away from him.

Anyone who has ever worked with cattle knows that if a cow does not want to move it takes a lot of work to get her to move. Even with a rope around its neck a cow will set its legs at such an angle as to prevent you from moving her. She begins to back up digging her hooves in and straightening her legs as to really fight against you and what you want her to do. God describes Israel as a backsliding heifer. Israel was just like this as God describes her as she so often did following other idols.

Hosea 4:15 Though thou, Israel, play the harlot, *yet* let not Judah offend; and come not ye unto Gilgal, neither go ye up to Bethaven, nor swear, The LORD liveth.

Hosea 4:16 For Israel slideth back as a backsliding heifer: now the LORD will feed them as a lamb in a large place.

Hosea 4:17 Ephraim *is* joined to idols: let him alone.

God says certain things happen in heaven when a lesson is learned by a child of God. The child already belongs to the Father. But when the child becomes disobedient or unresponsive to the will of the Father, he does not disown them or kick them out of the family. Instead, God chastises them to bring them to repent. When repentance takes place, it is seen as a time of rejoicing by those already in heaven, those who know best. Staying on the straight and narrow path is what the angels know all too well.

Luke 15:9 And when she hath found *it,* she calleth *her* friends and *her* neighbours together, saying, Rejoice with me; for I have found the piece which I had lost.
Luke 15:10 Likewise, I say unto you, there is joy in the presence of the angels of God over one sinner that repenteth.

We cannot see the joy in heaven over someone who has not kept themselves blameless and has seen the error of their way in this life and turned from it (repented). But it is assuring to know that the word of God here in Luke chapter fifteen expresses this over and over. If you are born again you are adopted into the family of God, and nothing can take that away not even you!

The Prodigal Son

Luke is the only writer to have this true story. This is no longer a part of the parable above. However, the two parables above are very important to see where Jesus is going with this true story. Christ does not mention this as a parable. He only mentions the above illustrations as a parable. This is because of the conjunction of "either" in verse eight. As discussed in the previous statements by Christ when He speaks in parables, he mentions that it is a parable and in verse three of this chapter "parable" is singular. Now it is said that there really was a "certain man."

So begins the true story of the prodigal son. As this is read you can apply it to your understanding of the Gospel in almost every conceivable way and every doctrine you can think of.

1. God loves the family

2. That we are to have assurance of salvation

3. That God is love

4. That man can go his own way (sovereignty)

5. That once you are born again you are permanently a child of God

6. That saved children still have problems with God

7. That repentance is needed to come back to the Father

8. God had to redeem both children, good or bad

9. That God is a rewarder of them that diligently seek Him

10. That without staying close to God, the world system will consume a man

Luke 15:11 And he said, A certain man had two sons:

The first thing Jesus says is that there are two sons. Remember who Jesus is talking to. In the room there are basically two types of men that Jesus is talking to. Publicans and sinners (represented by the younger son) and Pharisees and scribes (represented by the older son). It is not revealed that anyone in the room is saved but this lecture is designed to get these two groups of men to think about their salvation. They needed to understand that they first must become a child of the Father! How about you? Do you relate to one of these two sons? Are you a child of the Father? Both sons are born of the Father. Throughout this whole account they never stop being a child of the Father. So, it is true of a man being born again. Being born again you become a new child of the Father.

John 3:3 Jesus answered and said unto him, Verily, verily, I say unto thee, Except a man be born again, he cannot see the kingdom of God.

John 3:4 Nicodemus saith unto him, How can a man be born when he is old? can he enter the second time into his mother's womb, and be born?

John 3:5 Jesus answered, Verily, verily, I say unto thee, Except a man be born of water and *of* the Spirit, he cannot enter into the kingdom of God.

1Peter 1:23 Being born again, not of corruptible seed, but of incorruptible, by the word of God, which liveth and abideth for ever

Luke 15:12 And the younger of them said to *his* father, Father, give me the portion of goods that falleth *to me*. And he divided unto them *his* living.

Sometimes we all make wrong decisions. Is this you? Have you ever made a wrong decision and then let life's circumstances keep you out of the Father's will? I think as the father was dividing up the portion of goods, he was saying this Proverb. Proverbs 10 is all about sons making decisions that should be centered around wisdom.

Proverbs 10:1 The proverbs of Solomon. A wise son maketh a glad father: but a foolish son *is* the heaviness of his mother.

Proverbs 10:2 Treasures of wickedness profit nothing: but righteousness delivereth from death.

Proverbs 10:3 The LORD will not suffer the soul of the righteous to famish: but he casteth away the substance of the wicked.

Proverbs 10:4 He becometh poor that dealeth *with* a slack hand: but the hand of the diligent maketh rich.

Proverbs 10:5 He that gathereth in summer *is* a wise son: *but* he that sleepeth in harvest *is* a son that causeth shame.

Proverbs 10:6 Blessings *are* upon the head of the just: but violence covereth the mouth of the wicked.

In this case God gave the son what he wanted. God does that and allows us to see the error of our ways.

Proverbs 10:7 The memory of the just *is* blessed: but the name of the wicked shall rot.

Proverbs 10:8 The wise in heart will receive commandments: but a prating fool shall fall.

Proverbs 10:9 He that walketh uprightly walketh surely: but he that perverteth his ways shall be known.

Proverbs 10:10 He that winketh with the eye causeth sorrow: but a prating fool shall fall.

Proverbs 10:11 The mouth of a righteous *man is* a well of life: but violence covereth the mouth of the wicked.

Proverbs 10:12 Hatred stirreth up strifes: but love covereth all sins.

And the younger opened his mouth and said to the Father "give me the portion of goods."

Proverbs 10:13 In the lips of him that hath understanding wisdom is found: but a rod *is* for the back of him that is void of understanding.

This youngest son was void of understanding. The father allowed the choice of the younger and it became a "rod upon his back".

Proverbs 10:14 Wise *men* lay up knowledge: but the mouth of the foolish *is* near destruction.

Proverbs 10:15 The rich man's wealth *is* his strong city: the destruction of the poor *is* their poverty.

Proverbs 10:16 The labour of the righteous *tendeth* to life: the fruit of the wicked to sin.

Proverbs 10:17 He *is in* the way of life that keepeth instruction: but he that refuseth reproof erreth.

Proverbs 10:18 He that hideth hatred *with* lying lips, and he that uttereth a slander, *is* a fool.

Proverbs 10:19 In the multitude of words there wanteth not sin: but he that refraineth his lips *is* wise.

Proverbs 10:20 The tongue of the just *is as* choice silver: the heart of the wicked *is* little worth.

Proverbs 10:21 The lips of the righteous feed many: but fools die for want of wisdom.

He did not know it, but he was about to do a very foolish thing. Without wisdom, the youngest son was a fool. The father knew it but he allowed this foolishness to take place.

Luke 15:13 And not many days after the younger son gathered all together, and took his journey into a far country, and there wasted his substance with riotous living.

At first it always looks so enjoyable; so enticing; so desirous. This is how it appeared to this youngest son. He faced the three-fold enemy all at once here. The world, the flesh, and the devil all came together to destroy any testimony this younger son had.

Proverbs 10:22 The blessing of the LORD, it maketh rich, and he addeth no sorrow with it.

Proverbs 10:23 *It is* as sport to a fool to do mischief: but a man of understanding hath wisdom.

It is sport to a fool to do mischief! The youngest son did nothing but mischief. He wasted his substance with riotous living.

Proverbs 10:24 The fear of the wicked, it shall come upon him: but the desire of the righteous shall be granted.

The fear of the wicked was about to come upon the youngest son.

Luke 15:14 And when he had spent all, there arose a mighty famine in that land; and he began to be in want.

He began to be in want. When you have nothing and there is nothing in sight, fear sets in.

Proverbs 10:25 As the whirlwind passeth, so *is* the wicked no *more:* but the righteous *is* an everlasting foundation.

Proverbs 10:26 As vinegar to the teeth, and as smoke to the eyes, so *is* the sluggard to them that send him.

Proverbs 10:27 The fear of the LORD prolongeth days: but the years of the wicked shall be shortened.

Proverbs 10:28 The hope of the righteous *shall be* gladness: but the expectation of the wicked shall perish.

Proverbs 10:29 The way of the LORD *is* strength to the upright: but destruction *shall be* to the workers of iniquity.

Freedom is something everyone wants in their lifetime. But freedom without wisdom is never a good thing. The youngest son did not sneak off. He did not go without the OK of the father.

The father allowed him to go. However, freedom with the riotous living resulted in the destruction of the life of this young man. God will give us what we ask for even if He knows it will not be good for us. It is always a lesson to reflect on and a tremendous teaching tool in the hand of someone who is wise.

Proverbs 10:30 The righteous shall never be removed: but the wicked shall not inhabit the earth.

Proverbs 10:31 The mouth of the just bringeth forth wisdom: but the froward tongue shall be cut out.

Proverbs 10:32 The lips of the righteous know what is acceptable: but the mouth of the wicked *speaketh* frowardness.

The end result of this freedom and riotous living without wisdom:

Luke 15:15 And he went and joined himself to a citizen of that country; and he sent him into his fields to feed swine.

The youngest son undoubtedly never had anything to do with swine as they were considered unclean animals and the father would never eat pork or have anything to do with the care, feeding, control and or slaughter of a pig. Leviticus spells this out:

Leviticus 11:7 And the swine, though he divide the hoof, and be clovenfooted, yet he cheweth not the cud; he *is* unclean to you.

Leviticus 11:8 Of their flesh shall ye not eat, and their carcase shall ye not touch; they *are* unclean to you.

The way to a man's heart is through his stomach!

Luke 15:16 And he would fain have filled his belly with the husks that the swine did eat: and no man gave unto him.

This is not a biblical saying but it sure pulled a lot of weight in this man's thinking. He was hungry. He now understands the wisdom he should have had to stay home with a loving father.

Luke 15:17 And when he came to himself, he said, How many hired servants of my father's have bread enough and to spare, and I perish with hunger!

Repentance again becomes the main focal point in this lecture by Christ. This son demonstrates the complete repentance spoken of by the Savior in the last parable. Notice the change of mind. Notice the turning from this way of life. Understand that if he stops at this point, he will never have the life he desires. Repentance alone is not enough to save you. Sincerity will not get you into heaven. This son must follow with a belief in his heart by returning to the father who has provided what's needed to have that old lifestyle back. That new eternal life is available with his father.

Luke 15:18 I will arise and go to my father, and will say unto him, Father, I have sinned against heaven, and before thee,
Luke 15:19 And am no more worthy to be called thy son: make me as one of thy hired servants.

This is where repentance and belief go hand in hand. Belief is what is needed to receive the new life. Many say that just saying the words "I believe" is good enough. But if the young man in this story never arose and went back to the father, would he have that life? Belief is real when it causes a man to act. I use the story of General Lee and General Grant at the Appomattox courthouse. General Lee knew in his heart that there was nothing that the south could do to win another battle in the civil war. He believed with all his heart that the south was not going to win. What was his only recourse? He had to do something. If he just believed this and did nothing many more troops would die. So, what did he do? He believed and decided against every instinct in his body to move to action by surrendering.

Luke 15:20 And he arose, and came to his father. But when he was yet a great way off, his father saw him, and had compassion, and ran, and fell on his neck, and kissed him.

The youngest son belongs back in the family as the father displays. He has been and continues to be a child of the father where interaction will occur. There is repentance by confession with him saying:

Luke 15:21 And the son said unto him, Father, I have sinned against heaven, and in thy sight, and am no more worthy to be called thy son.

David knew of this confession. He confessed nearly the same thing in the Psalms:
Psalms 51:3 For I acknowledge my transgressions: and my sin *is* ever before me.
Psalms 51:4 Against thee, thee only, have I sinned, and done *this* evil in thy sight: that thou mightest be justified when thou speakest, *and* be clear when thou judgest.
One of the great verses in the Bible we use for confession and belief is Romans 10:9-10. Confess and believe! But what does belief have to bring? Belief must bring righteousness!
Romans 10:9 That if thou shalt confess with thy mouth the Lord Jesus, and shalt believe in thine heart that God hath raised him from the dead, thou shalt be saved.
Romans 10:10 For with the heart man believeth unto righteousness; and with the mouth confession is made unto salvation.
As the prodigal son repents, with a change of mind and heart, which is seen by his returning and confessing of his sin is this. His belief has invoked him to action. And just as our Father will do for us when we repent, he put on the younger his best robe.

Luke 15:22 But the father said to his servants, Bring forth the best robe, and put *it* on him; and put a ring on his hand, and shoes on *his* feet:
Luke 15:23 And bring hither the fatted calf, and kill *it;* and let us eat, and be merry:

To eat drink and be merry is one of the great results of honest labor. The father knew it from the scriptures he had access to.
Ecclesiastes 8:15 Then I commended mirth, because a man hath no better thing under the sun, than to eat, and to drink, and to

be merry: for that shall abide with him of his labour the days of his life, which God giveth him under the sun.

Luke 15:24 For this my son was dead, and is alive again; he was lost, and is found. And they began to be merry.

Remember that this true story is addressed to two groups of people that were assembled. Turning from the publicans and sinners, Jesus now speaks to the Pharisee's and scribes.

Luke 15:25 Now his elder son was in the field: and as he came and drew nigh to the house, he heard musick and dancing.
Luke 15:26 And he called one of the servants, and asked what these things meant.
Luke 15:27 And he said unto him, Thy brother is come; and thy father hath killed the fatted calf, because he hath received him safe and sound.

"Thy brother is come" makes him angry. What kind of an attitude is this? It is like the murmuring of verse two where the religious leaders say, "This man receiveth sinners, and eateth with them."

Luke 15:28 And he was angry, and would not go in: therefore came his father out, and intreated him.

The angry elder brother is wanting to get something off his chest. It has to do with jealousy and resentment.

Luke 15:29 And he answering said to *his* father, Lo, these many years do I serve thee, neither transgressed I at any time thy commandment: and yet thou never gavest me a kid, that I might make merry with my friends:

The eldest son states his case. He Speaks to the father as one who is bitter towards his brother.

Luke 15:30 But as soon as this thy son was come, which hath devoured thy living with harlots, thou hast killed for him the fatted calf.

To the older brother, killing the fatted calf is not the problem. Favoritism to the younger brother is the problem. The father sees this immediately and responds with a warm, loving statement.

Luke 15:31 And he said unto him, Son, thou art ever with me, and all that I have is thine.

Remember that the youngest son already received his inheritance from the father. So, he tells the oldest that all is thine. The oldest son knew this. But the sin of jealousy ran deeper than the inheritance. It was a heart problem. The father addressed this by saying:

Luke 15:32 It was meet that we should make merry, and be glad: for this thy brother was dead, and is alive again; and was lost, and is found.

Was the eldest son, right? Was the younger son, right? We are left to consider for ourselves what the two sons did. They were already sons of the father. But it is worth repeating that they both still needed to repent. Repentance is an ongoing thing that we need to do daily. God discussed this in heaven earlier in this chapter as Luke records:

Luke 15:10 Likewise, I say unto you, there is joy in the presence of the angels of God over one sinner that repenteth.

Paul discusses repentance in another way. He says that we must die to the old man. To please our Father which is in heaven, we must die daily.

1Corinthians 15:31 I protest by your rejoicing which I have in Christ Jesus our Lord, I die daily.

LUKE CHAPTER 16

Highlights:

Chapter sixteen has Jesus Christ speaking to His disciples and Jesus Christ speaking to the Pharisees. Jesus gives the most vivid look at hell.

Main Participants:

Jesus Christ v.1,
His Disciples v.1,
The Pharisees v.14,

In Brief:

Jesus Christ speaks of a certain man who had an unjust steward who wasted his goods. Jesus speaks to the Pharisees about their evil hearts. Jesus speaks about adultery. Jesus speaks about a certain rich man and Lazarus in the heart of the earth. Hell and Abraham's Bosom are there.

Only in Luke's Gospel

Luke 16:1 And he said also unto his disciples, There was a certain rich man, which had a steward; and the same was accused unto him that he had wasted his goods.

A PERFECT UNDERSTANDING
FRED A. KUYPERS

Jesus is continually instructing His disciples. He is in His final year of public ministry and may even be approaching His final month of public ministry. He has continually discussed His death with His disciples even though they have not understood what He is talking about. But also, along His trek through the promised land He always speaks of what is right and what is wrong. He now gives a story that is very strange. It is the first time that He indicates that the world may have something that His followers could understand and use. It is all about being faithful and not neglecting the things of God.

Luke 16:2 And he called him, and said unto him, How is it that I hear this of thee? give an account of thy stewardship; for thou mayest be no longer steward.

Jesus is not talking about losing salvation here. Jesus is talking about being in the world and losing an appointed position because of a worldly situation causing unfaithfulness. Soon Jesus will discuss what it takes for this or any rich man to make it into heaven. He will show how hard it is for a rich man to get into heaven later in chapter eighteen of Luke.

Luke 16:3 Then the steward said within himself, What shall I do? for my lord taketh away from me the stewardship: I cannot dig; to beg I am ashamed.
Luke 16:4 I am resolved what to do, that, when I am put out of the stewardship, they may receive me into their houses.
Luke 16:5 So he called every one of his lord's debtors *unto him,* and said unto the first, How much owest thou unto my lord?
Luke 16:6 And he said, An hundred measures of oil. And he said unto him, Take thy bill, and sit down quickly, and write fifty.

The steward uses earthly logic to at least retrieve something. This is saying something like "one in the hand is worth two in the bush". If you are a hunter, you know exactly what that means.

Luke 16:7 Then said he to another, And how much owest thou? And he said, An hundred measures of wheat. And he said unto him, Take thy bill, and write fourscore.

Now most of us would not be happy with losing 50% or even 20% of what we have. But sometimes in life it is known to take what you can out of a losing situation and cut your losses. In this case even the lord knew that the return of 50% of what was rightfully his or he would probably see nothing. So, the lord looks on this as a wise and good thing to do.

Luke 16:8 And the lord commended the unjust steward, because he had done wisely: for the children of this world are in their generation wiser than the children of light.

What Jesus is trying to get across here is that this steward considered wisely as far as material things go and acted in saving his own neck. If you are in the world and you don't belong to Jesus perhaps you need to be as wise as the world. But the real answer when you seek the wisdom of this world is that you will fail.

Luke 16:9 And I say unto you, Make to yourselves friends of the mammon of unrighteousness; that, when ye fail, they may receive you into everlasting habitations.

Jesus clearly says those who remain friends with mammon will fail.
1Timothy 6:10 For the love of money is the root of all evil: which while some coveted after, they have erred from the faith, and pierced themselves through with many sorrows.
In this world if you fail to trust Christ as your Savior, you will turn to mammon, and He says you will receive an everlasting habitation for this. Later in this chapter Jesus will expound on this habitation.

Luke 16:10 He that is faithful in that which is least is faithful also in much: and he that is unjust in the least is unjust also in much.

The only two relationships are one of righteousness and one of unrighteousness. Just and Unjust. Faithful and unfaithful or saved and unsaved. Jesus points out that what God is looking for in a man is that he be found faithful.

> 1Corinthians 4:1 Let a man so account of us, as of the ministers of Christ, and stewards of the mysteries of God.
>
> 1Corinthians 4:2 Moreover it is required in stewards, that a man be found faithful.

Luke 16:11 If therefore ye have not been faithful in the unrighteous mammon, who will commit to your trust the true *riches?*

God is who deals in true riches. This lesson that Jesus just gave us is about faithfulness. How important it is even in the world.

Luke 16:12 And if ye have not been faithful in that which is another man's, who shall give you that which is your own?

Luke 16:13 No servant can serve two masters: for either he will hate the one, and love the other; or else he will hold to the one, and despise the other. Ye cannot serve God and mammon.

There can only be one master to serve. Joshua knew this all too well in the Old Testament. He declared whom he would serve.

> Joshua 24:15 And if it seem evil unto you to serve the LORD, choose you this day whom ye will serve; whether the gods which your fathers served that *were* on the other side of the flood, or the gods of the Amorites, in whose land ye dwell: but as for me and my house, we will serve the LORD.

Mammon is a transliterated word that means wealth. It can mean money, but it can also refer to possessions. God is not saying you cannot have these things, but He is saying that you cannot have earthly possessions and wealth to the point where you serve them and love them.

Luke 16:14 And the Pharisees also, who were covetous, heard all these things: and they derided him.

God dealt with covetousness in that it is in the top ten of the commandments. Number ten actually:

Exodus 20:17 Thou shalt not covet thy neighbour's house, thou shalt not covet thy neighbour's wife, nor his manservant, nor his maidservant, nor his ox, nor his ass, nor any thing that *is* thy neighbour's.

Luke 16:15 And he said unto them, Ye are they which justify yourselves before men; but God knoweth your hearts: for that which is highly esteemed among men is abomination in the sight of God.

God always gives man direction and instruction. Sometimes man even asks for what God has for them and He gives it to them. The entire age or dispensation of law was about to be fulfilled by Jesus. The Hebrews had asked God to give them this time of law and for the prophets who declare the law. God gave them what they asked for with this age of law.

Exodus 19:4 Ye have seen what I did unto the Egyptians, and *how* I bare you on eagles' wings, and brought you unto myself.

Exodus 19:5 Now therefore, if ye will obey my voice indeed, and keep my covenant, then ye shall be a peculiar treasure unto me above all people: for all the earth *is* mine:

Exodus 19:6 And ye shall be unto me a kingdom of priests, and an holy nation. These *are* the words which thou shalt speak unto the children of Israel.

Exodus 19:7 And Moses came and called for the elders of the people, and laid before their faces all these words which the LORD commanded him.

Exodus 19:8 And all the people answered together, and said, All that the LORD hath spoken we will do. And Moses returned the words of the people unto the LORD.

Exodus 19:9 And the LORD said unto Moses, Lo, I come unto thee in a thick cloud, that the people may hear when I speak with thee, and believe thee for ever. And Moses told the words of the people unto the LORD.

The people spoke "all that the LORD hath spoken we will do." They asked for the age of law to begin. God did not want this. God wanted His creation to turn to Him by faith in Him.

Luke 16:16 The law and the prophets *were* until John: since that time the kingdom of God is preached, and every man presseth into it.

Jesus is now developing God's plan by explaining to the disciples that the way to God is not through the law and the prophets but through what John is beginning to preach as he prepares the way of the Lord. That message of course is REPENT!

Matthew 3:1 In those days came John the Baptist, preaching in the wilderness of Judaea,

Matthew 3:2 And saying, Repent ye: for the kingdom of heaven is at hand.

Repentance against sin prepares the heart for belief. Belief has always been the way to be saved and declared righteous with God. It's only that man wanted to show God that he could be righteous in his own merit. So, God sent the Law and the prophets by Moses to prove to man one thing. That man could not keep them. Now Abraham's time came around 2000BC. He believed God and it was counted unto him for righteousness.

Genesis 15:6 And he believed in the LORD; and he counted it to him for righteousness.

God declared that belief was the way to righteousness. Being right with God. All a man needed to do was believe that God would provide a way to forgive their sin. But, as it is stated above in Exodus, Moses declared to God the message that the people could accomplish God's requirements on their own. Today there is no difference with man. He thinks and says that he is banking his life on his good deeds. That his good deeds will outweigh his bad deeds.

God had a reply for that. God loves His creation of man. All God wanted was for man to love Him back. When the people ordered Moses to meet with God:

Deuteronomy 5:27 Go thou near, and hear all that the LORD our God shall say: and speak thou unto us all that the LORD our God shall speak unto thee; and we will hear *it,* and do *it.*

The people told Moses, whatever "God shall speak; we will hear it and do it! The Lord heard this communication from the people:

Deuteronomy 5:28 And the LORD heard the voice of your words, when ye spake unto me; and the LORD said unto me, I have heard the voice of the words of this people, which they have spoken unto thee: they have well said all that they have spoken.

God loves man so much, but He knew that man would not keep his words. After all, how difficult was it for Adam and Eve not to sin? Just one command from God! And not a difficult one at that. But in love God wished that His creation of man would have a heart that would not sin but love and listen to Him. God would have something to say about this desire of man:

Deuteronomy 5:29 O that there were such an heart in them, that they would fear me, and keep all my commandments always, that it might be well with them, and with their children for ever!

God gave the people what they asked for. God is still merciful as He knows man cannot keep his word to God. He gave the law at this point, but not for the reason man wanted. Paul expounds on this when he writes:

Galatians 3:22 But the scripture hath concluded all under sin, that the promise by faith of Jesus Christ might be given to them that believe.

Galatians 3:23 But before faith came, we were kept under the law, shut up unto the faith which should afterwards be revealed.

Galatians 3:24 Wherefore the law was our schoolmaster *to bring us* unto Christ, that we might be justified by faith.

Galatians 3:25 But after that faith is come, we are no longer under a schoolmaster. Galatians 3:26 For ye are all the children of God by faith in Christ Jesus.

The promise from God is that He would provide what to believe in. His provision of what to believe in is His Son, the Lord

Jesus Christ. Jesus declared this by saying it is now time to press toward the kingdom of God which in just one short chapter He will declare is "within you." That is the message of being born again, that you bring Jesus Christ into your heart and receive Him. What must a man do to keep the entire law and make his own way into heaven? Jesus says if you live by the law you cannot fail by the law.

Luke 16:17 And it is easier for heaven and earth to pass, than one tittle of the law to fail.

Perhaps the worst lawbreaking that was being done by the Pharisees listening this day was commandment number seven. Jesus points this out:

Luke 16:18 Whosoever putteth away his wife, and marrieth another, committeth adultery: and whosoever marrieth her that is put away from *her* husband committeth adultery.

The law has many elements. Here Jesus gives a couple of ways to look at the seventh commandment and what not to do. The seventh commandment just says:
Exodus 20:14 Thou shalt not commit adultery.
God expounds in many parts of the Bible ways to interpret this command. From premarital sex called "fornication" in the Bible to divorce, the Holy Spirit has many ways to work in the heart of a man when it comes to what adultery involves. It is not hard to know about adultery in your heart. Whether or not you are following God's design for you as His child in obeying Him when it comes to this commandment. The Pharisees would have nothing to do with this command either. Earlier they set the tone as they were called out for their covetousness. We read in verse 14 that they "derided Him". This means that they snubbed Him. They looked down their noses at Him. They sneered at Him. Their preexisting attitude toward Jesus would not change. The

Pharisees were going to get even with Jesus one way or another. Jesus decided to go right to the heart of the matter. He began to speak to them about hell and the result that they could expect.

It is now that Jesus gives what is the clearest and most precise explanation of hell in all of scripture. Not only does Jesus give a clear picture of what it looks like, or where hell is located, but he gives us the emotional and physical aspect of what you will experience if you are hell bound. Of course, the goal with this passage is to convince the reader not to go to hell. You need to figure out the only way acceptable to God to not go to this dreadful and eternal place of torment. That way is only through Jesus Christ who said:

John 14:6 Jesus saith unto him, I am the way, the truth, and the life: no man cometh unto the Father, but by me.

Luke 16:19 There was a certain rich man, which was clothed in purple and fine linen, and fared sumptuously every day:

Luke 16:20 And there was a certain beggar named Lazarus, which was laid at his gate, full of sores,

Luke 16:21 And desiring to be fed with the crumbs which fell from the rich man's table: moreover the dogs came and licked his sores.

The rich man was not having a problem because he was rich. He was having a problem because he had no love. There was no compassion for the beggar, Lazarus. Jesus declares this in His condensed version of the commandments and how to live to please God:

Matthew 22:37 Jesus said unto him, Thou shalt love the Lord thy God with all thy heart, and with all thy soul, and with all thy mind.

Matthew 22:38 This is the first and great commandment.

Matthew 22:39 And the second *is* like unto it, Thou shalt love thy neighbour as thyself.

Matthew 22:40 On these two commandments hang all the law and the prophets.

Luke 16:22 And it came to pass, that the beggar died, and was carried by the angels into Abraham's bosom: the rich man also died, and was buried;

It is at this point in both the lives of Lazarus and the rich man that they have crossed the vail of death. Many times, I have said that when you die, you cross from life to death and nothing about you changes. Here in hell, which is where the rich man immediately went, the reader can see that he still has eyes, he still has a mouth, he still has feelings, he still has a tongue.

Luke 16:23 And in hell he lift up his eyes, being in torments, and seeth Abraham afar off, and Lazarus in his bosom.

The word is hell. Modern versions change this word to hades. Hades is the Greek transliterated word for hell. Not everyone knows what hades means. If you asked 10 people what hades means only a few would know it means an unseen place where souls and spirits go. It is a way of softening the horrible result of dying without Christ. Hell is a word that everyone knows, and its meaning is not a good thing. One thing that is prevalent today is if you asked 10 people what the word "hell" means you would get 10 different answers, all of them bad. Hollywood has truly messed this up. Scripture is where to look for an accurate view of hell. Here, a picture is starting to unveil as to what hell is like. The rich man is in torments. The word torment has a meaning of going down to the bottom of a place with torture. The rich man can see that there are some people a great distance away from him. He can recognize certain people but only on the Abraham's bosom side.

Hell is described in scripture as being in the heart of the earth. Jesus was to go to this place.

Matthew 12:39 But he answered and said unto them, An evil and adulterous generation seeketh after a sign; and there shall no sign be given to it, but the sign of the prophet Jonas:

Matthew 12:40 For as Jonas was three days and three nights in the whale's belly; so shall the Son of man be three days and three nights in the heart of the earth.

Scripture says that Jesus would descend into the lower parts of the earth.

Ephesians 4:9 (Now that he ascended, what is it but that he also descended first into the lower parts of the earth?

Ephesians 4:10 He that descended is the same also that ascended up far above all heavens, that he might fill all things.)

The Old Testament declares that David's soul would not be left in hell.

Psalms 16:10 For thou wilt not leave my soul in hell; neither wilt thou suffer thine Holy One to see corruption.

Now, the New Testament clears this up in the Acts of the Apostles by quoting what David says here. When the Lord went down into the heart of the earth for three days and three nights, He would be with David who was with Abraham and with Lazarus and with all Old Testament saints gathered on the correct side of the chasm.

Acts 2:25 For David speaketh concerning him, I foresaw the Lord always before my face, for he is on my right hand, that I should not be moved:

Acts 2:26 Therefore did my heart rejoice, and my tongue was glad; moreover also my flesh shall rest in hope:

Acts 2:27 Because thou wilt not leave my soul in hell, neither wilt thou suffer thine Holy One to see corruption.

Jesus's body never would see corruption. He was three days and three nights in the grave, but during this time He also was three days and three nights in the heart of the earth. Jesus could have been in the grave for longer and He still would have never seen the corruption or decay of the body.

Acts 2:29 Men *and* brethren, let me freely speak unto you of the patriarch David, that he is both dead and buried, and his sepulchre is with us unto this day.

Acts 2:30 Therefore being a prophet, and knowing that God had sworn with an oath to him, that of the fruit of his loins, according to the flesh, he would raise up Christ to sit on his throne;

Acts 2:31 He seeing this before spake of the resurrection of Christ, that his soul was not left in hell, neither his flesh did see corruption.

Acts 2:32 This Jesus hath God raised up, whereof we all are witnesses.

After three days and three nights, Jesus would ascend to the Father to sprinkle His blood on the mercy seat. He told Mary not to touch Him at this time when He first appeared to her:

John 20:16 Jesus saith unto her, Mary. She turned herself, and saith unto him, Rabboni; which is to say, Master.

John 20:17 Jesus saith unto her, Touch me not; for I am not yet ascended to my Father: but go to my brethren, and say unto them, I ascend unto my Father, and your Father; and *to* my God, and your God.

Once the Blood sacrifice was made, Jesus went back to hell to "lead captivity captive" all those who were on the correct side of the chasm and bring them to heaven:

Ephesians 4:8 Wherefore he saith, When he ascended up on high, he led captivity captive, and gave gifts unto men.

Once those who were captive in Abraham's Bosom were led up to heaven there was room now for hell to become larger. God never intended man to go there. Now with Abraham's bosom gone, room was made so hell could be made bigger. There is a verse in the Bible that says that hell had to be enlarged:

Isaiah 5:13 Therefore my people are gone into captivity, because *they have* no knowledge: and their honourable men *are* famished, and their multitude dried up with thirst.

Isaiah 5:14 Therefore hell hath enlarged herself, and opened her mouth without measure: and their glory, and their multitude, and their pomp, and he that rejoiceth, shall descend into it.

Isaiah 5:15 And the mean man shall be brought down, and the mighty man shall be humbled, and the eyes of the lofty shall be humbled:

Perhaps at this time, when Jesus emptied Abraham's Bosom that hell would be enlarged. However, with Lazarus and the rich man, both the correct side and the wrong side are still in the heart of the earth. The rich man is on the wrong side.

Luke 16:24 And he cried and said, Father Abraham, have mercy on me, and send Lazarus, that he may dip the tip of his finger in water, and cool my tongue; for I am tormented in this flame.

There is no other communication with anyone else here. The only thing that the rich man wants is to have Lazarus help him. The rich man is in complete isolation. Hell is not a place where you will go to be with your buddies. Hell is not a place where you will be free to live how you want to. There is a song that says "I'd rather laugh with the sinners than cry with the saints the sinners have much more fun:" how the world has it wrong. Hell is a place that no one would want to experience. Jesus describes this torment to His followers when He says:

Mark 9:43 And if thy hand offend thee, cut it off: it is better for thee to enter into life maimed, than having two hands to go into hell, into the fire that never shall be quenched:

Mark 9:44 Where their worm dieth not, and the fire is not quenched.

Hell used here is the Greek word "Geenna". Strong's Concordance says it is the valley of Hinnom; gehenna (or Ge-Hinnom), a valley of Jerusalem, used (figuratively) as a name for the place (or state) of everlasting punishment: - hell.

The valley of Hinnom (called Gehenna) was on the south side of the temple mount. It was used for garbage, a land fill. After several hundred years of dumping the garbage out of the dung gate, the people of Jerusalem realized that their enemy could attack by just walking over the garbage that had piled up in this deep valley. So they lit the garbage and the garbage would burn 24/7 and was still burning in Jesus' day. So Jesus used this fire as an example of the fire that would never be quenched.

Luke 16:25 But Abraham said, Son, remember that thou in thy lifetime receivedst thy good things, and likewise Lazarus evil things: but now he is comforted, and thou art tormented.

There are only two possible outcomes when you die. We say today that it is heaven or hell. But God will not allow any sin in heaven. No one went to heaven until God took care of man's sin problem. At this point in time, man's sin problem had not been taken care of. Jesus was still presenting Himself as the Messiah. He had not paid the offering that God required for man's sin. A blood offering just like what He described and did for the first sinners, Adam and Eve. He had to kill a lamb and shed its blood to make the coats of skin to cover up their sin problem. And that is all it did was to cover the problem up.

Genesis 3:21 Unto Adam also and to his wife did the LORD God make coats of skins, and clothed them.

The covering of man's sin never took the sin away. It took this shedding of a perfect blood to eradicate our sin problem. Now God gives some insight as to where those who "believed God" have been held in preparation to go to heaven up to this point in time. They should be in heaven. But their sin keeps them out. Christ's sacrifice can free them and open heavens gates but that has not happened yet.

Luke 16:26 And beside all this, between us and you there is a great gulf fixed: so that they which would pass from hence to you cannot; neither can they pass to us, that *would come* from thence.

In the heart of the earth during this time there are two areas where spirits are being held. Jesus gives the picture of this and says a great gulf separates them. I think of standing on the rim of the Grand Canyon and looking across to the other rim and thinking that there is no way you can get from one side to the other. God is holding two sets of spirits. One side has people who followed in Abraham's footsteps. They are people who believed God and God

counted it to them for righteousness. Lazarus did not go to this location because he was poor or because he was a beggar. He went to this location because in his life he must have believed God. He believed that God would provide for him even if the rich man did not. And now God is providing eternal life for Lazarus. However, Abraham makes note that there is no way out of hell. It is eternal.

Luke 16:27 Then he said, I pray thee therefore, father, that thou wouldest send him to my father's house:
Luke 16:28 For I have five brethren; that he may testify unto them, lest they also come into this place of torment.

The rich man wants Lazarus to go to his five brothers. HE knows the lifestyle they are living and are in big trouble if they don't repent. That is the only reason the rich man wants someone to go to his brothers. He wants to warn them about the fire as Jude says.

Jude 1:21 Keep yourselves in the love of God, looking for the mercy of our Lord Jesus Christ unto eternal life.

Jude 1:22 And of some have compassion, making a difference:

Jude 1:23 And others save with fear, pulling *them* out of the fire; hating even the garment spotted by the flesh.

Jude 1:24 Now unto him that is able to keep you from falling, and to present *you* faultless before the presence of his glory with exceeding joy,

Jude 1:25 To the only wise God our Saviour, *be* glory and majesty, dominion and power, both now and ever. Amen.

He wants to scream "REPENT! REPENT! REPENT!

Luke 16:29 Abraham saith unto him, They have Moses and the prophets; let them hear them.

Abraham says they have the scriptures. That is what Moses, and the prophets represent.

Luke 16:30 And he said, Nay, father Abraham: but if one went unto them from the dead, they will repent.

All the rich man wants to do is argue with Abraham. This is an indication of what hell will be like. Man is forever arguing with God in hell. Telling God, He was not fair with him. Telling God that he was not given a chance. Arguing with God that no one told him about Jesus. Could someone be in hell screaming that you or I did not tell him about Jesus when God gave us that opportunity to witness. Can we live for eternity with a lost person saying:

"Why didn't you tell me about Jesus."

Luke 16:31 And he said unto him, If they hear not Moses and the prophets, neither will they be persuaded, though one rose from the dead.

Abraham states why the rich man went to hell. Not because he did evil deeds but, because he did not believe God. Anything evil is possible without believing in the living God.

Hebrews 3:12 Take heed, brethren, lest there be in any of you an evil heart of unbelief, in departing from the living God.

LUKE CHAPTER 17

Highlights:

Chapter seventeen has Jesus Christ speaking to His disciples. His Apostles question Jesus. The ten lepers healed. Jesus speaks of His second coming.

Main Participants:

Jesus Christ v.1,
His Disciples v.1,
His Apostles v.5,
Ten Lepers v.12,
Samaritan leper v.16,
Pharisees v.20,

In Brief:

Jesus Christ speaks about offenses that will always come. Jesus speaks to His Apostles about having faith and their service for Christ. Jesus uses ten lepers to prove what faith should look like as one comes back to worship. He declares what the Kingdom of God is all about and that it must be within you. Jesus points to the days of Noah and Lot representing His second coming.

Synoptic in Matthew, Mark, and Luke's Gospel

Luke 17:1 Then said he unto the disciples, It is impossible but that offences will come: but woe *unto him,* through whom they come!

This chapter in the Gospel of Luke starts with a warning. The word "offences" is the word for a stumbling block or snare. Jesus is saying that many stumbling blocks and snares are going to stand in the way of reaching a lost soul for Christ.

The word "woe" is a word that should bring fear into the heart of anyone. Jesus is saying that stumbling blocks and snares are offences that stand in the way and perhaps were what led to the rich man going to hell. Jesus is also saying that if you are one of those who bring about these stumbling blocks, (that is blocking the Gospel from going forth) this does not bode well. WOE to you if this describes what you do to stop Christ's gospel.

Luke 17:2 It were better for him that a millstone were hanged about his neck, and he cast into the sea, than that he should offend one of these little ones.

Jesus is not talking about little children here. A "little one" here is a babe in Christ. Everyone who is born again is a newborn baby in Christ, desiring the sincere milk of the word. This is one of God's first principles in the Church age we live in.

Hebrews 5:12 For when for the time ye ought to be teachers, ye have need that one teach you again which *be* the first principles of the oracles of God; and are become such as have need of milk, and not of strong meat.

Hebrews 5:13 For every one that useth milk *is* unskilful in the word of righteousness: for he is a babe.

Hebrews 5:14 But strong meat belongeth to them that are of full age, *even* those who by reason of use have their senses exercised to discern both good and evil.

This word "millstone" only appears in the Gospels at this location. Matthew, Mark and Luke speak of this millstone, but John is silent. It is such a vivid way of describing someone who is in big trouble with God and has no way out.

Matthew describes this:

> Matthew 18:6 But whoso shall offend one of these little ones which believe in me, it were better for him that a millstone were hanged about his neck, and *that* he were drowned in the depth of the sea.
>
> Matthew 18:7 Woe unto the world because of offences! for it must needs be that offences come; but woe to that man by whom the offence cometh!

And Mark describes this:

> Mark 9:42 And whosoever shall offend one of *these* little ones that believe in me, it is better for him that a millstone were hanged about his neck, and he were cast into the sea.
>
> Mark 9:43 And if thy hand offend thee, cut it off: it is better for thee to enter into life maimed, than having two hands to go into hell, into the fire that never shall be quenched:
>
> Mark 9:44 Where their worm dieth not, and the fire is not quenched.

Luke 17:3 Take heed to yourselves: If thy brother trespass against thee, rebuke him; and if he repent, forgive him.

Luke 17:4 And if he trespass against thee seven times in a day, and seven times in a day turn again to thee, saying, I repent; thou shalt forgive him.

This chapter in the Gospel of Luke will start to intensify and explain the reason that Jesus Christ came to this earth. He will start to discuss what the Apostles will experience soon in this life. Jesus will instruct as to what they can expect in this lifetime and what is yet to come. This can be applied to the Christian today. We may not see what is yet to come either! That is the powerful return of the King of kings. Later in this chapter, He will say to His disciples:

"The days will come, when ye shall desire to see one of the days of the Son of man, and ye shall not see it."

Matthew adds this:

Matthew 18:21 Then came Peter to him, and said, Lord, how oft shall my brother sin against me, and I forgive him? till seven times?

Matthew 18:22 Jesus saith unto him, I say not unto thee, Until seven times: but, Until seventy times seven.

Jesus is teaching the value of forgiveness. Sometimes forgiving is a hard thing to do. But if we are to be like our Father in heaven then we must forgive continually.

Only in Matthew and Luke's Gospel

Luke and Matthew speak of faith as a mustard seed. However, they are not synoptic. It is not at the same time and is not about the same topic. Matthew exclaims that Jesus said that mustard seed faith can move a mountain.

Matthew 17:19 Then came the disciples to Jesus apart, and said, Why could not we cast him out?

Matthew 17:20 And Jesus said unto them, Because of your unbelief: for verily I say unto you, If ye have faith as a grain of mustard seed, ye shall say unto this mountain, Remove hence to yonder place; and it shall remove; and nothing shall be impossible unto you.

Matthew 17:21 Howbeit this kind goeth not out but by prayer and fasting.

Luke describes something totally different. He starts with the apostles asking:

Luke 17:5 And the apostles said unto the Lord, Increase our faith.

When the apostles say to increase our faith, they are asking Jesus to consummate more on this subject of faith. They are not

saying give us more substance or quantity of faith but quality of faith. Jesus is about to explain what kind of "faith" God is looking for. Quality faith not Quantity faith.

Luke 17:6 And the Lord said, If ye had faith as a grain of mustard seed, ye might say unto this sycamine tree, Be thou plucked up by the root, and be thou planted in the sea; and it should obey you.

Only in Luke's Gospel

Luke 17:7 But which of you, having a servant plowing or feeding cattle, will say unto him by and by, when he is come from the field, Go and sit down to meat?
Luke 17:8 And will not rather say unto him, Make ready wherewith I may sup, and gird thyself, and serve me, till I have eaten and drunken; and afterward thou shalt eat and drink?
Luke 17:9 Doth he thank that servant because he did the things that were commanded him? I trow not.

It is expected for us to obey the Master. After all Jesus said "If ye love Me, keep My commandments." There is no "atta boy" for doing what we are supposed to be doing. By not swearing, not idle worshipping, not stealing, not lying, and not coveting these should be expected of a Christian. There is no profit just because you follow Jesus. It is our duty. Some are faithful in their entire lives and never see any possessions on earth come their way.

Luke 17:10 So likewise ye, when ye shall have done all those things which are commanded you, say, We are unprofitable servants: we have done that which was our duty to do.

There are ten lepers in the story to follow and only one who shows this correct and quality faith. It is one thing to be healed in the flesh in the "here and now." It is another blessed event that by faith Jesus may say "Arise, go thy way: thy faith hath made thee whole."

Luke 17:11 And it came to pass, as he went to Jerusalem, that he passed through the midst of Samaria and Galilee.
Luke 17:12 And as he entered into a certain village, there met him ten men that were lepers, which stood afar off:
Luke 17:13 And they lifted up *their* voices, and said, Jesus, Master, have mercy on us.
Luke 17:14 And when he saw *them,* he said unto them, Go shew yourselves unto the priests. And it came to pass, that, as they went, they were cleansed.

God shows mercy continually to everyone over their lifetime. But what should be done in return for Him? Man was created for the worship of God. To glorify and to worship the God who created us!

Luke 17:15 And one of them, when he saw that he was healed, turned back, and with a loud voice glorified God,
Luke 17:16 And fell down on *his* face at his feet, giving him thanks: and he was a Samaritan.
Luke 17:17 And Jesus answering said, Were there not ten cleansed? but where *are* the nine?
Luke 17:18 There are not found that returned to give glory to God, save this stranger.
Luke 17:19 And he said unto him, Arise, go thy way: thy faith hath made thee whole.

The "kingdom of God" is what Jesus was demanded of to speak about. This is what the religious leaders of the day were asking for. They wanted a glorious kingdom now! They wanted it here so that they could be a big part of. They were looking for a king, like unto David, that would appoint these Pharisees to a high position. The Pharisees "demanded" this, but Jesus explained what His kingdom would be comprised of. Not with observation, that is nothing you could see, but something that must take place in the heart of every man.

Luke 17:20 And when he was demanded of the Pharisees, when the kingdom of God should come, he answered them and said, The kingdom of God cometh not with observation:
Luke 17:21 Neither shall they say, Lo here! or, lo there! for, behold, the kingdom of God is within you.

Though everyone wanted to see and experience the kingdom age, Jesus said that ye shall not see it. It is future. At least not yet during the disciple's lifetime.

Luke 17:22 And he said unto the disciples, The days will come, when ye shall desire to see one of the days of the Son of man, and ye shall not see *it.*

Jesus gives just a glimpse of what it will look like and when to expect the kingdom age but not now; not here. The warnings of false prophets and false lifestyles are given by Jesus.

Luke 17:23 And they shall say to you, See here; or, see there: go not after *them,* nor follow *them.*
Luke 17:24 For as the lightning, that lighteneth out of the one *part* under heaven, shineth unto the other *part* under heaven; so shall also the Son of man be in his day.

Jesus again foretells of the horrible suffering He will face on the cross. This whole generation and the whole world at this time will reject Him.

Luke 17:25 But first must he suffer many things, and be rejected of this generation.
Luke 17:26 And as it was in the days of Noe, so shall it be also in the days of the Son of man.

God is giving a warning. As it was in the days of Noe? What were those days like? Full of corruption! Full of violence! Sound familiar??

Genesis 6:11 The earth also was corrupt before God, and the earth was filled with violence.

Genesis 6:12 And God looked upon the earth, and, behold, it was corrupt; for all flesh had corrupted his way upon the earth.

Genesis 6:13 And God said unto Noah, The end of all flesh is come before me; for the earth is filled with violence through them; and, behold, I will destroy them with the earth.

Luke 17:27 They did eat, they drank, they married wives, they were given in marriage, until the day that Noe entered into the ark, and the flood came, and destroyed them all.

Luke 17:28 Likewise also as it was in the days of Lot; they did eat, they drank, they bought, they sold, they planted, they builded;

Luke 17:29 But the same day that Lot went out of Sodom it rained fire and brimstone from heaven, and destroyed *them* all.

Another warning is now given. What happened in the days of Lot?

Genesis 18:20 And the LORD said, Because the cry of Sodom and Gomorrah is great, and because their sin is very grievous;

Genesis 18:21 I will go down now, and see whether they have done altogether according to the cry of it, which is come unto me; and if not, I will know.

Were the people of Sodom involved in disobeying God? Were they proud to disobey God? What caused this to happen to Sodom? Ezekiel tells us what leads to the sin of sodomy:

Ezekiel 16:49 Behold, this was the iniquity of thy sister Sodom, pride, fulness of bread, and abundance of idleness was in her and in her daughters, neither did she strengthen the hand of the poor and needy.

Ezekiel 16:50 And they were haughty, and committed abomination before me: therefore I took them away as I saw *good.*

God has given two things to look for when the Son of man is about to be revealed. Remember that the world does not know Him. But Christians know Him. This should be shouted from every house top today as both these conditions of Noah and Lot

are now being called good and what little law and order are left is being called evil.

> Isaiah 5:20 Woe unto them that call evil good, and good evil; that put darkness for light, and light for darkness; that put bitter for sweet, and sweet for bitter!

A prophecy revealing the Son of man is now given. The Son of man has not been believed by the Jew. That day is still yet future. Currently they are blinded by their own rejection of the Messiah. Jesus promises this:

Luke 17:30 Even thus shall it be in the day when the Son of man is revealed.

Luke 17:31 In that day, he which shall be upon the housetop, and his stuff in the house, let him not come down to take it away: and he that is in the field, let him likewise not return back.

Luke 17:32 Remember Lot's wife.

God promises that Jesus will be revealed to Israel. However, Jesus is not revealed to Israel as a nation until after the church is raptured or taken out of the way. At this point there is not one saved person left on the earth. At this point, Antichrist is revealed and all will follow him.

During this time also known as Jacob's trouble of seven years, the Jews who realize that they missed Jesus Christ as their Messiah will face hardships like never before. They will have to flee to be hidden away from Antichrist. Antichrist will begin to hunt down any and all those who accept Jesus Christ as their Savior. After the rapture of the church it will cost your life to believe upon Jesus during that seven-year period.

Luke 17:33 Whosoever shall seek to save his life shall lose it; and whosoever shall lose his life shall preserve it.

Luke 17:34 I tell you, in that night there shall be two *men* in one bed; the one shall be taken, and the other shall be left.

Luke 17:35 Two *women* shall be grinding together; the one shall be taken, and the other left.

Luke 17:36 Two *men* shall be in the field; the one shall be taken, and the other left.

Luke 17:37 And they answered and said unto him, Where, Lord? And he said unto them, Wheresoever the body *is,* thither will the eagles be gathered together.

There will be nowhere to run and nowhere to hide during these seven years of tribulation. The gathering of the saints to God at the last day ended at the moment of the rapture. Only 144,000 Jews will be saved from the Antichrist and the rest of the Gentiles and Jews who decide to trust Christ, this will cost them their lives.

The commentator John Gill says it like this:

> ***"These words can by no means be understood of sinners fleeing to Christ for eternal life and salvation; nor of the gathering of saints to him, at the last day."***

I agree!

LUKE CHAPTER 18

Highlights:

Chapter eighteen has Jesus Christ speaking to His disciples. Jesus Christ speaking to His Apostles. Jesus Christ speaking to the ten lepers. And Jesus Christ speaking to the Pharisees.

Main Participants:

Jesus Christ v.1,
His Disciples v.1,
His Apostles v.5,
Ten Lepers v.12,
Some Pharisees v.20,

In Brief:

Jesus Christ speaks about offenses that will always come. Jesus speaks to His Apostles about having faith and their service for Christ. Jesus uses ten lepers to prove what faith should look like. He declares what the Kingdom of God is all about and points this out to His Disciples.

Only in Luke's Gospel

Luke 18:1 And he spake a parable unto them *to this end,* that men ought always to pray, and not to faint;

Jesus is making His way back to Judea. The Bible tells us that He has left Samaria and Galilee and is making His way back to Jerusalem which is in Judea. Luke brought this out earlier.

Luke 17:11 And it came to pass, as he went to Jerusalem, that he passed through the midst of Samaria and Galilee.

Remember that when Jesus speaks in parables the bible calls it a parable.

Luke 18:2 Saying, There was in a city a judge, which feared not God, neither regarded man:

Luke 18:3 And there was a widow in that city; and she came unto him, saying, Avenge me of mine adversary.

Luke 18:4 And he would not for a while: but afterward he said within himself, Though I fear not God, nor regard man;

Luke 18:5 Yet because this widow troubleth me, I will avenge her, lest by her continual coming she weary me.

Jesus will now explain the parable for that is what a parable is, a short story that will have a moral application.

Luke 18:6 And the Lord said, Hear what the unjust judge saith.

Luke 18:7 And shall not God avenge his own elect, which cry day and night unto him, though he bear long with them?

Are things so bad that crying day and night is taking place? Jesus says it must get to this point. The rapture will come not when we are on flowery beds of ease but when we cry day and night for Christ to come. Jesus has a statement for us to live by when evil and unjust judges that fear not God will prevail:

Romans 12:17 Recompense to no man evil for evil. Provide things honest in the sight of all men.

Romans 12:18 If it be possible, as much as lieth in you, live peaceably with all men.

Romans 12:19 Dearly beloved, avenge not yourselves, but *rather* give place unto wrath: for it is written, Vengeance *is* mine; I will repay, saith the Lord.

Heaping coals of fire on the head of those that persecute us: that is get them thinking about their eternal life after death. Help them to understand that they will be either in heaven or hell! And Jesus says how shall we win them? Well, here is the answer;

Romans 12:20 Therefore if thine enemy hunger, feed him; if he thirst, give him drink: for in so doing thou shalt heap coals of fire on his head.

Romans 12:21 Be not overcome of evil, but overcome evil with good.

This is such a truth in the Word of God. Overcoming evil with good. I really need this instruction in today's world. As a Christian I need to overcome evil with good.

Luke 18:8 I tell you that he will avenge them speedily. Nevertheless when the Son of man cometh, shall he find faith on the earth?

Jesus is speaking here. He is the Son of man. Obviously, this is in reference to His second coming. And His second coming is preceded by the rapture. This return Christ is talking about is His return for His saints at the rapture. At this time Jesus asks the question "Shall He find faith". This is almost demanding a NO answer. He will find very little faith out there. Remember that the moment the rapture occurs not one person will be left behind on earth with any saving faith. Every person left will believe the lie of the Antichrist.

Matthew 7:14 Because strait is the gate, and narrow is the way, which leadeth unto life, and few there be that find it.

That is why so few will be raptured. Only a remnant will go that have truly made Jesus Christ their Lord and Master and Savior.

Luke 18:9 And he spake this parable unto certain which trusted in themselves that they were righteous, and despised others:

Jesus directs this parable to a certain type of people; those who trusted in themselves. The best way to witness is to get people to look at themselves. Most think that they are pretty good. In fact they think their good deeds by far out way their bad deeds.

Luke 18:10 Two men went up into the temple to pray; the one a Pharisee, and the other a publican.

Luke 18:11 The Pharisee stood and prayed thus with himself, God, I thank thee, that I am not as other men *are,* extortioners, unjust, adulterers, or even as this publican.

Luke 18:12 I fast twice in the week, I give tithes of all that I possess.

Luke 18:13 And the publican, standing afar off, would not lift up so much as *his* eyes unto heaven, but smote upon his breast, saying, God be merciful to me a sinner.

Jesus now explains the moral truth of this parable. Pride is the sin that God wants us to look at first.

Proverbs 16:18 Pride *goeth* before destruction, and an haughty spirit before a fall.

He will not have a boaster in heaven.

Ephesians 2:8 For by grace are ye saved through faith; and that not of yourselves: *it is* the gift of God:

Ephesians 2:9 Not of works, lest any man should boast.

And humbleness is what God looks for in a man:

Luke 18:14 I tell you, this man went down to his house justified *rather* than the other: for every one that exalteth himself shall be abased; and he that humbleth himself shall be exalted.

Synoptic in Matthew, Mark, and Luke's Gospel

Jesus at this point has come to a city beyond Jordan that is to say on the east side of the Jordan river opposite of Jerusalem. He is now back in Judea. How do we know that? Matthew says this:

Matthew 19:1 And it came to pass, *that* when Jesus had finished these sayings, he departed from Galilee, and came into the coasts of Judaea beyond Jordan;

The Gospel of Mark describes it as this:

Mark 10:1 And he arose from thence, and cometh into the coasts of Judaea by the farther side of Jordan: and the people resort unto him again; and, as he was wont, he taught them again.

The Gospel of John describes this place further.

John 10:40 And went away again beyond Jordan into the place where John at first baptized; and there he abode.

The place where John first baptized is the city of Bethabara.

John 1:28 These things were done in Bethabara beyond Jordan, where John was baptizing.

The new versions of scripture have changed this city to Bethany. Modern scholars have said that Bethabara was not a city but a location. However, in recent years archaeologists have discovered the name of Bethabara on mosaic artifacts uncovered proving that it was a name of a place on the east side of the Jordan River. The King James Bible, NKJB and Young's Literal Bible are the only ones to call the city Bethabara.

Jesus is at Bethabara, and this is the place for baptisms.

Luke 18:15 And they brought unto him also infants, that he would touch them: but when *his* disciples saw *it,* they rebuked them.

Infant comes from the Greek word brephos **which can literally mean unborn or just born. Now an important question arises. Why did Jesus not baptize every infant that came into His hands? If baptism saves you why did not Jesus partake in this ritual? After all that is the reason Jesus came was it not? In the next chapter it is clearly said why Jesus came:**

Luke 19:10 For the Son of man is come to seek and to save that which was lost.

Luke 18:16 But Jesus called them *unto him,* and said, Suffer little children to come unto me, and forbid them not: for of such is the kingdom of God.

Jesus changes the age of the little ones being brought to Him by saying "little children". The Greek word here is paidion meaning an infant but older to a young child. Jesus takes the emphasis off of the infant or just born and places it on a child that is entering his/her learning years. Half-grown but old enough to understand the words of Jesus. This is the same word in the next verse translated "little child".

Luke 18:17 Verily I say unto you, Whosoever shall not receive the kingdom of God as a little child shall in no wise enter therein.

Jesus is very clear. He says what John said in his gospel:
John 1:12 But as many as received him, to them gave he power to become the sons of God, *even* to them that believe on his name:

In Bethabara, Jesus is walking on the main traveled road called "the way" in Mark 10:17 and a rich ruler approaches Him. All three gospels have the same narration currently.

Luke 18:18 And a certain ruler asked him, saying, Good Master, what shall I do to inherit eternal life?

Matthew Mark and Luke all say the same as this ruler says "Good Master". Jesus completely sets the ruler in his place.

Luke 18:19 And Jesus said unto him, Why callest thou me good? none *is* good, save one, *that is,* God.
Luke 18:20 Thou knowest the commandments, Do not commit adultery, Do not kill, Do not steal, Do not bear false witness, Honour thy father and thy mother.

This ruler missed the meaning of the ten commandments by so much that Jesus skipped right over the first five of them. Jesus went straight for the root problem and that is the love of money more than the love of God.

1Ti 6:9 But they that will be rich fall into temptation and a snare, and *into* many foolish and hurtful lusts, which drown men in destruction and perdition.

1Ti 6:10 For the love of money is the root of all evil: which while some coveted after, they have erred from the faith, and pierced themselves through with many sorrows.

1Ti 6:11 But thou, O man of God, flee these things; and follow after righteousness, godliness, faith, love, patience, meekness.

Luke 18:21 And he said, All these have I kept from my youth up.

Luke 18:22 Now when Jesus heard these things, he said unto him, Yet lackest thou one thing: sell all that thou hast, and distribute unto the poor, and thou shalt have treasure in heaven: and come, follow me.

The one thing Jesus says he is not doing and that is putting God first in his life. He put his possessions first in his life.

Luke 18:23 And when he heard this, he was very sorrowful: for he was very rich.

Matthew says he went away sorrowful:

Matthew 19:22 But when the young man heard that saying, he went away sorrowful: for he had great possessions.

Mark says he went away grieved:

Mark 10:22 And he was sad at that saying, and went away grieved: for he had great possessions.

Luke says he was sorrowful:

Luke 18:24 And when Jesus saw that he was very sorrowful, he said, How hardly shall they that have riches enter into the kingdom of God!

All three synoptic gospels say the same thing now:

Luke 18:25 For it is easier for a camel to go through a needle's eye, than for a rich man to enter into the kingdom of God.

Luke 18:26 And they that heard *it* said, Who then can be saved?

Matthew and Mark say that His disciples where astonished and amazed with what Jesus said.

Luke 18:27 And he said, The things which are impossible with men are possible with God.

One of the most comforting statements by Jesus is this one. It gives everyone of us hope. It is a lifetime of learning that we keep the first five commandments which this rich ruler missed completely. But God makes it possible. The very first of all of God's commands is:
Exodus 20:3 Thou shalt have no other gods before me.

Luke 18:28 Then Peter said, Lo, we have left all, and followed thee.

Peter may think he has left all. But has he? In a little less than two weeks he will deny Jesus three times. At that point he is putting his own self before God just as this ruler had done.

Luke 18:29 And he said unto them, Verily I say unto you, There is no man that hath left house, or parents, or brethren, or wife, or children, for the kingdom of God's sake,
Luke 18:30 Who shall not receive manifold more in this present time, and in the world to come life everlasting.

Only in Luke's Gospel

Luke 18:31 Then he took *unto him* the twelve, and said unto them, Behold, we go up to Jerusalem, and all things that are written by the prophets concerning the Son of man shall be accomplished.

Jesus decides to go "UP" to Jerusalem. But this decision was made after several things had to occur in Bethabara. He has been in Bethabara for 2 or 3 days. The month of Nisan is upon them and this important month is when Passover occurs on the 14th of Nisan. Some things happen during this time in Bethabara that only

John's Gospel talks about. Jesus, still in Bethabara, received word that Lazarus is sick. And Lazarus lives in the town of Bethany.

John 11:1 Now a certain *man* was sick, *named* Lazarus, of Bethany, the town of Mary and her sister Martha.

As Jesus receives this word He says:

John 11:4 When Jesus heard *that,* he said, This sickness is not unto death, but for the glory of God, that the Son of God might be glorified thereby.

When Jesus heard this about Lazarus, He hoped that the Apostles would just believe Him. So, to prove to them that this was not Lazarus's final death Jesus decided to sojourn in Bethabara for two more days with Lazarus being sick in Bethany.

John 11:6 When he had heard therefore that he was sick, he abode two days still in the same place where he was.

So two days go by and John's Gospel is at the exact point in time as above in Luke 18:31.

John 11:7 Then after that saith he to *his* disciples, Let us go into Judaea again.

All things are written by the prophets. It is the entire Old Testament that points to the promised *Kinsman Redeemer* spoken of by Ruth. The promised *BRANCH* by Zachariah. The one called *Immanuel* by Isaiah. However, the name of Jesus was never revealed in the Old Testament. So those who knew the Old Testament completely could not understand the death that Jesus will now explain again to His disciples. This death not by stoning:

John 11:8 *His* disciples say unto him, Master, the Jews of late sought to stone thee; and goest thou thither again?

But by the insult of the cross:

Luke 18:32 For he shall be delivered unto the Gentiles, and shall be mocked, and spitefully entreated, and spitted on:

Luke 18:33 And they shall scourge *him,* and put him to death: and the third day he shall rise again.

Jesus declares why this type of death must be performed. Jesus is crystal clear about all the things He will be going through

in two weeks on the 14th of Nisan. He knows He will not die by stoning. He will be the sacrificial lamb. He will be cursed and die the death on the tree:

> Galatians 3:13 Christ hath redeemed us from the curse of the law, being made a curse for us: for it is written, Cursed *is* every one that hangeth on a tree:

Quoted from Deuteronomy:

> Deuteronomy 21:22 And if a man have committed a sin worthy of death, and he be to be put to death, and thou hang him on a tree:
>
> Deuteronomy 21:23 His body shall not remain all night upon the tree, but thou shalt in any wise bury him that day; (for he that is hanged *is* accursed of God;) that thy land be not defiled, which the LORD thy God giveth thee *for* an inheritance.

Luke 18:34 And they understood none of these things: and this saying was hid from them, neither knew they the things which were spoken.

Once again, the process by which Jesus is put to death flies over the head of all His disciples. They understood nothing about what He was saying. But they do know that the Jews have been looking for Jesus. They do know that the Jews want to stone Him. They do know that Jerusalem could be very dangerous for Jesus at this time, and They hear that Lazarus sleeps. Jesus says He is sleeping. But why would Jesus have to go to wake him out of his sleep? To show to the world that He is the light of the world!

> John 11:9 Jesus answered, Are there not twelve hours in the day? If any man walk in the day, he stumbleth not, because he seeth the light of this world.
>
> John 11:10 But if a man walk in the night, he stumbleth, because there is no light in him.
>
> John 11:11 These things said he: and after that he saith unto them, Our friend Lazarus sleepeth; but I go, that I may awake him out of sleep.

Jesus must begin His travel back to Jerusalem for the last time. It is less than two weeks before the Passover of Nisan 14th.

Jesus will use this statement about Lazarus to get His disciples to agree to all go with Him back to Jerusalem. In a few days, Jesus will be in Jerusalem and to travel to Bethany is only 15 furlongs, a little less than two miles from Jerusalem as John declares.

John 11:12 Then said his disciples, Lord, if he sleep, he shall do well.

John 11:13 Howbeit Jesus spake of his death: but they thought that he had spoken of taking of rest in sleep.

John 11:14 Then said Jesus unto them plainly, Lazarus is dead.

Perhaps a Saturday Sabbath occurs at this time. No travel can be done of this great distance on a Sabbath. Jesus decides to leave after this Sabbath. Jericho is only a short distance from Bethabara and Jesus will encounter blind men both going into Jericho and a day later when He leaves Jericho. Luke again will be the only Gospel that will speak of this next day stop in Jericho.

Luke 18:35 And it came to pass, that as he was come nigh unto Jericho, a certain blind man sat by the way side begging:

Luke 18:36 And hearing the multitude pass by, he asked what it meant.

Luke 18:37 And they told him, that Jesus of Nazareth passeth by.

Luke 18:38 And he cried, saying, Jesus, *thou* Son of David, have mercy on me.

Luke 18:39 And they which went before rebuked him, that he should hold his peace: but he cried so much the more, *Thou* Son of David, have mercy on me.

This should be preached often by pastors. This blind man is reaching out to Jesus by importunity. Importunity draws the attention of our Lord! Luke spoke of this back in Chapter eleven verse eight:

Luke 11:8 I say unto you, Though he will not rise and give him, because he is his friend, yet because of his importunity he will rise and give him as many as he needeth.

Luke 18:40 And Jesus stood, and commanded him to be brought unto him: and when he was come near, he asked him,

Luke 18:41 Saying, What wilt thou that I shall do unto thee? And he said, Lord, that I may receive my sight.

Luke 18:42 And Jesus said unto him, Receive thy sight: thy faith hath saved thee.

Luke 18:43 And immediately he received his sight, and followed him, glorifying God: and all the people, when they saw *it,* gave praise unto God.

Importunity requires a small quantity of faith but a large heart to express the quality of that faith.

Matthew 17:20 And Jesus said unto them, Because of your unbelief: for verily I say unto you, If ye have faith as a grain of mustard seed, ye shall say unto this mountain, Remove hence to yonder place; and it shall remove; and nothing shall be impossible unto you.

LUKE CHAPTER 19

Highlights:

Chapter nineteen Jesus Christ enters Jericho. Jesus Christ speaks to Zacchaeus. Jesus Christ walks to Jerusalem. And Jesus Christ has His triumphal entry into Jerusalem.

Main Participants:

Jesus Christ v.1,
Zacchaeus v.2,
Those around Him v.7,
Two of His Disciples v.29,
Owners of the colt v.33,
Multitudes of disciples v.37,
Pharisees v.39,
Chief Priests and scribes v.47.

In Brief:

Jesus Christ speaks to Zacchaeus about salvation. Jesus speaks as to the reason He came to earth. To seek and to save that which is lost. Jesus presents parable of ten pounds and the loss of kingdom blessings. He enters Jerusalem as the King of kings and then weeps over Jerusalem. He cleanses the temple for the second time.

Only in Luke's Gospel

Luke 19:1 And *Jesus* entered and passed through Jericho.

This first, single, blind man was encountered on the road into Jericho. In the last chapter, Luke 18:35 speaks of a blind man as Jesus was coming near to entering into Jericho. This is completely different from Matthew and Mark as they describe Jesus coming out of Jericho.

Matthew says:

Matthew 20:29 And as they departed from Jericho, a great multitude followed him.

Matthew 20:30 And, behold, two blind men sitting by the way side, when they heard that Jesus passed by, cried out, saying, Have mercy on us, O Lord, *thou* Son of David.

And Mark says:

Mark 10:46 And they came to Jericho: and as he went out of Jericho with his disciples and a great number of people, blind Bartimaeus, the son of Timaeus, sat by the highway side begging.

Only Luke has the encounter with Zacchaeus. As Jesus begins to walk and enter into Jericho after having the first encounter with a blind man, Jesus has almost walked clear out of town; that is, He passed through most of Jericho:

Luke 19:2 And, behold, *there was* a man named Zacchaeus, which was the chief among the publicans, and he was rich.

Zacchaeus must have been well known in Jericho. He was a publican and not just a publican but the chief among publicans. He was rich, famous, but nevertheless lost as will be seen by his own testimony.

Luke 19:3 And he sought to see Jesus who he was; and could not for the press, because he was little of stature.

Luke 19:4 And he ran before, and climbed up into a sycamore tree to see him: for he was to pass that *way.*

Luke 19:5 And when Jesus came to the place, he looked up, and saw him, and said unto him, Zacchaeus, make haste, and come down; for to day I must abide at thy house.

Jesus looks directly at Zacchaeus. He says today I must abide at thy house. I must abide. Why? Why does Jesus have to abide in Zacchaeus's house? Because another day must expire that Lazarus is in the tomb. Today is the second day that Lazarus is in the tomb. He must be in the tomb for four days.

John 11:17 Then when Jesus came, he found that he had *lain* in the grave four days already.

Luke 19:6 And he made haste, and came down, and received him joyfully.

Jesus eating and spending the night with a publican? A sinner? How dare He!

Luke 19:7 And when they saw *it,* they all murmured, saying, That he was gone to be guest with a man that is a sinner.

What makes Zacchaeus lost is his faith in his own good works. Zacchaeus begins an immediate defense of his actions thinking that his good works will impress the Lord. Have we ever done that?

Luke 19:8 And Zacchaeus stood, and said unto the Lord; Behold, Lord, the half of my goods I give to the poor; and if I have taken any thing from any man by false accusation, I restore *him* fourfold.
Luke 19:9 And Jesus said unto him, This day is salvation come to this house, forsomuch as he also is a son of Abraham.

The Lord Jesus spends no time to not addressing Zacchaeus' good works. He in no way acknowledges them. Instead, He immediately gives the answer to eternal life. And the fact that eternal life was offered to the Jew first. Being a Jew, Zacchaeus is given the plan by God as to why Jesus came to this world.

Luke 19:10 For the Son of man is come to seek and to save that which was lost.

This is the new message that will begin to go out to the whole world. Back in Luke 18:31-33, the Gospel was given to the Apostles, and Luke 18:34 says it was not understood at all. Zacchaeus, who is one of the first to hear what the new message that Christ brings. is about to be addressed. Now everyone who is within ear shot are presented with this truth.

Romans 1:16 For I am not ashamed of the gospel of Christ: for it is the power of God unto salvation to every one that believeth; to the Jew first, and also to the Greek.

Romans 1:17 For therein is the righteousness of God revealed from faith to faith: as it is written, The just shall live by faith.

Christ now begins to open up and proclaim that salvation will be solely by Him. The Old Testament spoke many times of salvation, but it was only presented to God's chosen people, the Jews. Jesus never had His Apostles go to anyone but the Jew. It was offered to them alone:

Matthew 10:5 These twelve Jesus sent forth, and commanded them, saying, Go not into the way of the Gentiles, and into *any* city of the Samaritans enter ye not:

Matthew 10:6 But go rather to the lost sheep of the house of Israel.

Do you think that the Samaritans did not know what was going on? Do you think maybe they felt snubbed? He is about to open the door of heaven to everyone. Remember what Jesus said to the Samaritan woman? In John 4:22 salvation (the only time the word *salvation* is mentioned in the gospels except by Luke who mentions it 5 times) is presented to a Gentile.

John 4:19 The woman saith unto him, Sir, I perceive that thou art a prophet.

John 4:20 Our fathers worshipped in this mountain; and ye say, that in Jerusalem is the place where men ought to worship.

John 4:21 Jesus saith unto her, Woman, believe me, the hour cometh, when ye shall neither in this mountain, nor yet at Jerusalem, worship the Father.

John 4:22 Ye worship ye know not what: we know what we worship: for salvation is of the Jews.

John 4:23 But the hour cometh, and now is, when the true worshippers shall worship the Father in spirit and in truth: for the Father seeketh such to worship him.

John 4:24 God *is* a Spirit: and they that worship him must worship *him* in spirit and in truth.

Luke 19:11 And as they heard these things, he added and spake a parable, because he was nigh to Jerusalem, and because they thought that the kingdom of God should immediatcly appear.

Once again God declares a parable by Jesus. So, we need to look for a parallel meaning with this.

Luke 19:12 He said therefore, A certain nobleman went into a far country to receive for himself a kingdom, and to return.

Luke 19:13 And he called his ten servants, and delivered them ten pounds, and said unto them, Occupy till I come.

Luke 19:14 But his citizens hated him, and sent a message after him, saying, We will not have this *man* to reign over us.

Luke 19:15 And it came to pass, that when he was returned, having received the kingdom, then he commanded these servants to be called unto him, to whom he had given the money, that he might know how much every man had gained by trading.

Luke 19:16 Then came the first, saying, Lord, thy pound hath gained ten pounds.

Luke 19:17 And he said unto him, Well, thou good servant: because thou hast been faithful in a very little, have thou authority over ten cities.

Luke 19:18 And the second came, saying, Lord, thy pound hath gained five pounds.

Luke 19:19 And he said likewise to him, Be thou also over five cities.

Luke 19:20 And another came, saying, Lord, behold, *here is* thy pound, which I have kept laid up in a napkin:

Luke 19:21 For I feared thee, because thou art an austere man: thou takest up that thou layedst not down, and reapest that thou didst not sow.

Luke 19:22 And he saith unto him, Out of thine own mouth will I judge thee, *thou* wicked servant. Thou knewest that I was an austere man, taking up that I laid not down, and reaping that I did not sow:

Luke 19:23 Wherefore then gavest not thou my money into the bank, that at my coming I might have required mine own with usury?

Luke 19:24 And he said unto them that stood by, Take from him the pound, and give *it* to him that hath ten pounds.

Luke 19:25 (And they said unto him, Lord, he hath ten pounds.)

Jesus now gives the parallel, actual real meaning of this parable. It has nothing to do with pounds or monetary earnings. It has everything to do with the rewards received from our service on this earth. The only riches to take to heaven from this earth are OTHER SOULS!

If God gives a talent someway, somehow for a "citizen" to witness to others and to give them the Gospel and all that "citizen" does is just "lays it up in a napkin:" God says He will take away any reward and give it to those who did witness.

Luke 19:26 For I say unto you, That unto every one which hath shall be given; and from him that hath not, even that he hath shall be taken away from him.

Notice Jesus never says, him that hath not will lose his place or his life with God, but rather he will lose "all that he hath." Not as those citizens mentioned in verse 14 who were enemies and reject taking any pounds. They are considered Christ's enemies who hate Him. Christ is offered as a gift to every citizen of earth. But, you must receive Him.

John 1:10 He was in the world, and the world was made by him, and the world knew him not.

John 1:11 He came unto his own, and his own received him not.

John 1:12 But as many as received him, to them gave he power to become the sons of God, *even* to them that believe on his name:

Without Christ every citizen of earth will die a death of eternal separation from God by unbelief. Today there are people who wish to be *slain in the spirit.* Perhaps the next verse is what God means by "being slain in the spirit." Not such a good thing!

Luke 19:27 But those mine enemies, which would not that I should reign over them, bring hither, and slay *them* before me.

After Jesus spends this day and night with Zacchaeus, which is the second full day of Lazarus dead in the tomb, the third day of Lazarus's being in the tomb begins. This will be the day Jesus walks the 30-35 kilometers to Jerusalem from Jericho.

Luke 19:28 And when he had thus spoken, he went before, ascending up to Jerusalem.

Only in Matthew and Mark's Gospel

Luke spoke of a blind man who Jesus healed because of his importunity going "into" Jericho. Word had spread about this healing power of Jesus. Now leaving Jericho, Jesus will heal two more men of blindness not mentioned in Luke as He begins by traveling out of Jericho the next morning.

Matthew 20:29 And as they departed from Jericho, a great multitude followed him.

Matthew 20:30 And, behold, two blind men sitting by the way side, when they heard that Jesus passed by, cried out, saying, Have mercy on us, O Lord, *thou* Son of David.

Mark says one of these blind men is named Bartimaeus.

Mark 10:46 And they came to Jericho: and as he went out of Jericho with his disciples and a great number of people, blind Bartimaeus, the son of Timaeus, sat by the highway side begging.

Only in John's Gospel

The following day, that is the fourth day of Lazarus being dead and buried in the tomb, Jesus will make the short trip from Jerusalem to Bethany where Lazarus tomb is located.

John 11:17 Then when Jesus came, he found that he had *lain* in the grave four days already.

John 11:18 Now Bethany was nigh unto Jerusalem, about fifteen furlongs off:

John 11:19 And many of the Jews came to Martha and Mary, to comfort them concerning their brother.

John 11:20 Then Martha, as soon as she heard that Jesus was coming, went and met him: but Mary sat *still* in the house.

John 11:21 Then said Martha unto Jesus, Lord, if thou hadst been here, my brother had not died.

John 11:22 But I know, that even now, whatsoever thou wilt ask of God, God will give *it* thee.

The raising of Lazarus takes place only according to Chapter 11 in John's Gospel and only in John's Gospel. Jesus will then spend this night in Ephraim.

John 11:54 Jesus therefore walked no more openly among the Jews; but went thence unto a country near to the wilderness, into a city called Ephraim, and there continued with his disciples.

John 11:55 And the Jews' passover was nigh at hand: and many went out of the country up to Jerusalem before the passover, to purify themselves.

Jesus makes His way to the mount of Olives after this night in Ephraim.

Luke 19:29 And it came to pass, when he was come nigh to Bethphage and Bethany, at the mount called *the mount* of Olives, he sent two of his disciples,

Bethphage and Bethany are located on the Mount of Olives. Bethany is to the south and Bethphage is to the north. Here is

where the Gospels become Synoptic again but each saying this in an entirely different way.

In Matthew, Mark, Luke and John's Gospel

The triumphal entry into Jerusalem. Jesus is about to fulfill a well-known scripture from the TaNaKh or what the Jews follow known as the Torah (Instruction, or Law, also called the Pentateuch), the Nevi'im (Prophets), and the Ketuvim (Writings). In the Jewish Nevi'im is a prophecy by Zechariah that speaks of the Messiah:

> Zechariah 9:9 Rejoice greatly, O daughter of Zion; shout, O daughter of Jerusalem: behold, thy King cometh unto thee: he *is* just, and having salvation; lowly, and riding upon an ass, and upon a colt the foal of an ass.

It seems that Zechariah is mentioning two animals. An ass or a donkey, which is an animal of burden, and a colt, young, wild and untamed.

Matthew says they were to look for two animals just as Zechariah says and backs him up:

> Matthew 21:1 And when they drew nigh unto Jerusalem, and were come to Bethphage, unto the mount of Olives, then sent Jesus two disciples,
> Matthew 21:2 Saying unto them, Go into the village over against you, and straightway ye shall find an ass tied, and a colt with her: loose *them,* and bring *them* unto me.

Mark mentions only the wild colt where no man had sat:

> Mark 11:1 And when they came nigh to Jerusalem, unto Bethphage and Bethany, at the mount of Olives, he sendeth forth two of his disciples,
> Mark 11:2 And saith unto them, Go your way into the village over against you: and as soon as ye be entered into it, ye shall find a colt tied, whereon never man sat; loose him, and bring *him.*

Luke speaks of the same wild colt where no man had sat:

Luke 19:30 Saying, Go ye into the village over against *you;* in the which at your entering ye shall find a colt tied, whereon yet never man sat: loose him, and bring *him hither.*

Luke 19:31 And if any man ask you, Why do ye loose *him?* thus shall ye say unto him, Because the Lord hath need of him.

Notice that Luke only discusses the colt and not the donkey. Why? Because Luke is the Gospel primarily to the Gentiles. Matthew is the Gospel mainly to the Jews. The Jews need to see their prophesies fulfilled and Matthew gives them this explanation. The Gentiles only need to know that Jesus rode in on an animal untamed. This is so Gentiles understand that Jesus will begin to use them to present the Gospel to the world.

John mentions only a young ass but clarifies it as an ass's colt:
John 12:14 And Jesus, when he had found a young ass, sat thereon; as it is written,

John 12:15 Fear not, daughter of Sion: behold, thy King cometh, sitting on an ass's colt.

Only Zechariah and Matthew speak of two animals. Matthew is the Gospel to the Jew and therefore had to explain the animals in detail to answer the prophet's prediction. The other three gospels speaking to Gentiles need only to point out what Christ was trying to show with two animals.

Let's take a closer look.

All four gospels mention a colt, young, wild and untamed where no man had sat upon. This is the animal that Jesus sat on as He approached the gate to the city. Could this colt, unridden, wild, never used before represent Jesus switching to the Gentiles to reach the world with the gospel? Paul seemed to think so:
Romans 11:13 For I speak to you Gentiles, inasmuch as I am the apostle of the Gentiles, I magnify mine office:

Romans 11:14 If by any means I may provoke to emulation *them which are* my flesh, and might save some of them.

Romans 11:15 For if the casting away of them *be* the reconciling of the world, what *shall* the receiving *of them be,* but life from the dead?

Romans 11:16 For if the firstfruit *be* holy, the lump *is* also *holy:* and if the root *be* holy, so *are* the branches.

Romans 11:17 And if some of the branches be broken off, and thou, being a wild olive tree, wert graffed in among them, and with them partakest of the root and fatness of the olive tree;

Paul here speaks to the Gentiles as they have been brought in (grafted) into the church by God's plan of saving the world through Jesus Christ and His work on the cross. He is that holy root and that holy firstfruit that some of the branches have been broken off (that is unbelieving Jews) and wild branches (that is Gentiles) that have been grafted in.

Romans 11:18 Boast not against the branches. But if thou boast, thou bearest not the root, but the root thee.

Romans 11:19 Thou wilt say then, The branches were broken off, that I might be graffed in.

Romans 11:20 Well; because of unbelief they were broken off, and thou standest by faith. Be not highminded, but fear:

Romans 11:21 For if God spared not the natural branches, *take heed* lest he also spare not thee.

God's plan has been to always save everyone. His method has always been the same. To believe God and it would be counted for righteousness. Adam and Eve knew it. They had to believe God and they failed at the start. Abraham had to believe. David had to believe. By this time His Apostles had to believe. And today we must believe in the Death, burial, and resurrection of Jesus Christ.

Romans 11:22 Behold therefore the goodness and severity of God: on them which fell, severity; but toward thee, goodness, if thou continue in *his* goodness: otherwise thou also shalt be cut off.

The Jews are given a promise even though God has switched to the Gentiles to get the message of the cross out, God will keep a

Jew grafted in when they believe that their long awaited Messiah is Jesus Christ.

> Romans 11:23 And they also, if they abide not still in unbelief, shall be graffed in: for God is able to graff them in again.
>
> Romans 11:24 For if thou wert cut out of the olive tree which is wild by nature, and wert graffed contrary to nature into a good olive tree: how much more shall these, which be the natural *branches,* be graffed into their own olive tree?

God explains that the Children of Israel have been blinded until every Gentile that will be grafted in, is grafted in.

> Romans 11:25 For I would not, brethren, that ye should be ignorant of this mystery, lest ye should be wise in your own conceits; that blindness in part is happened to Israel, until the fulness of the Gentiles be come in.

His disciples carry through with finding the colt, loosing it and bringing the colt to Jesus.

> Luke 19:32 And they that were sent went their way, and found even as he had said unto them.

Just as Jesus predicted, the owner asks why they are taking the colt? The disciples give the reply as Jesus had instructed.

> Luke 19:33 And as they were loosing the colt, the owners thereof said unto them, Why loose ye the colt?
>
> Luke 19:34 And they said, The Lord hath need of him.
>
> Luke 19:35 And they brought him to Jesus: and they cast their garments upon the colt, and they set Jesus thereon.
>
> Luke 19:36 And as he went, they spread their clothes in the way.

John is the only Gospel to mention Palm branches. This is where the Catholic term *Palm Sunday* comes from. However, this day did not occur on a Sunday or as the Jews would say, on the first day of the week.

> John 12:12 On the next day much people that were come to the feast, when they heard that Jesus was coming to Jerusalem,

John 12:13 Took branches of palm trees, and went forth to meet him, and cried, Hosanna: Blessed *is* the King of Israel that cometh in the name of the Lord.

His disciples carry through with finding the colt, loosing it and bringing the colt to Jesus.

Luke 19:37 And when he was come nigh, even now at the descent of the mount of Olives, the whole multitude of the disciples began to rejoice and praise God with a loud voice for all the mighty works that they had seen;
Luke 19:38 Saying, Blessed *be* the King that cometh in the name of the Lord: peace in heaven, and glory in the highest.

Only in Luke's Gospel

When Jesus left Bethpage, He was on an ass known today as a donkey. The terrain coming down the Mt of Olives was very steep, down into the Kidron valley. Perhaps after crossing the river Kidron, Jesus switches from the ass to the wild colt. Now, as Jesus is riding on the untamed colt, they lay out their garments and palm tree branches and shout the King is coming. In just 6 days they will be shouting "Crucify Him! Crucify Him!"

Luke 19:39 And some of the Pharisees from among the multitude said unto him, Master, rebuke thy disciples.
Luke 19:40 And he answered and said unto them, I tell you that, if these should hold their peace, the stones would immediately cry out.

The Pharisees hate the fact that Jesus has so many followers. His followers cry Hosanna! The three other gospels use this term, Hosanna. Hosanna means *Oh Save!* It is the only time that the word appears in the King James Bible. Here at the entry of our Lord into Jerusalem. Showing that it was understood why Jesus came to this earth. Jesus says that even the stones would cry out

if the people did not understand. Paul mentioned this about all of creation also:

> Romans 8:21 Because the creature itself also shall be delivered from the bondage of corruption into the glorious liberty of the children of God.
> Romans 8:22 For we know that the whole creation groaneth and travaileth in pain together until now.

Luke 19:41 And when he was come near, he beheld the city, and wept over it,
Luke 19:42 Saying, If thou hadst known, even thou, at least in this thy day, the things *which belong* unto thy peace! but now they are hid from thine eyes.

Jesus is not weeping over the buildings or the monuments. He knows that in just forty years all these buildings will be cast down and not one stone left upon another by Titus of Rome. He is weeping over the lost condition of God's chosen people, the Jews. Soon they will reject Him and God will fulfill the prediction of switching from the Jews to the Gentiles to proclaim the salvation of the Lord. The things of God are going to be hid from the Jew's eyes. Because of their rejection of Christ, God will blind them to the truth of the Messiah. Paul later writes:

> Romans 11:25 For I would not, brethren, that ye should be ignorant of this mystery, lest ye should be wise in your own conceits; that blindness in part is happened to Israel, until the fulness of the Gentiles be come in.

Jesus speaks of the terrible times to come upon the Jews. Their enemies shall surround them. Their children will suffer.

Luke 19:43 For the days shall come upon thee, that thine enemies shall cast a trench about thee, and compass thee round, and keep thee in on every side,
Luke 19:44 And shall lay thee even with the ground, and thy children within thee; and they shall not leave in thee one stone upon another; because thou knewest not the time of thy visitation.

And why did all this happen to the Jew? Because they rejected their Messiah and missed the first coming of Jesus Christ as their Messiah. For the second time, at the time of Passover, Jesus will cleanse the temple. He did this earlier in His ministry:

John 2:13 And the Jews' passover was at hand, and Jesus went up to Jerusalem,

John 2:14 And found in the temple those that sold oxen and sheep and doves, and the changers of money sitting:

John 2:15 And when he had made a scourge of small cords, he drove them all out of the temple, and the sheep, and the oxen; and poured out the changers' money, and overthrew the tables;

John 2:16 And said unto them that sold doves, Take these things hence; make not my Father's house an house of merchandise.

And He does it again at the very last Passover that will ever have to take place. The perfect sacrifice to complete the requirements of God will be accomplished in just a few days. This upcoming Passover will take care of our sin problem, and is about to be accomplished.

Luke 19:45 And he went into the temple, and began to cast out them that sold therein, and them that bought;

Luke 19:46 Saying unto them, It is written, My house is the house of prayer: but ye have made it a den of thieves.

Luke 19:47 And he taught daily in the temple. But the chief priests and the scribes and the chief of the people sought to destroy him,

Jesus could not and would not stop the progression to His crucifixion from this point. He will be hated by the chief priests and others seeking to destroy Him. Remember the parable above in this chapter. The scriptures would start to reveal who really hated Him.

Luke 19:14 But his citizens hated him, and sent a message after him, saying, We will not have this *man* to reign over us.

Some who were given talents, (that is knowledge as depicted in this parable) understood this one to be the Messiah. They would listen to Jesus but, where would they be just 6 days from now?

Luke 19:48 And could not find what they might do: for all the people were very attentive to hear him.

Faith comes by hearing the words of our Savior the Lord Jesus Christ. He is the truth that everyone should seek after. Today, we should be so very attentive to hear Him as he tells us:

John 14:6 Jesus saith unto him, I am the way, the truth, and the life: no man cometh unto the Father, but by me.

John 14:7 If ye had known me, ye should have known my Father also: and from henceforth ye know him, and have seen him.

LUKE CHAPTER 20

Highlights:

Chapter twenty has Jesus Christ answering questions. Jesus Christ speaking more parables. Jesus answering the Sadducees and the scribes.

Main Participants:

Jesus Christ v.1,
Chief Priests and scribes v.1,
Spies v.20,
Sadducees v.27,
His Disciples v.45.

In Brief:

Jesus Christ's authority is questioned by the chief priests and scribes. Jesus tells the Parable of the vineyard. Jesus uses a penny to address the chief priests. The Sadducees try to trap Jesus with a foolish question about the resurrection. The Sadducees don't even believe in a resurrection! Jesus uses Psalms 110 to explain truth to the scribes.

Synoptic in Matthew, Mark, and Luke's Gospel

Luke 20:1 And it came to pass, *that* on one of those days, as he taught the people in the temple, and preached the gospel, the chief priests and the scribes came upon *him* with the elders,

Luke 20:2 And spake unto him, saying, Tell us, by what authority doest thou these things? or who is he that gave thee this authority?

It is early on the morning of the Olivet discourse. The three synoptic gospels all have this question by the religious leaders. They are trying to trap Him. Jesus invariably answered His critics with another question. Here He asks a question that they cannot answer.

Luke 20:3 And he answered and said unto them, I will also ask you one thing; and answer me:

Luke 20:4 The baptism of John, was it from heaven, or of men?

Luke 20:5 And they reasoned with themselves, saying, If we shall say, From heaven; he will say, Why then believed ye him not?

Luke 20:6 But and if we say, Of men; all the people will stone us: for they be persuaded that John was a prophet.

Luke 20:7 And they answered, that they could not tell whence *it was.*

Luke 20:8 And Jesus said unto them, Neither tell I you by what authority I do these things.

Paul said in the book of Romans that the scribes and the elders are going to be held accountable for what they know of the scriptures. Every man is going to be held accountable to God for the scriptures. The moral law of God is written in the hearts of man:

Romans 2:11 For there is no respect of persons with God.

Romans 2:12 For as many as have sinned without law shall also perish without law: and as many as have sinned in the law shall be judged by the law;

Romans 2:13 (For not the hearers of the law *are* just before God, but the doers of the law shall be justified.

Romans 2:14 For when the Gentiles, which have not the law, do by nature the things contained in the law, these, having not the law, are a law unto themselves:

Romans 2:15 Which shew the work of the law written in their hearts, their conscience also bearing witness, and *their* thoughts the mean while accusing or else excusing one another;)

Jesus now speaks in a parable again. Very few parables are synoptic to all three gospels. This is one of them because it goes back to the prophet Isaiah:

Luke 20:9 Then began he to speak to the people this parable; A certain man planted a vineyard, and let it forth to husbandmen, and went into a far country for a long time.

Isaiah speaks of this vineyard and sheds much light on what the religious leaders should have already known. Jesus was talking about the house of Israel:

Isaiah 5:1 Now will I sing to my wellbeloved a song of my beloved touching his vineyard. My wellbeloved hath a vineyard in a very fruitful hill:

Isaiah 5:2 And he fenced it, and gathered out the stones thereof, and planted it with the choicest vine, and built a tower in the midst of it, and also made a winepress therein: and he looked that it should bring forth grapes, and it brought forth wild grapes.

Isaiah 5:3 And now, O inhabitants of Jerusalem, and men of Judah, judge, I pray you, betwixt me and my vineyard.

Isaiah 5:4 What could have been done more to my vineyard, that I have not done in it? wherefore, when I looked that it should bring forth grapes, brought it forth wild grapes?

Isaiah 5:5 And now go to; I will tell you what I will do to my vineyard: I will take away the hedge thereof, and it shall be eaten up; *and* break down the wall thereof, and it shall be trodden down:

Now, Jesus will expound on this vineyard. Luke has a very satisfying way of telling this parable.

Luke 20:10 And at the season he sent a servant to the husbandmen, that they should give him of the fruit of the vineyard: but the husbandmen beat him, and sent *him* away empty.

Luke 20:11 And again he sent another servant: and they beat him also, and entreated *him* shamefully, and sent *him* away empty.

Luke 20:12 And again he sent a third: and they wounded him also, and cast *him* out.

Luke 20:13 Then said the lord of the vineyard, What shall I do? I will send my beloved son: it may be they will reverence *him* when they see him.

Luke 20:14 But when the husbandmen saw him, they reasoned among themselves, saying, This is the heir: come, let us kill him, that the inheritance may be ours.

Luke 20:15 So they cast him out of the vineyard, and killed *him.* What therefore shall the lord of the vineyard do unto them?

Luke 20:16 He shall come and destroy these husbandmen, and shall give the vineyard to others. And when they heard *it,* they said, God forbid.

Seeing that Jesus is just stating the scriptures from Isaiah, He talks of giving the vineyard to another. That other is you and me, the Gentiles! The chief priests and scribes and elders of verse one, should have already known. Isaiah said what Jesus is about to tell them. Isaiah explains what the vineyard is and who is represented by the plants.

Isaiah 5:6 And I will lay it waste: it shall not be pruned, nor digged; but there shall come up briers and thorns: I will also command the clouds that they rain no rain upon it.

Isaiah 5:7 For the vineyard of the LORD of hosts *is* the house of Israel, and the men of Judah his pleasant plant: and he looked for judgment, but behold oppression; for righteousness, but behold a cry

Jesus gives the meaning of this parable. It has everything to do with Jesus going to the house of Israel (vineyard) and the rejection of the Son of God (Jesus) who was sent to the chief priests (husbandmen) and how they intend to kill him.

Luke 20:17 And he beheld them, and said, What is this then that is written, The stone which the builders rejected, the same is become the head of the corner?

This is taken from Psalms as David speaks about this stone:
Psalms 118:22 The stone *which* the builders refused is become the head *stone* of the corner.

Jesus points directly at the chief priests and elders and says they are rejecting the Christ who is the head of the corner. Later, after Pentecost, Peter will expand on this.

Acts 4:10 Be it known unto you all, and to all the people of Israel, that by the name of Jesus Christ of Nazareth, whom ye crucified, whom God raised from the dead, *even* by him doth this man stand here before you whole.

Acts 4:11 This is the stone which was set at nought of you builders, which is become the head of the corner.

Acts 4:12 Neither is there salvation in any other: for there is none other name under heaven given among men, whereby we must be saved.

Only in Matthew and Luke's Gospel

Luke 20:18 Whosoever shall fall upon that stone shall be broken; but on whomsoever it shall fall, it will grind him to powder.

In Matthew it reads like this:
Matthew 21:44 And whosoever shall fall on this stone shall be broken: but on whomsoever it shall fall, it will grind him to powder.

Notice the "stone." This stone is Jesus, the rock! Daniel calls Him the stone that was cut out of the mountain without hands in Daniel 2:44. He is that "head of the corner" stone referred to in verse seventeen and taken from Psalm 118:22 above.

What does this passage in Matthew and Luke mean? This passage explains that there are two ways to approach Christ.

First is to turn to Him and fall on Him with a broken heart and a contrite spirit (Psalm 34:18). If a man learns the truth and truly believes that Christ's death, burial, and resurrection is the answer to life's eternal question that man will fall on the stone and be broken in heart and in spirit. But, if during this life that man does not fall on the stone by turning to Christ, He will in the end time judgement to come, have Jesus the Stone fall on him, and it will grind him to powder and destroy him in hell forever.

Luke 20:19 And the chief priests and the scribes the same hour sought to lay hands on him; and they feared the people: for they perceived that he had spoken this parable against them.
Luke 20:20 And they watched *him,* and sent forth spies, which should feign themselves just men, that they might take hold of his words, that so they might deliver him unto the power and authority of the governor.

The chief priests and elders were running scared of the people. They were so upset with Christ that they sent spies as phony "just" men to trap Jesus in His own words.

Synoptic in Matthew, Mark, and Luke's Gospel

Several groups of men now step up to try and trap Christ in His own words. The first group is a group of legalists trying to trap Jesus with government rules:

Luke 20:21 And they asked him, saying, Master, we know that thou sayest and teachest rightly, neither acceptest thou the person *of any,* but teachest the way of God truly:
Luke 20:22 Is it lawful for us to give tribute unto Caesar, or no?

Here as before, Jesus answers with a question of His own.

Luke 20:23 But he perceived their craftiness, and said unto them, Why tempt ye me?

Luke 20:24 Shew me a penny. Whose image and superscription hath it? They answered and said, Caesar's.

Luke 20:25 And he said unto them, Render therefore unto Caesar the things which be Caesar's, and unto God the things which be God's.

Luke 20:26 And they could not take hold of his words before the people: and they marvelled at his answer, and held their peace.

Up step the Sadducees. These are the religious leaders of the day who say there is no resurrection. The Sadducees have several beliefs different than the Pharisees:

Luke 20:27 Then came to *him* certain of the Sadducees, which deny that there is any resurrection; and they asked him,

Luke 20:28 Saying, Master, Moses wrote unto us, If any man's brother die, having a wife, and he die without children, that his brother should take his wife, and raise up seed unto his brother.

Luke 20:29 There were therefore seven brethren: and the first took a wife, and died without children.

Luke 20:30 And the second took her to wife, and he died childless.

Luke 20:31 And the third took her; and in like manner the seven also: and they left no children, and died.

Luke 20:32 Last of all the woman died also.

Luke 20:33 Therefore in the resurrection whose wife of them is she? for seven had her to wife.

Jesus, in Matthew and Mark, speaks out loud that the Sadducees do err.

> Matthew 22:29 Jesus answered and said unto them, Ye do err, not knowing the scriptures, nor the power of God.

In all three synoptic gospels Jesus straightens out the thinking of the unsaved religious leaders.

Luke 20:34 And Jesus answering said unto them, The children of this world marry, and are given in marriage:

Luke 20:35 But they which shall be accounted worthy to obtain that world, and the resurrection from the dead, neither marry, nor are given in marriage:

Luke 20:36 Neither can they die any more: for they are equal unto the angels; and are the children of God, being the children of the resurrection.

Jesus will set the Sadducees straight by quoting scripture from Exodus:

> Exodus 3:6 Moreover he said, I *am* the God of thy father, the God of Abraham, the God of Isaac, and the God of Jacob. And Moses hid his face; for he was afraid to look upon God.

Jesus explains what was really meant when He declared "I am the God of Abraham, The God of Isaac, and the God of Jacob." Our God is not the God of the dead but of the living!

Luke 20:37 Now that the dead are raised, even Moses shewed at the bush, when he calleth the Lord the God of Abraham, and the God of Isaac, and the God of Jacob.

Luke 20:38 For he is not a God of the dead, but of the living: for all live unto him.

In Matthew and Mark, the Pharisees step up and question Jesus. However, Luke goes directly to the next group, the scribes. They are left speechless!

Luke 20:39 Then certain of the scribes answering said, Master, thou hast well said.

Luke 20:40 And after that they durst not ask him any *question at all.*

Jesus decides to turn the tables and asks the religious leaders a question to stump them. They presented Jesus with Jewish fables. There was nothing pure in their thoughts. Paul described them perfectly in his letter to Titus.

> Titus 1:14 Not giving heed to Jewish fables, and commandments of men, that turn from the truth.
>
> Titus 1:15 Unto the pure all things *are* pure: but unto them that are defiled and unbelieving *is* nothing pure; but even their mind and conscience is defiled.

Titus 1:16 They profess that they know God; but in works they deny *him,* being abominable, and disobedient, and unto every good work reprobate.

Jesus quotes from the Psalms here, showing that the Old Testament scriptures are the words of God. Notice the harmony of the synoptic Gospels here, with each narrative quoting David in Psalm 110:1.

Psalms 110:1 **A Psalm of David.** The LORD said unto my Lord, Sit thou at my right hand, until I make thine enemies thy footstool.

Each writer quotes this passage from Psalms in their own words: Matthew says:

Matthew 22:44 The LORD said unto my Lord, Sit thou on my right hand, till I make thine enemies thy footstool?

Mark says:

Mark 12:36 For David himself said by the Holy Ghost, The LORD said to my Lord, Sit thou on my right hand, till I make thine enemies thy footstool.

And Luke says:

Luke 20:41 And he said unto them, How say they that Christ is David's son?

Luke 20:42 And David himself saith in the book of Psalms, The LORD said unto my Lord, Sit thou on my right hand,

Luke 20:43 Till I make thine enemies thy footstool.

Luke 20:44 David therefore calleth him Lord, how is he then his son?

Luke 20:45 Then in the audience of all the people he said unto his disciples,

Jesus calls out the scribes, but this is meant for all the leaders that tried to trap Him. It became a game of cat and mouse as every type of religious leader would seek to entrap Jesus with His own words. Imagine trying to outthink the Saviour!

Luke 20:46 Beware of the scribes, which desire to walk in long robes, and love greetings in the markets, and the highest seats in the synagogues, and the chief rooms at feasts;

Luke 20:47 Which devour widows' houses, and for a shew make long prayers: the same shall receive greater damnation.

Jesus continually had a problem with religious leaders. It did not matter if they were high priests, or leaders, or even scribes and lawyers. Wanting the titles of "Doctor" or "Reverend" or "Master Rabbi" they love to be seen and heard in their long prayer vigils and rituals. How easy is it to be trapped into thinking as these men did, that they have the upper hand.

Isaiah 31:1 Woe to them that go down to Egypt for help; and stay on horses, and trust in chariots, because *they are* many; and in horsemen, because they are very strong; but they look not unto the Holy One of Israel, neither seek the LORD!

Isaiah 31:2 Yet he also *is* wise, and will bring evil, and will not call back his words: but will arise against the house of the evildoers, and against the help of them that work iniquity.

LUKE CHAPTER 21

Highlights:

Chapter twenty-one Jesus Christ preaches the gospel. Jesus Christ speaks in parables. Jesus answers the Sadducees and the scribes.

Main Participants:

Jesus Christ v.1,
Rich men v.1,
Poor Widow v.2,
The disciples v.7.

In Brief:

Jesus Christ speaks that the widow's mite was a larger gift than that of the rich men. Jesus begins His famous Olivet Discourse. Jesus prophesies of the destruction of Jerusalem. He speaks of His second coming. He speaks another parable, this time of the fig tree. Jesus gives warnings in view of His second coming.

Only in Mark and Luke's Gospel

Luke 21:1 And he looked up, and saw the rich men casting their gifts into the treasury.
Luke 21:2 And he saw also a certain poor widow casting in thither two mites.

Jesus sat over against the treasury and took note of a widow who had come to the temple on the Sabbath to pay her tribute to God. Jesus is about to explain the true essence of giving. The widow's mite has been used many times to teach the error of the love of money.

Luke 21:3 And he said, Of a truth I say unto you, that this poor widow hath cast in more than they all:
Luke 21:4 For all these have of their abundance cast in unto the offerings of God: but she of her penury hath cast in all the living that she had.

The word penury is called archaic by many. Most modern translations change this word to poverty. But the word goes much deeper than that. It is giving what you know you need to live. Mark tells it so:

Mark 12:42 And there came a certain poor widow, and she threw in two mites, which make a farthing.
Mark 12:43 And he called *unto him* his disciples, and saith unto them, Verily I say unto you, That this poor widow hath cast more in, than all they which have cast into the treasury:
Mark 12:44 For all *they* did cast in of their abundance; but she of her want did cast in all that she had, *even* all her living.

Synoptic in Matthew, Mark, and Luke's Gospel

Jesus makes His way out of the temple and begins a walk to the mount of Olives. This starts His most famous talk called the Olivet Discourse. The synoptic gospels each give an account of this speech, and in so doing bring us to the same moment in time when Jesus starts the discourse by addressing the disciples and their view of how beautiful the temple appears. He begins with describing the end of the current age or dispensation.

Luke 21:5 And as some spake of the temple, how it was adorned with goodly stones and gifts, he said,

Luke 21:6 *As for* these things which ye behold, the days will come, in the which there shall not be left one stone upon another, that shall not be thrown down.

Luke 21:7 And they asked him, saying, Master, but when shall these things be? and what sign *will there be* when these things shall come to pass?

Matthew is the book that is quoted from the most for the Olivet Discourse.

Matthew 24:1 And Jesus went out, and departed from the temple: and his disciples came to *him* for to shew him the buildings of the temple.

Matthew 24:2 And Jesus said unto them, See ye not all these things? verily I say unto you, There shall not be left here one stone upon another, that shall not be thrown down.

Matthew 24:3 And as he sat upon the mount of Olives, the disciples came unto him privately, saying, Tell us, when shall these things be? and what *shall be* the sign of thy coming, and of the end of the world?

The question needs some explanation. The "end of the world" here uses a different Greek word for the word "world."

It is not the word *oikoumenē*, the created earth or planet or globe limited by the fact that it is a circle. Interestingly the word *oikoumenē* is used in verse 14 of this chapter of Matthew, indicating that over the entire planet or to every corner of the inhabited earth. North, south, east, or west, the Gospel of the kingdom will be preached:

Matthew 24:14 And this gospel of the kingdom shall be preached in all the world for a witness unto all nations; and then shall the end come.

It is not the word *kosmos*, meaning inhabitants or the adorning people on this globe. *Kosmos* is used in verse 21 of this chapter in Matthew, describing that the great tribulation that would come

on the people will be greater than anything since Adam and Eve at the beginning of mankind.

> Matthew 24:21 For then shall be great tribulation, such as was not since the beginning of the world to this time, no, nor ever shall be.

It is not the word *ghay*, meaning the solid part or the ground or land. *Ghay* is used in Revelation 13:3 where all the land wondered at the beast.

> Revelation 13:3 And I saw one of his heads as it were wounded to death; and his deadly wound was healed: and all the world wondered after the beast.

However, it is the word *aion* or an "age" or a particular period of time. So, the disciples are questioning our Lord about the end of the age of time that will usher in His coming again, or as most call it the second coming of Jesus Christ. Putting this into perspective, what age is being talked about at this point? It cannot be the church age or the age of grace (the same age) because that age had not started at this time. It must be the age of law which began at the moment the Jews requested the law of God be given to them in Exodus 19:8:

> Exodus 19:8 And all the people answered together, and said, All that the LORD hath spoken we will do. And Moses returned the words of the people unto the LORD.

Can anyone guess what term is used in the most famous verse in the Bible? It is not the same as the word *world* used here in Matthew 24:3!

> John 3:16 For God so loved the world, that he gave his only begotten Son, that whosoever believeth in him should not perish, but have everlasting life.

Here in John 3:16 world is the Greek word_____! Hint: it's COSMOS!

Luke 21:8 And he said, Take heed that ye be not deceived: for many shall come in my name, saying, I am *Christ;* and the time draweth near: go ye not therefore after them.

The "Ye" referred to here is the Jewish race. These are the people who for the last three years Jesus has ordered His disciples to preach to.

Matthew 10:5 These twelve Jesus sent forth, and commanded them, saying, Go not into the way of the Gentiles, and into *any* city of the Samaritans enter ye not:

Matthew 10:6 But go rather to the lost sheep of the house of Israel.

This prophecy of the end time events is 100% about the Jew. All who happen to be living with the Jews during these last days will see and experience the buildup of God haters. This buildup to the seven years yet to commence from the book of Daniel:.

Daniel 9:27 And he shall confirm the covenant with many for one week: and in the midst of the week he shall cause the sacrifice and the oblation to cease, and for the overspreading of abominations he shall make *it* desolate, even until the consummation, and that determined shall be poured upon the desolate.

However, just before this seven-year period begins, the rapture will occur as the church is taken! These next few verses are during this build up and all those on earth are still a part of this. Then this "era" (Greek word aion) or dispensation of time will come to an end. The church, which is the temple of the Holy Ghost will be removed and will not extend into the last seven years of Daniel's vision.

Luke 21:9 But when ye shall hear of wars and commotions, be not terrified: for these things must first come to pass; but the end *is* not by and by.

Luke 21:10 Then said he unto them, Nation shall rise against nation, and kingdom against kingdom:

Luke 21:11 And great earthquakes shall be in divers places, and famines, and pestilences; and fearful sights and great signs shall there be from heaven.

Matthew says it in this way:

Matthew 24:7 For nation shall rise against nation, and kingdom against kingdom: and there shall be famines, and pestilences, and earthquakes, in divers places.

Mark also:

Mark 13:8 For nation shall rise against nation, and kingdom against kingdom: and there shall be earthquakes in divers places, and there shall be famines and troubles: these *are* the beginnings of sorrows.

The church is on the earth up to this moment. Jesus will now talk about things that have happened and are still happening to His followers during the church age. It is at this point that Jesus describes the times as the beginning of sorrows.

Matthew 24:8 All these *are* the beginning of sorrows.

Modern versions change the word "sorrows" to birth-pangs (RSV) or birth pains (ESV). That is very limiting. Men cannot understand the pain of birth-pangs. But all can understand the pain or pang being described here. It is the pang of remorse and of guilt and of disappointment and of hunger and of death. Jesus says that before all this His followers will be persecuted:

Luke 21:12 But before all these, they shall lay their hands on you, and persecute *you,* delivering *you* up to the synagogues, and into prisons, being brought before kings and rulers for my name's sake.
Luke 21:13 And it shall turn to you for a testimony.

Given to the disciples at this time but applicable to all who are on the earth at the end times, Jesus tells how to handle this attack on all His followers. *But before all these things* as it says in verse 12 means these last statements still apply to those on earth (the church age) just before the final week of Daniel's vision begins for his people, the Jews.

Luke 21:14 Settle *it* therefore in your hearts, not to meditate before what ye shall answer:
Luke 21:15 For I will give you a mouth and wisdom, which all your adversaries shall not be able to gainsay nor resist.
Luke 21:16 And ye shall be betrayed both by parents, and brethren, and kinsfolks, and friends; and *some* of you shall they cause to be put to death.

Luke 21:17 And ye shall be hated of all *men* for my name's sake.

Jews and Christians alike shall be hated of all. Matthew says the same:
> Matthew 24:9 Then shall they deliver you up to be afflicted, and shall kill you: and ye shall be hated of all nations for my name's sake.

And Mark says the same:
> Mark 13:9 But take heed to yourselves: for they shall deliver you up to councils; and in the synagogues ye shall be beaten: and ye shall be brought before rulers and kings for my sake, for a testimony against them.

Only in Luke's Gospel

God gives a promise here found only in Luke. Could it be that Luke being the Gospel to the Gentiles that it is to the Gentile church that this promise is for?

Luke 21:18 But there shall not an hair of your head perish.
Luke 21:19 In your patience possess ye your souls.

The church is commanded by God to build patience. This is evident in James:
> James 1:2 My brethren, count it all joy when ye fall into divers temptations;
> James 1:3 Knowing *this,* that the trying of your faith worketh patience.
> James 1:4 But let patience have *her* perfect work, that ye may be perfect and entire, wanting nothing.

Patience has always been a mark of knowing God. Noah possessed his salvation through the ark by his patience for seven days. Job possessed his life by his enormous patience in waiting on God to answer his problems of which there were many. Today in the end times, patience is needed as we approach the end of the church age. Our souls depend on our patience waiting for Christ

to come for His bride, the church. Soon the rapture, followed by the revealing of Antichrist will mark the start of the tribulation period. Patience is needed up to this point. But after this moment action is required. As the abomination of desolation will occur at the midpoint of the final week of Daniel's vision.

> Daniel 9:26 And after threescore and two weeks shall Messiah be cut off, but not for himself: and the people of the prince that shall come shall destroy the city and the sanctuary; and the end thereof *shall be* with a flood, and unto the end of the war desolations are determined.

> Daniel 9:27 And he shall confirm the covenant with many for one week: and in the midst of the week he shall cause the sacrifice and the oblation to cease, and for the overspreading of abominations he shall make *it* desolate, even until the consummation, and that determined shall be poured upon the desolate.

At this point the tribulation has begun. The saved who were on earth will be gone. Not one saved person remains. God says so! Matthew and Mark speak of this moment:

> Matthew 24:15 When ye therefore shall see the abomination of desolation, spoken of by Daniel the prophet, stand in the holy place, (whoso readeth, let him understand:)

And Mark says:

> Mark 13:14 But when ye shall see the abomination of desolation, spoken of by Daniel the prophet, standing where it ought not, (let him that readeth understand,) then let them that be in Judaea flee to the mountains:

The tribulation period began three and a half years before the abomination of desolation takes place. This tribulation time starts with the rapture.

1. Rapture Revelation 4:1

2. Seven seals opened Revealing of antichrist Revelation 6:1-2

3. Seven trumpets contained in the seventh seal.

4. Mid-trib and antichrist sitting at the throne in the third temple.

2Thessalonians 2:3 Let no man deceive you by any means: for *that day shall not come,* except there come a falling away first, and that man of sin be revealed, the son of perdition;
2Thessalonians 2:4 Who opposeth and exalteth himself above all that is called God, or that is worshipped; so that he as God sitteth in the temple of God, shewing himself that he is God.

5.   "Great" tribulation begins with the seven vials contained in the seventh seal opened.

6.   After the last three and a half years, Armageddon

7.   Finally, the return of the Lord in power and great glory.

Only in Luke does Jesus point out problems for Jews beginning with the destruction of Jerusalem. Verses 20-24 are not given in Matthew or Mark.

Luke 21:20 And when ye shall see Jerusalem compassed with armies, then know that the desolation thereof is nigh.

Jesus explains to the Jews that their precious Jerusalem will be destroyed again. The Jews will face many days of vengeance, being accused of killing the Messiah. Jews will be led away captive culminating with the holocaust when 6 million were killed.

Luke 21:21 Then let them which are in Judaea flee to the mountains; and let them which are in the midst of it depart out; and let not them that are in the countries enter thereinto.
Luke 21:22 For these be the days of vengeance, that all things which are written may be fulfilled.
Luke 21:23 But woe unto them that are with child, and to them that give suck, in those days! for there shall be great distress in the land, and wrath upon this people.
Luke 21:24 And they shall fall by the edge of the sword, and shall be led away captive into all nations: and Jerusalem shall be trodden down of the Gentiles, until the times of the Gentiles be fulfilled.

Jerusalem was trodden down of the Gentiles starting with Babylon and King Nebuchadnezzar. Then the Gentile world powers continued to rule over Jerusalem. King Nebuchadnezzar's dream established these world empires that would rule over Jerusalem. Nebuchadnezzar was the first world empire to have control over Jerusalem.

Daniel 2:36 This *is* the dream; and we will tell the interpretation thereof before the king.

Daniel 2:37 Thou, O king, *art* a king of kings: for the God of heaven hath given thee a kingdom, power, and strength, and glory.

Daniel 2:38 And wheresoever the children of men dwell, the beasts of the field and the fowls of the heaven hath he given into thine hand, and hath made thee ruler over them all. Thou *art* this head of gold.

Then came the world empires of the Medes and the Persians and Alexander the Great from Greece.

Daniel 2:39 And after thee shall arise another kingdom inferior to thee, and another third kingdom of brass, which shall bear rule over all the earth.

Then came the world empire of Rome that ruled with an iron fist.

Daniel 2:40 And the fourth kingdom shall be strong as iron: forasmuch as iron breaketh in pieces and subdueth all *things:* and as iron that breaketh all these, shall it break in pieces and bruise.

Now comes a world empire comprised of ten nations represented by Rome (iron) and weaker nations (clay).

Daniel 2:41 And whereas thou sawest the feet and toes, part of potters' clay, and part of iron, the kingdom shall be divided; but there shall be in it of the strength of the iron, forasmuch as thou sawest the iron mixed with miry clay.

The feet and toes are a divided group that cannot agree on a way to handle the Jewish nation or a way to have them live in their promised land. This Cabal, this Illuminate today known as a New World Order will come into being. It will be of ten members,

perhaps ten nations. They will come under the one who will unite these ten toes with his covenant which is confirmed for a week as explained in chapter nine of Daniel. Here is the vision that Daniel interpreted about the feet and toes.

Daniel 2:42 And *as* the toes of the feet *were* part of iron, and part of clay, *so* the kingdom shall be partly strong, and partly broken.

Daniel 2:43 And whereas thou sawest iron mixed with miry clay, they shall mingle themselves with the seed of men: but they shall not cleave one to another, even as iron is not mixed with clay.

And then Christ's kingdom will come:

Daniel 2:44 And in the days of these kings shall the God of heaven set up a kingdom, which shall never be destroyed: and the kingdom shall not be left to other people, *but* it shall break in pieces and consume all these kingdoms, and it shall stand for ever.

Daniel 2:45 Forasmuch as thou sawest that the stone was cut out of the mountain without hands, and that it brake in pieces the iron, the brass, the clay, the silver, and the gold; the great God hath made known to the king what shall come to pass hereafter: and the dream *is* certain, and the interpretation thereof sure.

This dream is about the length of the "times of the Gentiles" which was fulfilled when Jerusalem went back into the hands of the Jews. This happened in the six-day war of 1967.

Only in Matthew and Luke's Gospel

Here is Luke's description of what it will be like during these seven years of tribulation.

Luke 21:25 And there shall be signs in the sun, and in the moon, and in the stars; and upon the earth distress of nations, with perplexity; the sea and the waves roaring;

Luke 21:26 Men's hearts failing them for fear, and for looking after those things which are coming on the earth: for the powers of heaven shall be shaken.

Many who are moving toward mid-trib or a pos-trib rapture miss-apply these seven years of tribulation at this point. Matthew uses the term tribulation here.

Matthew 24:29 Immediately after the tribulation of those days shall the sun be darkened, and the moon shall not give her light, and the stars shall fall from heaven, and the powers of the heavens shall be shaken:

The word says "and after the tribulation" meaning it is over. That is correct. But since this prophecy is for the Jew, the Jew is still on this earth. The seven-year time of Jacob's Trouble (Jeremiah 30:7) is this time of tribulation. This is not for the church. Every saved person from the church age is already up in heaven. We are living throughout heaven in our mansions built for us by Christ.

John 14:1 Let not your heart be troubled: ye believe in God, believe also in me.

John 14:2 In my Father's house are many mansions: if *it were* not *so,* I would have told you. I go to prepare a place for you.

John 14:3 And if I go and prepare a place for you, I will come again, and receive you unto myself; that where I am, *there* ye may be also.

The appearing of Christ at His second coming now takes place. The 12 tribes of Israel shall mourn as they see the Messiah whom they rejected:

Matthew 24:30 And then shall appear the sign of the Son of man in heaven: and then shall all the tribes of the earth mourn, and they shall see the Son of man coming in the clouds of heaven with power and great glory.

Christ coming in power and great glory is not the same as a thief in the night.

The angels are to gather His elect, that is those who have made Him their Lord, from one end of heaven, and I add in their

mansions prepared by Jesus, from one end of HEAVEN to the other. This indicates we are already in heaven when this second coming occurs.

> Matthew 24:31 And he shall send his angels with a great sound of a trumpet, and they shall gather together his elect from the four winds, from one end of heaven to the other.

And here is Luke's description of the second coming of Jesus Christ.

Luke 21:27 And then shall they see the Son of man coming in a cloud with power and great glory.
Luke 21:28 And when these things begin to come to pass, then look up, and lift up your heads; for your redemption draweth nigh.

Synoptic in Matthew, Mark, and Luke's Gospel

Again, very few parables are synoptic to all three gospels. This is one of them because it goes back to the prophet Isaiah:

Luke 21:29 And he spake to them a parable; Behold the fig tree, and all the trees;

Commentators who wrote in earlier years, before the Jews were being allowed to return to Jerusalem for the first time (1917 Balfour Declaration), had no idea as to this parable. In 1948 most Bible followers looked on the formation of the new nation of Israel as an impossible miracle of scripture being revealed right before their eyes. Three hundred years earlier, Matthew Henry wrote:

> *Christ appoints his disciples to observe the signs of the times, which they might judge by, if they had an eye to the foregoing directions, with as much certainty and assurance as they could judge of the approach of summer by the budding forth of the trees, Luk 21:29-31. As in the kingdom of nature there is a chain of causes, so in the kingdom of providence there is a*

consequence of one event upon another. When we see a nation filling up the measure of their iniquity, we may conclude that their ruin is nigh; when we see the ruin of persecuting powers hastening on, we may thence infer that the kingdom of God is nigh at hand, that when the opposition given to it is removed it shall gain ground. As we may lawfully prognosticate the change of the seasons when second causes have begun to work, so we may, in the disposal of events, expect something uncommon when God is already raised up out of his holy habitation (Zechariah 2:13); then stand still and see his salvation.

Absolutely no vision by these early commentators of this parable referring to the Jews back in the homeland. Two hundred and fifty years ago John Gill wrote very little about this passage as to it being prophetic about the Jews returning to their land:

Now learn a parable of the fig tree. Take a similitude, or comparison from the fig tree, which was a tree well known in Judea; and the putting forth of its branches, leaves, and fruit, fell under the observation of everyone:

when its branch is yet tender; through the influence of the sun, and the motion of the sap, which was bound up, and congealed in the winter season:

and putteth forth leaves; from the tender branches, which swell, and open, and put forth buds, leaves, and fruit:

ye know the summer is nigh; spring being already come: the fig tree putting forth her green figs, is a sign that the winter is past, the spring is come, and summer is at hand;

Most Commentaries just rambled on about the return of the Jew to the land. These early commentators did not fully understand that the fig tree represented the Jews and Jerusalem. The Jews, who are now back in control of the holy city of Jerusalem that had been trodden down of the Gentiles since Babylon!

Luke 21:30 When they now shoot forth, ye see and know of your own selves that summer is now nigh at hand.
Luke 21:31 So likewise ye, when ye see these things come to pass, know ye that the kingdom of God is nigh at hand.

This parable describes what Christ said earlier in chapter seventeen that the kingdom of God must be within you. Since Christ had not gone to the cross yet and the Gospel message of the death, burial, and resurrection of our Lord was not understood at this moment Jesus used the term the kingdom of God is "nigh at hand." The "kingdom of God" that Jesus mentions is near at hand is just a few days away, that is the death, burial, and resurrection of Christ when it actually occurs. This is what is called the Gospel message by Paul declaring it to the churches. Jesus described that the generation that sees this parable come to pass; that is the figs shooting forth once again from Jerusalem, will see the signs Jesus spoke of in the last days.

Luke 21:32 Verily I say unto you, This generation shall not pass away, till all be fulfilled.
Luke 21:33 Heaven and earth shall pass away: but my words shall not pass away.
Luke 21:34 And take heed to yourselves, lest at any time your hearts be overcharged with surfeiting, and drunkenness, and cares of this life, and so that day come upon you unawares.

The church is on earth for many reasons. But one of the main reasons is to study the scriptures together. Parables are given with story plots that have an ulterior motive. The ulterior motive with this parable was not known by early commentators. But now as scripture is being revealed by the Holy Spirit in these last days the truths are becoming evident. The truth that will be the rapture is what a church member should be looking for. Those left behind will be snared and will not be able to escape all these things.

Luke 21:35 For as a snare shall it come on all them that dwell on the face of the whole earth.
Luke 21:36 Watch ye therefore, and pray always, that ye may be accounted worthy to escape all these things that shall come to pass, and to stand before the Son of man.

Here is the command of Jesus as to how church people are to react to this parable. We are to watch and pray. Watch for Jerusalem to be no longer in the hands of the Gentiles. Watch for the figs (figs are Jews as described in Jeremiah 24) to shoot forth from the Fig tree. We are also to pray for those who hear the Gospel during these last days. The kingdom of God that is within you must center on a belief in the death, burial, and resurrection that was preached by Paul to all the churches.

Luke 21:37 And in the day time he was teaching in the temple; and at night he went out, and abode in the mount that is called *the mount* of Olives.

After this day on the mount of Olives, Christ would return to the temple to continue His preaching that He must suffer many things and be killed, and remember, they understood not.

Luke 21:38 And all the people came early in the morning to him in the temple, for to hear him.

Willing to come early to hear Him? Is this the attitude of the followers of Christ today? The Gospel of Christ must be heard. His death, burial, and resurrection must be proclaimed. Seek Him early the scriptures say.

Psalms 63:1 O God, thou *art* my God; early will I seek thee: my soul thirsteth for thee, my flesh longeth for thee in a dry and thirsty land, where no water is;

Early in the day, and early in life Christ is to be sought after.

Proverbs 8:17 I love them that love me; and those that seek me early shall find me.

The command from God is to hear what Jesus has said, but the reality is are we obeying and walking in that truth?

2John 1:4 I rejoiced greatly that I found of thy children walking in truth, as we have received a commandment from the Father.

LUKE CHAPTER 22

Highlights:

Chapter twenty-two has Jesus Christ at the last supper. Heads to the garden of Gethsemane with the betrayal of Judas. The denial of Jesus Christ by Peter.

Main Participants:

Jesus Christ v.2,
Chief priests and Scribes v.2,
Satan v.3,
Judas Iscariot v.3,
Peter and John v.8,
The Twelve v.14,
Captains of the Temple and Elders v.52,
The High Priest v.54,
A Certain Maid who had seen Peter v.56,
Another who saw Peter v.58,
Another who saw Peter v.59,
The men that held Jesus v.63,
The Elders v.66.

In Brief:

Judas Iscariot covenants to betray Jesus for thirty pieces of silver. Jesus has His Apostles prepare for the last supper. The Lord's Supper is instituted. His followers strive with each other as to who is the greatest. Jesus predicts Peter's denial. Jesus goes to the Garden of Gethsemane. Jesus is arrested. Jesus is brought before the High Priest. Peter denies Jesus three times and weeps. Jesus is brought before the council.

Only in Luke's Gospel

Luke 22:1 Now the feast of unleavened bread drew nigh, which is called the Passover.

Within a couple of days, Christ will be offered as the Passover "Lamb of God which taketh away the sin of the world."
John 1:29 The next day John seeth Jesus coming unto him, and saith, Behold the Lamb of God, which taketh away the sin of the world.

Luke 22:2 And the chief priests and scribes sought how they might kill him; for they feared the people.

Before Jesus goes to the cross, in the days between the tenth of Nisan and the fourteenth of Nisan, the chief priests will try to figure out "how" they might kill Him. According to scripture, it is on the tenth of Nisan (Abib) that the Passover Lamb is to be chosen:
Exodus 12:3 Speak ye unto all the congregation of Israel, saying, In the tenth *day* of this month they shall take to them every man a lamb, according to the house of *their* fathers, a lamb for an house:
It is on this day, the tenth of Nisan, that Matthew says Christ was selected to be that Lamb:
Matthew 26:3 Then assembled together the chief priests, and the scribes, and the elders of the people, unto the palace of the high priest, who was called Caiaphas,
Matthew 26:4 And consulted that they might take Jesus by subtilty, and kill *him.*
Luke begins his discussion of Judas Iscariot's betrayal of Jesus Christ:

Luke 22:3 Then entered Satan into Judas surnamed Iscariot, being of the number of the twelve.

Luke 22:4 And he went his way, and communed with the chief priests and captains, how he might betray him unto them.

Luke 22:5 And they were glad, and covenanted to give him money.

Only in Matthew's Gospel

In Mark, Luke, and John the price for the betrayal of Christ is never mentioned. Thirty Pieces of silver as stated in the Old Testament by Zachariah 11:12-13. It is only mentioned in Matthew. Again, as in times before, Matthew is the Gospel to the Jew and in so doing Matthew seeks to show the fulfillment of all passages from the Old Testament. He has done this time and time again.

Matthew 26:14 Then one of the twelve, called Judas Iscariot, went unto the chief priests,

Matthew 26:15 And said *unto them,* What will ye give me, and I will deliver him unto you? And they covenanted with him for thirty pieces of silver.

Just recently Matthew was the only Gospel writer to claim Jesus came into Jerusalem triumphantly on two animals. Matthew agreed with the Old Testament prophecy of Zachariah 9:9 as both claim Jesus rode in on two animals. First, He rode to Jerusalem on a donkey (a beast of burden representing the burden of the law) and secondly, Jesus had ridden on the young untamed colt (representing the Gentiles being a wild olive tree, which was grafted in among them into the work of God to spread the good news of Christ). Mark, Luke, and John do not mention the donkey, but only speak of the young colt. Thus, declaring the message that God would now use the Gentiles who had never been used of God in the past to present His word. Shortly after Pentecost, Jesus brought in this plan with Cornelious, to use the Gentiles to win souls for Christ in His church.

Luke 22:6 And he promised, and sought opportunity to betray him unto them in the absence of the multitude.

Luke 22:7 Then came the day of unleavened bread, when the passover must be killed.

The Passover must be killed at even **on the fourteenth of Nisan (Nisan was called Abib before the Babylonian captivity).**

Exodus 12:5 Your lamb shall be without blemish, a male of the first year: ye shall take *it* out from the sheep, or from the goats:

Exodus 12:6 And ye shall keep it up until the fourteenth day of the same month: and the whole assembly of the congregation of Israel shall kill it in the evening.

The fourteenth of Nisan is the day that Jesus is to be killed at even (3pm in the Jewish day). This eternal day will begin at 6pm the night before. The Passover meal will be eaten for supper, at 6pm, when the fourteenth of Nisan begins. To be ready for this timing, Jesus orders two apostles to locate the upper room. This is done the day before on the thirteenth of Nisan. The room to be prepared is where this last meal would take place.

Luke 22:8 And he sent Peter and John, saying, Go and prepare us the passover, that we may eat.

Luke says their names and Mark is the only other Gospel to say there were two of them. Matthew refers to the disciples in plural but does not limit it to the two. Only Luke names the two. Now, Peter and John ask Jesus a question. Time is of the utmost importance as the Fourteenth of Nisan approaches.

Synoptic in Matthew, Mark, and Luke's Gospel

Luke 22:9 And they said unto him, Where wilt thou that we prepare?

Luke 22:10 And he said unto them, Behold, when ye are entered into the city, there shall a man meet you, bearing a pitcher of water; follow him into the house where he entereth in.

Luke 22:11 And ye shall say unto the goodman of the house, The Master saith unto thee, Where is the guestchamber, where I shall eat the passover with my disciples?

Luke 22:12 And he shall shew you a large upper room furnished: there make ready.

Luke 22:13 And they went, and found as he had said unto them: and they made ready the passover.

Jesus says to locate a large upper room and make it ready for the 6pm Passover meal. At this point it is approx. 24 hours before the even of the Passover when the Lamb is to be slain. Matthew says when the even was come (that is the even of the thirteenth of Nisan) they sat down:

Matthew 26:20 Now when the even was come, he sat down with the twelve.

This is anytime from 3pm till 5:59pm on the thirteenth of Nisan. It is obvious that the disciples assembled in the upper room moments before the actual seating and preparation to start the last supper. This would be at the end of the day, the thirteenth of Nisan, in preparation for the Fourteenth of Nisan to begin. At 6pm this night, the Fourteenth of Nisan, the eventful day begins. The last supper, that is this meal eaten at 6pm as the Jews start their new day has come. The supper meal is eaten and then they should rest for the night to prepare for the day of work ahead. But there will be no rest tonight. For it is written that His hour has come. He has been desiring for this moment that His disciples understood not.

Luke 22:14 And when the hour was come, he sat down, and the twelve apostles with him.

Luke 22:15 And he said unto them, With desire I have desired to eat this passover with you before I suffer:

The word *suffer* here (paschō to experience a sensation usually painful, passion) is totally different than the word *suffer* (aphiēmi- to send or to send forth) as used by Jesus about little

children. There are many other distinct different Greek words for suffer also.

Jesus was about to go through the torture that He would give His blood to rescue all mankind from sin and hell. Luke will give the most graphic and humanly description of what will happen to Jesus in the next 24 hours.

Luke 22:16 For I say unto you, I will not any more eat thereof, until it be fulfilled in the kingdom of God.

God's plan of salvation, the kingdom of God which must be within you (Luke 17:21), is about to take place. Jesus is about to fulfill what every age has been waiting for. He will fulfill what our age looks back to. The Gospel or good news for all of mankind is about to take place. The death, burial, and resurrection of Christ will be understood when Jesus rises after three days, on the first day of the week and meets with them in that evening.

Luke 22:17 And he took the cup, and gave thanks, and said, Take this, and divide *it* among yourselves:
Luke 22:18 For I say unto you, I will not drink of the fruit of the vine, until the kingdom of God shall come.

Jesus will not eat, verse 16, nor will He drink, verse 18, until He has done the Father's will, and the kingdom of God comes to fruition. Some versions change this wording to wine. Fruit of the vine is good, wholesome grape juice. Christ spoke of the events about to take place as the kingdom of God that shall come.

Luke 22:19 And he took bread, and gave thanks, and brake *it,* and gave unto them, saying, This is my body which is given for you: this do in remembrance of me.

The last supper is all about remembrance. It is for a memorial to the events Christ would now go through. God's plan for the ages began this night.

Luke 22:20 Likewise also the cup after supper, saying, This cup *is* the new testament in my blood, which is shed for you.

The cup, symbolizing His shed blood, according to Matthew,

Matthew 26:28 For this is my blood of the new testament, which is shed for many for the remission of sins.

and Mark.

Mark 14:24 And he said unto them, This is my blood of the new testament, which is shed for many.

While they were eating, Matthew and Mark discuss the betrayal of Jesus.

Matthew 26:21 And as they did eat, he said, Verily I say unto you, that one of you shall betray me.

Matthew 26:22 And they were exceeding sorrowful, and began every one of them to say unto him, Lord, is it I?

Matthew 26:23 And he answered and said, He that dippeth *his* hand with me in the dish, the same shall betray me.

Matthew 26:24 The Son of man goeth as it is written of him: but woe unto that man by whom the Son of man is betrayed! it had been good for that man if he had not been born.

Mark says:

Mark 14:18 And as they sat and did eat, Jesus said, Verily I say unto you, One of you which eateth with me shall betray me.

But Luke discusses the betrayal differently. Jesus speaking differently at this point:

Luke 22:21 But, behold, the hand of him that betrayeth me *is* with me on the table.

Luke 22:22 And truly the Son of man goeth, as it was determined: but woe unto that man by whom he is betrayed!

Luke 22:23 And they began to enquire among themselves, which of them it was that should do this thing.

Only in Luke's Gospel

It does not take long for the Apostles to go off topic and continue to discuss worldly things. So much so that Luke describes this as a strife or a dispute among them.

Luke 22:24 And there was also a strife among them, which of them should be accounted the greatest.

Luke 22:25 And he said unto them, The kings of the Gentiles exercise lordship over them; and they that exercise authority upon them are called benefactors.

Luke 22:26 But ye *shall* not *be* so: but he that is greatest among you, let him be as the younger; and he that is chief, as he that doth serve.

Luke 22:27 For whether *is* greater, he that sitteth at meat, or he that serveth? *is* not he that sitteth at meat? but I am among you as he that serveth.

Jesus is again explaining that to follow Him, you must be willing to serve your fellow man. He was showing this by example and not just speaking it. He talked the talk and He walked the walk!

Luke 22:28 Ye are they which have continued with me in my temptations.

Luke 22:29 And I appoint unto you a kingdom, as my Father hath appointed unto me;

Luke 22:30 That ye may eat and drink at my table in my kingdom, and sit on thrones judging the twelve tribes of Israel.

Luke 22:31 And the Lord said, Simon, Simon, behold, Satan hath desired *to have* you, that he may sift *you* as wheat:

Luke 22:32 But I have prayed for thee, that thy faith fail not: and when thou art converted, strengthen thy brethren.

Jesus at this point makes a declaring revelation. Peter is not yet converted! He must be converted to have the gift of the Holy Ghost and be baptized (placed into) the body of Christ, that is

the church. It is still future when he will be converted and turn to Christ. Jesus spoke of starting His church back in Matthew.

Matthew 16:17 And Jesus answered and said unto him, Blessed art thou, Simon Barjona: for flesh and blood hath not revealed it unto thee, but my Father which is in heaven.

Matthew 16:18 And I say also unto thee, That thou art Peter, and upon this rock I will build my church; and the gates of hell shall not prevail against it.

Matthew 16:19 And I will give unto thee the keys of the kingdom of heaven: and whatsoever thou shalt bind on earth shall be bound in heaven: and whatsoever thou shalt loose on earth shall be loosed in heaven.

Peter will be the main player in presenting the church. He will have the keys. The one who has the keys is usually the first one in. But it cannot happen yet. He is not converted. The keys (which will be the Gospel to both the Jews first and then to the Gentiles) have not been used. And cannot be used until the gift of the Holy Ghost is given as Jesus is about to explain in John's gospel.

Peter thinks he is ready:

Luke 22:33 And he said unto him, Lord, I am ready to go with thee, both into prison, and to death.

Synoptic in Matthew, Mark, Luke, and John's Gospel

Jesus sets him in his place:

Luke 22:34 And he said, I tell thee, Peter, the cock shall not crow this day, before that thou shalt thrice deny that thou knowest me.

This is a very intense conversation that the Apostles are having with Jesus. Peter is entirely put in his place by Jesus Christ. You will deny me three times Jesus said. Before this night is over and the cock crows you will deny me three times Jesus states. If someone in my church was to deny Jesus Christ time

and time again, either he would have to go, or I would have to come out from among them as the scripture orders me to do. All four Gospels have a record of this. Jesus may have said it more than once to Peter as we read the different ways it is quoted in the Gospels.

Matthew:

Matthew 26:34 Jesus said unto him, Verily I say unto thee, That this night, before the cock crow, thou shalt deny me thrice.

Mark:

Mark 14:30 And Jesus saith unto him, Verily I say unto thee, That this day, *even* in this night, before the cock crow twice, thou shalt deny me thrice.

John:

John 13:38 Jesus answered him, Wilt thou lay down thy life for my sake? Verily, verily, I say unto thee, The cock shall not crow, till thou hast denied me thrice.

Only in Luke's Gospel

Luke 22:35 And he said unto them, When I sent you without purse, and scrip, and shoes, lacked ye any thing? And they said, Nothing.
Luke 22:36 Then said he unto them, But now, he that hath a purse, let him take *it,* and likewise *his* scrip: and he that hath no sword, let him sell his garment, and buy one.

Jesus says to sell your garment and buy a sword which of course is the weapon of choice in that day and age. Not to use for attack or offense as Jesus will soon explain to Peter who chops off Malchus's ear. But to be used for a deterrent and defense of family and home.

Luke 22:37 For I say unto you, that this that is written must yet be accomplished in me, And he was reckoned among the transgressors: for the things concerning me have an end.

Jesus beaten and crucified with the transgressors is expressed so much in the Old Testament. Here the fulfillment of Isaiah 53 will take place on this day.

Isaiah 53:12 Therefore will I divide him *a portion* with the great, and he shall divide the spoil with the strong; because he hath poured out his soul unto death: and he was numbered with the transgressors; and he bare the sin of many, and made intercession for the transgressors.

Luke 22:38 And they said, Lord, behold, here *are* two swords. And he said unto them, It is enough.

The Apostles declare that they have two swords. Jesus says two are enough. This is an obvious statement meaning the sword is for defensive measures only. Not offensive equipment.

Luke 22:39 And he came out, and went, as he was wont, to the mount of Olives; and his disciples also followed him.

Synoptic in Matthew, Mark, Luke, and John's Gospel

Jesus will now lead them to the garden of Gethsemane. The garden is located on the western slope of the Mount of Olives. The Gospels, especially John, will now have much to say about this. Many activities took place in the upper room that are not in Luke's Gospel. Judas leaving to betray Jesus John (13:2); The washing of the feet of the Apostles by the Lord (John 13:4); and Jesus declaring that all will betray Him must be accomplished to fulfill the Old Testament prophecy of Zechariah in chapter thirteen.

As they make their way from the western side of Jerusalem (which is where the two- story homes were located) Jesus begins His speech on the Comforter that can only come down to earth after Jesus goes back to heaven. John speaks much of the need for Christ to return to heaven so that the Holy Spirit may come down and indwell the believer. This would mark the beginning of the Church.

> John 14:16 And I will pray the Father, and he shall give you another Comforter, that he may abide with you for ever;

Again in John:

> John 14:26 But the Comforter, *which is* the Holy Ghost, whom the Father will send in my name, he shall teach you all things, and bring all things to your remembrance, whatsoever I have said unto you.

And again in John:

> John 15:26 But when the Comforter is come, whom I will send unto you from the Father, *even* the Spirit of truth, which proceedeth from the Father, he shall testify of me:

And once more in John:

> John 16:7 Nevertheless I tell you the truth; It is expedient for you that I go away: for if I go not away, the Comforter will not come unto you; but if I depart, I will send him unto you.

All this talk about the Holy Ghost known as the Comforter who will have to come according to John's Gospel, is taking place on this walk to the Garden of Gethsemane which is on the western slope of the Mount of Olives. During this walk, Jesus prays His prayer to the Father recorded in John chapter 17. Walking past the temple and crossing to the mount of Olives is known because John 18:1 speaks of the crossing of the brook Cedron (Kidron Valley) from the eastern gate on the side of Jerusalem to the western side of the Mount of Olives and into the Garden of Gethsemane. Luke now refers to this as the place where He will begin to pray.

Luke 22:40 And when he was at the place, he said unto them, Pray that ye enter not into temptation.

Using words that Jesus Himself taught His disciples on how to pray in Luke 11:2-4 Jesus is very consistent with His instructions.

Luke 22:41 And he was withdrawn from them about a stone's cast, and kneeled down, and prayed,

Luke names one time when Jesus went off to pray on His own, but Matthew and Mark mention that this happened 3 times for approximately one hour each time.

Only in Luke's Gospel

Luke 22:42 Saying, Father, if thou be willing, remove this cup from me: nevertheless not my will, but thine, be done.
Luke 22:43 And there appeared an angel unto him from heaven, strengthening him.

Is Jesus strengthened here? He is strengthened Only in His human form. Being God, Jesus certainly did not need an angel to strengthen Him. After all He created the angels:
Revelation 4:11 Thou art worthy, O Lord, to receive glory and honour and power: for thou hast created all things, and for thy pleasure they are and were created.
Each believer should know God cares enough to have guardian angels watching over us continually.

Luke 22:44 And being in an agony he prayed more earnestly: and his sweat was as it were great drops of blood falling down to the ground.

Luke alone describes the great drops of blood falling to the ground. Jesus sweats "as it were great drops of blood" because He is at the height of His concern about the soon separation that would occur between Him and His Father who is in heaven above. Again, it is Luke the physician who describes the events of the human side of Jesus as He sweats blood." This is holy blood. It is the beginning of the longest, hardest day in history and the shedding of blood on this day for man's sins!

This key verse in Luke has four uniquely used words that only occur once in the New Testament. They are 1-agony, 2-more earnestly, 3-sweat, and 4-great drops. It is a tremendously emotional passage proving Jesus was truly man, manifested in the flesh:

1John 3:5 And ye know that he was manifested to take away our sins; and in him is no sin.

The shedding of the innocent Christ's blood begins. This is the price of my redemption as it says in Colossians. The blood is declared clearly in the King James Version but not as clear in many others:

Colossians 1:14 In whom we have redemption through his blood, even the forgiveness of sins:

This would be when He takes upon Himself the sins of each one of us as it says in Galatians:

Galatians 1:4 Who gave himself for our sins, that he might deliver us from this present evil world, according to the will of God and our Father:

And again in 1 John, it says Jesus paid for the sins of the whole world:

1John 2:2 And he is the propitiation for our sins: and not for ours only, but also for the sins of the whole world.

Luke 22:45 And when he rose up from prayer, and was come to his disciples, he found them sleeping for sorrow,
Luke 22:46 And said unto them, Why sleep ye? rise and pray, lest ye enter into temptation.

During this time, Luke only mentions Jesus going to prayer once. However, the other Gospels mention that He went to prayer three times. Each time for about one hour.

Matthew 26:40 And he cometh unto the disciples, and findeth them asleep, and saith unto Peter, What, could ye not watch with me one hour?
Matthew 26:41 Watch and pray, that ye enter not into temptation: the spirit indeed *is* willing, but the flesh *is* weak.

Synoptic in Matthew, Mark, Luke, and John's Gospel

Luke 22:47 And while he yet spake, behold a multitude, and he that was called Judas, one of the twelve, went before them, and drew near unto Jesus to kiss him.

Judas and a great multitude of men arrive at the garden and approach Jesus. In Psalm 41 it states:
Psalms 41:9 Yea, mine own familiar friend, in whom I trusted, which did eat of my bread, hath lifted up *his* heel against me.

Luke 22:48 But Jesus said unto him, Judas, betrayest thou the Son of man with a kiss?

Luke describes how Jesus questions Judas in regards to this secret sign he has given to expose Christ. How Jesus phrases this question brings all the conviction down on Judas. God prophesied of this moment in Psalms:
Psalms 55:12 For *it was* not an enemy *that* reproached me; then I could have borne *it:* neither *was it* he that hated me *that* did magnify *himself* against me; then I would have hid myself from him:
Psalms 55:13 But *it was* thou, a man mine equal, my guide, and mine acquaintance.
Psalms 55:14 We took sweet counsel together, *and* walked unto the house of God in company.

Luke 22:49 When they which were about him saw what would follow, they said unto him, Lord, shall we smite with the sword?
Luke 22:50 And one of them smote the servant of the high priest, and cut off his right ear.

In John it is revealed that the one with the sword is Peter. It is Peter who will not listen to Jesus again at this time. Jesus said that Satan would sift him as wheat. And Peter is being played like a fiddle by Satan right now to the fullest. Also, John mentions that it is a man named Malchus who has his ear chopped off.

John 18:10 Then Simon Peter having a sword drew it, and smote the high priest's servant, and cut off his right ear. The servant's name was Malchus.

Luke 22:51 And Jesus answered and said, Suffer ye thus far. And he touched his ear, and healed him.

Luke 22:52 Then Jesus said unto the chief priests, and captains of the temple, and the elders, which were come to him, Be ye come out, as against a thief, with swords and staves?

Luke 22:53 When I was daily with you in the temple, ye stretched forth no hands against me: but this is your hour, and the power of darkness.

John has the best narrative of this moment. Judas steps back and rejoins the band of men, and Jesus brings the whole matter to a pinnacle by asking, "Who do you seek?"

John 18:4 Jesus therefore, knowing all things that should come upon him, went forth, and said unto them, Whom seek ye?

One of the bands of men makes it clear. It is "Jesus of Nazareth" that they are seeking:

John 18:5 They answered him, Jesus of Nazareth. Jesus saith unto them, I am *he.* And Judas also, which betrayed him, stood with them.

Three times Jesus will say "I AM" here in John's Gospel. In verse five He says, "I am" and notice the "he" is in italics meaning it was inserted by the translators for proper English and clarity. Three times in verses five, six, and eight Jesus declares that He is the great "I AM" that appeared to Moses at the burning bush in Exodus chapter three. Judas and the band of men show "fear" because they located this Jesus who showed "no fear". Jesus, with His love for you and me, was not about to hide from them on this special night:

John 18:6 As soon then as he had said unto them, I am *he,* they went backward, and fell to the ground.

Jesus would ask the band of men a second time as they were so startled about the fact that He was not running and hiding.

John 18:7 Then asked he them again, Whom seek ye? And they said, Jesus of Nazareth.

John 18:8 Jesus answered, I have told you that I am *he:* if therefore ye seek me, let these go their way:

Jesus is led to Annas first. The Gospel of John will describe the relationship here of Annas and Caiaphas. Annas is father-in-law to the current high priest, Caiaphas.

John 18:13 And led him away to Annas first; for he was father in law to Caiaphas, which was the high priest that same year.

John 18:14 Now Caiaphas was he, which gave counsel to the Jews, that it was expedient that one man should die for the people.

Luke 22:54 Then took they him, and led *him,* and brought him into the high priest's house. And Peter followed afar off.

Dealing with a man's pride! Even at a crucial time such as this, God in all His mercy will deal one on one with any person at any time. Are there any followers more faithful than Peter? Would it be possible knowing what Peter knew, and having just witnessed the miracle of reattaching the ear of Malchus that he had so carelessly chopped off, that Peter could deny the Lord Jesus Christ at this moment? Peter, who just a few hours earlier said to Jesus; "Though all men shall be offended because of thee, yet will I never be offended," is now keeping his distance. He looks for the comfort of the warm fire and has forsaken Jesus already in his heart. Also, in just a moment, he will begin to verbally deny Jesus three times. The High Priest's house is that of Caiaphas and Peter is about to show that he talked the talk, but he cannot walk the walk!

Luke 22:55 And when they had kindled a fire in the midst of the hall, and were set down together, Peter sat down among them.

Luke 22:56 But a certain maid beheld him as he sat by the fire, and earnestly looked upon him, and said, This man was also with him.

Luke 22:57 And he denied him, saying, Woman, I know him not.

First a maid confronts Peter. Mark said that a cock would crow twice. He is the only Gospel to say this. When this maid confronted Peter for the first time, a cock crowed according to Mark:

Mark 14:66 And as Peter was beneath in the palace, there cometh one of the maids of the high priest:

Mark 14:67 And when she saw Peter warming himself, she looked upon him, and said, And thou also wast with Jesus of Nazareth.

Mark 14:68 But he denied, saying, I know not, neither understand I what thou sayest. And he went out into the porch; and the cock crew.

This must have been very ominous to Peter. Hearing the cock crow at this first denial must have shaken Peter, but not enough to get him to be the man!

Luke 22:58 And after a little while another saw him, and said, Thou art also of them. And Peter said, Man, I am not.

Luke 22:59 And about the space of one hour after another confidently affirmed, saying, Of a truth this *fellow* also was with him: for he is a Galilaean.

Luke 22:60 And Peter said, Man, I know not what thou sayest. And immediately, while he yet spake, the cock crew.

At this point, Peter begins to realize that he has denied the Lord just as Jesus had predicted. However, the real *heart to heart* moment came next:

Luke 22:61 And the Lord turned, and looked upon Peter. And Peter remembered the word of the Lord, how he had said unto him, Before the cock crow, thou shalt deny me thrice.

This stare by Jesus was more than Peter could bear. Could any one of us bear it? This happens each time we sin! We need to remember the word of the Lord and repent of the evil deed. Peter could do nothing. All he could do is cry.

Luke 22:62 And Peter went out, and wept bitterly.

The insults and false accusations are now hurled at the Lord Jesus Christ.

Luke 22:63 And the men that held Jesus mocked him, and smote *him.*
Luke 22:64 And when they had blindfolded him, they struck him on the face, and asked him, saying, Prophesy, who is it that smote thee?
Luke 22:65 And many other things blasphemously spake they against him.

It is now 6am. Daytime has begun. the Lord is now retried; not by the written law of God, but by the religious leaders who will attempt to follow their own oral rules in the Jewish Mishnah:

Let a capital offense be tried during the day but suspended at night.

Luke 22:66 And as soon as it was day, the elders of the people and the chief priests and the scribes came together, and led him into their council, saying,
Luke 22:67 Art thou the Christ? tell us. And he said unto them, If I tell you, ye will not believe:
Luke 22:68 And if I also ask *you,* ye will not answer me, nor let *me* go.

Jesus has exhausted every phrase in the Hebrew language. He has told them over and over that He was the only begotten of the Father in Heaven.

Luke 22:69 Hereafter shall the Son of man sit on the right hand of the power of God.

Jesus told them over and over that He was the Lord. That He is God manifested in the flesh. He could say nothing less. So, Jesus reverts to and speaks of what God has always wanted to take place. His Son, the Lord Jesus Christ, seated at the right hand of the Father with power and great glory.

Luke 22:70 Then said they all, Art thou then the Son of God? And he said unto them, Ye say that I am.

The Lord continues to take the all-important name of God which is "I AM".

Luke 22:71 And they said, What need we any further witness? for we ourselves have heard of his own mouth.

The religious leaders follow their oral law but break the written law of God that specifically says:
Deuteronomy 17:6 At the mouth of two witnesses, or three witnesses, shall he that is worthy of death be put to death; *but* at the mouth of one witness he shall not be put to death.

Only in Matthew's Gospel

It is at this time, before the judgement hall opens at 9am on the Fourteenth of Nisan, the history of Judas is unveiled in Matthew:
Matthew 27:1 When the morning was come, all the chief priests and elders of the people took counsel against Jesus to put him to death:
Matthew 27:2 And when they had bound him, they led *him* away, and delivered him to Pontius Pilate the governor.
Conviction comes upon Judas, and he begins to realize the awful thing he did by betraying Jesus. His remorse is more than he can bear. This act of repentance alone does not save him. It is important to understand this. You can change your mind or repent about your sin, but if you could do this perfectly and become sinless then you do not need Christ the Saviour. When repentance takes place, a person turns from something. Faith is what God requires for a man to turn to Him. Since it is man's nature to sin, man should be in constant repentance.
Understand that man is not a sinner because he sins; man sins because he is a sinner!

The strain of constantly having to repent because of our sin by our old nature would kill us. It happened to Judas!

Matthew 27:3 Then Judas, which had betrayed him, when he saw that he was condemned, repented himself, and brought again the thirty pieces of silver to the chief priests and elders,

Matthew 27:4 Saying, I have sinned in that I have betrayed the innocent blood. And they said, What *is that* to us? see thou *to that.*

Matthew 27:5 And he cast down the pieces of silver in the temple, and departed, and went and hanged himself.

Repentance will not save a man. It did not save Judas. Sincerity will not save a man. Humility will not save a man. Though repentance is an important first step, along with sincerity and humility, the only way to be saved is to come to Jesus Christ by faith, to ask Him to personally save you and then you must believe the Gospel. The Gospel is the good news that Jesus Christ came and that He died and that He was buried, and that He rose again from the grave on the first day of the week, which is contained in the Bible, the Word of God. Repentance means to "turn from," and faith means to "turn to." Ye have not because ye ask not!

James 4:2 Ye lust, and have not: ye kill, and desire to have, and cannot obtain: ye fight and war, yet ye have not, because ye ask not.

The chief priests were afraid of what to do with this money. It was cast at their feet, and they decide to buy a plot in the potter's field. A potter's field is a place where clay is removed for making pottery. It then is useless to build on and commonly is referred to as a burial site for unknown or indigent people.

Matthew 27:6 And the chief priests took the silver pieces, and said, It is not lawful for to put them into the treasury, because it is the price of blood.

Matthew 27:7 And they took counsel, and bought with them the potter's field, to bury strangers in.

Matthew 27:8 Wherefore that field was called, The field of blood, unto this day.

Again, Bible prophesies are fulfilled, this time by Jeremiah:

Matthew 27:9 Then was fulfilled that which was spoken by Jeremy the prophet, saying, And they took the thirty pieces of silver, the price of him that was valued, whom they of the children of Israel did value;

Matthew 27:10 And gave them for the potter's field, as the Lord appointed me.

What a minute! This specific Bible prophesy is in Zechariah not in Jeremiah!

Zechariah 11:12 And I said unto them, If ye think good, give *me* my price; and if not, forbear. So they weighed for my price thirty *pieces* of silver.

Zechariah 11:13 And the LORD said unto me, Cast it unto the potter: a goodly price that I was prised at of them. And I took the thirty *pieces* of silver, and cast them to the potter in the house of the LORD.

However, the book of Jeremiah is where God really points out the problem of a people who have never turned to God and His Word. God used a comparison of the potter and the clay.

Jeremiah 18:1 The word which came to Jeremiah from the LORD, saying,

Jeremiah 18:2 Arise, and go down to the potter's house, and there I will cause thee to hear my words.

The potter's house would be the house of God. Where it is appropriate to hear the words of God.

Jeremiah 18:3 Then I went down to the potter's house, and, behold, he wrought a work on the wheels.

Who is the potter? Scripture tells us that God represents Himself as the Potter and that all of mankind is the clay. He formed man out of the dust of the ground.

Isaiah 64:8 But now, O LORD, thou *art* our father; we *are* the clay, and thou our potter; and we all *are* the work of thy hand.

God created Adam. He was the first vessel. He became marred with sin. God could not rework the old Adam. He had to create a new vessel. God would have to regenerate man. God did not just

change the old Adam but made him a new work via the new birth in Christ.

> Jeremiah 18:4 And the vessel that he made of clay was marred in the hand of the potter: so he made it again another vessel, as seemed good to the potter to make *it.*

God says through this prophesy in Jeremiah that these chief priests have totally forgotten the Messiah who they should have been looking for. Now that they have caused others to stumble, all God's people, the Jews, will be scattered, and all they will see is God's back:

> Jeremiah 18:15 Because my people hath forgotten me, they have burned incense to vanity, and they have caused them to stumble in their ways *from* the ancient paths, to walk in paths, *in* a way not cast up;
>
> Jeremiah 18:16 To make their land desolate, *and* a perpetual hissing; every one that passeth thereby shall be astonished, and wag his head.
>
> Jeremiah 18:17 I will scatter them as with an east wind before the enemy; I will shew them the back, and not the face, in the day of their calamity.

The two-thousand-year Jewish calamity was about to begin. A calamity like none other was about to take place. In just forty short years, Jerusalem would be destroyed, and the Jews would be scattered and hated even to this very day. God showed them His back and not His face, and it has been a horrible time for their race. But God is not through with the Jews yet. There is still the matter of the seven-year period or one week left from Daniel's seventy weeks to come to pass. Called a time of Jacob's trouble by Jeremiah, God will continue dealing with His people, the Jews at that seven-year time of tribulation.

LUKE CHAPTER 23

Highlights:

Chapter twenty-three has Jesus Christ before Pilate. Jesus Christ is condemned to die the death of crucifixion. He is buried in a tomb where never man was laid.

Main Participants:

Jesus Christ v.1,
Pontious Pilate v.1,
Herod v.7,
Chief priests and Scribes v.10,
Barabbas v.18,
Simon the Cyrenian v.26,
A great company v.27,
Two malefactors v.32,
The centurion v.47,
The women that followed v.49,
Joseph of Arimathaea v.50,

In Brief:

Jesus appears before Pontius Pilate. Jesus appears before Herod. Jesus before the chief priests who ask for Barabbas to be released instead of Jesus. Jesus carries His cross and will be assisted by Simon. He is crucified with two thieves. Jesus Christ dies at 3pm on the 14th of Nisan, Passover, the first month of the

Jewish religious year. Joseph of Arimathea begs the body of Jesus from Pilate and buries Him in a new tomb covered with a stone.

Synoptic in Matthew, Mark, and Luke's Gospel

Luke 23:1 And the whole multitude of them arose, and led him unto Pilate.

Pilate appeared many times before the crowd this morning with Jesus. In fact, at seven different times Pilate and Jesus meet before the people. Luke has four encounters, and John has three encounters with Pilate. The first encounter below is mentioned and is in fact listed in all the synoptic Gospels.

Pilate before the people in Luke's Gospel 1st encounter

Luke 23:2 And they began to accuse him, saying, We found this *fellow* perverting the nation, and forbidding to give tribute to Caesar, saying that he himself is Christ a King.
Luke 23:3 And Pilate asked him, saying, Art thou the King of the Jews? And he answered him and said, Thou sayest *it*.

Matthew says the same:
> Matthew 27:11 And Jesus stood before the governor: and the governor asked him, saying, Art thou the King of the Jews? And Jesus said unto him, Thou sayest.

Mark also says the same:
> Mar 15:2 And Pilate asked him, Art thou the King of the Jews? And he answering said unto him, Thou sayest *it*.

Luke 23:4 Then said Pilate to the chief priests and *to* the people, I find no fault in this man.

Luke 23:5 And they were the more fierce, saying, He stirreth up the people, teaching throughout all Jewry, beginning from Galilee to this place.

Only in Luke's Gospel

Pilate hears a key word, "Galilaean." Pilate then determines that Jesus is not part of his jurisdiction but instead belongs to Herod's jurisdiction.

Luke 23:6 When Pilate heard of Galilee, he asked whether the man were a Galilaean.
Luke 23:7 And as soon as he knew that he belonged unto Herod's jurisdiction, he sent him to Herod, who himself also was at Jerusalem at that time.

Herod receives Jesus and is excited but for an entirely different reason. Herod had heard of the miracles and healings that Jesus had worked in the past. He wanted some entertainment.

Luke 23:8 And when Herod saw Jesus, he was exceeding glad: for he was desirous to see him of a long *season,* because he had heard many things of him; and he hoped to have seen some miracle done by him.
Luke 23:9 Then he questioned with him in many words; but he answered him nothing.
Luke 23:10 And the chief priests and scribes stood and vehemently accused him.
Luke 23:11 And Herod with his men of war set him at nought, and mocked *him,* and arrayed him in a gorgeous robe, and sent him again to Pilate.

Interesting to note that in politics, even back in the day, Herod and Pilate had much to do with *Quid Pro Quo.*

Luke 23:12 And the same day Pilate and Herod were made friends together: for before they were at enmity between themselves.

Synoptic in Matthew, Mark, and Luke's Gospel

Pilate appears the second time this morning with Jesus. Pilate called for a special meeting with the chief priests. This second encounter below is only mentioned in the Gospel of Luke.

Pilate before the people in Luke's Gospel 2nd encounter

Luke 23:13 And Pilate, when he had called together the chief priests and the rulers and the people,

Luke 23:14 Said unto them, Ye have brought this man unto me, as one that perverteth the people: and, behold, I, having examined *him* before you, have found no fault in this man touching those things whereof ye accuse him:

Luke 23:15 No, nor yet Herod: for I sent you to him; and, lo, nothing worthy of death is done unto him.

Luke 23:16 I will therefore chastise him, and release *him.*

Luke 23:17 (For of necessity he must release one unto them at the feast.)

Only in Matthew's Gospel

It is approximately at this point in time, that Pilate sits down, and his wife approaches him. Luke says nothing about this strange encounter, but Matthew has much to say about it.

Matthew 27:19 When he was set down on the judgment seat, his wife sent unto him, saying, Have thou nothing to do with that just man: for I have suffered many things this day in a dream because of him.

Matthew 27:20 But the chief priests and elders persuaded the multitude that they should ask Barabbas, and destroy Jesus.

A PERFECT UNDERSTANDING

<u>Synoptic in Matthew, Mark, Luke, and John's Gospel</u>

All four Gospels speak of the murderer, robber, thief, and insurrectionist, Barabbas! The Gospel of Luke is sufficient to explain this.

Luke 23:18 And they cried out all at once, saying, Away with this *man,* and release unto us Barabbas:
Luke 23:19 (Who for a certain sedition made in the city, and for murder, was cast into prison.)

<u>Pilate before the people only in John's Gospel 3rd encounter</u>

John has a unique encounter with Pilate at this time. This is a third time that Pilate is before the people and a second encounter with Jesus. Notice that verse 33 says *Pilate entered into the judgement hall again.* Jesus gives a unique response only recorded by John.

John 18:31 Then said Pilate unto them, Take ye him, and judge him according to your law. The Jews therefore said unto him, It is not lawful for us to put any man to death:
John 18:32 That the saying of Jesus might be fulfilled, which he spake, signifying what death he should die.
John 18:33 Then Pilate entered into the judgment hall again, and called Jesus, and said unto him, Art thou the King of the Jews?
John 18:34 Jesus answered him, Sayest thou this thing of thyself, or did others tell it thee of me?

Pilate before the people in Luke's Gospel 4th encounter

Luke 23:20 Pilate therefore, willing to release Jesus, spake again to them.
Luke 23:21 But they cried, saying, Crucify *him,* crucify him.

Luke quickly has Pilate hear the cry, "Crucify him, crucify him" and it is not what Pilate wants to hear. After his wife scared him and after his personal questioning of Jesus and finding no fault in him, He continues with a fifth encounter with the crowd.

Pilate before the people in Luke's Gospel 5th encounter

Luke says that Pilate asked the same question three times. What evil hath he done? Pilate asked this question the first time in Luke 23:14 saying he, that is Pilate questioned the man and found no fault in Him. In Luke 23:20 Pilate again went before the people. Now for the third time and he asks Why? Why? Why?

Luke 23:22 And he said unto them the third time, Why, what evil hath he done? I have found no cause of death in him: I will therefore chastise him, and let *him* go.
Luke 23:23 And they were instant with loud voices, requiring that he might be crucified. And the voices of them and of the chief priests prevailed.

What happens next is the statement heard around the world! You have heard of the "shot heard around the world?' Well, the Jews brought continual condemnation upon their children for generations to follow. Even today, the Jews are hunted, and hated, and killed, and have been for generation after generation.

Matthew 27:25 Then answered all the people, and said, His blood *be* on us, and on our children.

Luke 23:24 And Pilate gave sentence that it should be as they required. Luke 23:25 And he released unto them him that for sedition and murder was cast into prison, whom they had desired; but he delivered Jesus to their will.

This is a terrible insult to God and His Son, the Lord Jesus Christ. the fact that a robber and a murderer would be allowed to go free instead of Jesus. Barabbas is released at this moment and Christ is turned over to the will of the people.

Only in Matthew, Mark, and John's Gospel not in Luke

The scourging of Christ is not in Luke's Gospel. This is interesting to note as Luke is the physician who would understand the pain of this moment. However, the scourging is mentioned in each of the other three Gospels.
In Matthew:
Matthew 27:26 Then released he Barabbas unto them: and when he had scourged Jesus, he delivered *him* to be crucified.
In Mark:
Mark 15:15 And *so* Pilate, willing to content the people, released Barabbas unto them, and delivered Jesus, when he had scourged *him,* to be crucified.
And in John:
John 19:1 Then Pilate therefore took Jesus, and scourged *him.*
Images in movies, and statues, and in paintings that depict Christ being whipped do not please God. In fact, God hates them. The fact is, God says if you bow down or worship any likeness that

347

appear before you, you hate God! I believe this is why God gave us the second commandment:

> Exodus 20:4 Thou shalt not make unto thee any graven image, or any likeness *of any thing* that *is* in heaven above, or that *is* in the earth beneath, or that *is* in the water under the earth:
>
> Exodus 20:5 Thou shalt not bow down thyself to them, nor serve them: for I the LORD thy God *am* a jealous God, visiting the iniquity of the fathers upon the children unto the third and fourth *generation* of them that hate me;
>
> Exodus 20:6 And shewing mercy unto thousands of them that love me, and keep my commandments.

God used 4 short words and that is; "he had scoured Him." This will go down for an eternity that Pilate, the coward that he was, ordered the scourging of Christ. And God spent absolutely no time dwelling on this point of scripture. Luke describes how Pilate gave the order for the sentence requiring it to take place.

Pilate before the people only in John's Gospel 6ᵗʰ encounter

After the scourging, Pilate goes out again for a sixth time before the People. Pilate, the coward that he is, makes some statements to perhaps please his wife. He again says he finds no fault in Jesus.

> John 19:4 Pilate therefore went forth again, and saith unto them, Behold, I bring him forth to you, that ye may know that I find no fault in him.

It's during this sixth encounter with the people that Pilate makes his famous statement of "Behold the Man!"

> John 19:5 Then came Jesus forth, wearing the crown of thorns, and the purple robe. And *Pilate* saith unto them, Behold the man!

For the first time in the scriptures, Pilate gives his permission to the chief priests to go ahead and crucify Him.

John 19:6 When the chief priests therefore and officers saw him, they cried out, saying, Crucify *him, crucify him.* Pilate saith unto them, Take ye him, and crucify *him:* for I find no fault in him.

John 19:7 The Jews answered him, We have a law, and by our law he ought to die, because he made himself the Son of God.

The true colors of Pilate finally come out. He is afraid! He doesn't know what to do!

John 19:8 When Pilate therefore heard that saying, he was the more afraid;

Pilate before the people only in John's Gospel 7ᵗʰ encounter

Pilate heads back into the judgement hall. He is a nervous wreck. He talks with Jesus

John 19:9 And went again into the judgment hall, and saith unto Jesus, Whence art thou? But Jesus gave him no answer.

John 19:10 Then saith Pilate unto him, Speakest thou not unto me? knowest thou not that I have power to crucify thee, and have power to release thee?

John 19:11 Jesus answered, Thou couldest have no power *at all* against me, except it were given thee from above: therefore he that delivered me unto thee hath the greater sin.

Pilate goes out to the people and thinks he is going to release Jesus. But the crowd has been swayed by the chief priests.

John 19:12 And from thenceforth Pilate sought to release him: but the Jews cried out, saying, If thou let this man go, thou art not Caesar's friend: whosoever maketh himself a king speaketh against Caesar.

John 19:13 When Pilate therefore heard that saying, he brought Jesus forth, and sat down in the judgment seat in a place that is called the Pavement, but in the Hebrew, Gabbatha.

It is just before noon, (The sixth hour of the day is noon) on the fourteenth of Abib (The name of the Jews first month if the year, Abib. This name, Abib, was changed to Nisan during the Babylonian captivity.) Pilate is giving the order to crucify Jesus at this point.

John 19:14 And it was the preparation of the passover, and about the sixth hour: and he saith unto the Jews, Behold your King!

Behold your King! Infuriates the chief priests. They state their disgust with Jesus:

John 19:15 But they cried out, Away with *him,* away with *him,* crucify him. Pilate saith unto them, Shall I crucify your King? The chief priests answered, We have no king but Caesar.

Synoptic in Matthew, Mark, Luke, and John's Gospel

The time is concurrent at this moment in all four gospels. Jesus is being led away to be crucified. This is a time sensitive moment in eternity.

Matthew says:

Matthew 27:31 And after that they had mocked him, they took the robe off from him, and put his own raiment on him, and led him away to crucify *him.*

Matthew 27:32 And as they came out, they found a man of Cyrene, Simon by name: him they compelled to bear his cross.

Mark says:

Mark 15:20 And when they had mocked him, they took off the purple from him, and put his own clothes on him, and led him out to crucify him.

Mark 15:21 And they compel one Simon a Cyrenian, who passed by, coming out of the country, the father of Alexander and Rufus, to bear his cross.

Luke says:

Luke 23:26 And as they led him away, they laid hold upon one Simon, a Cyrenian, coming out of the country, and on him they laid the cross, that he might bear *it* after Jesus.

John says:

John 19:16 Then delivered he him therefore unto them to be crucified. And they took Jesus, and led *him* away.

John 19:17 And he bearing his cross went forth into a place called *the place* of a skull, which is called in the Hebrew Golgotha:

John is the only Gospel that adds that Christ carried His own cross indicating that Simon the Cyrenian helped for a short period of time. Jesus was required to carry His own cross up the hill to Golgotha. Golgotha is called by the Greek name *Calvary* only in Luke's Gospel. Notice that in all four accounts of the gospels not one implies that Jesus fell to the ground. This is a man-made belief that Jesus fell under the weight of the cross.

Only in Luke's Gospel

Only the Gospel of Luke has this sincere exchange between Jesus and the Daughters of Jerusalem. It is the only account of Jesus speaking during the trip to Golgotha. This is a very intense statement for those who are still close to Him. They are following Jesus and weeping for Him.

Luke 23:27 And there followed him a great company of people, and of women, which also bewailed and lamented him.

Luke 23:28 But Jesus turning unto them said, Daughters of Jerusalem, weep not for me, but weep for yourselves, and for your children.

Luke 23:29 For, behold, the days are coming, in the which they shall say, Blessed *are* the barren, and the wombs that never bare, and the paps which never gave suck.

Luke 23:30 Then shall they begin to say to the mountains, Fall on us; and to the hills, Cover us.

Luke 23:31 For if they do these things in a green tree, what shall be done in the dry?

Jesus points out that the destruction of the living or green tree is taking place now. Jesus will be put to death. But, when He

is crucified; when all hope rested only in Him; when all the world would be blessed through Abraham; the rest of the world have no hope; no chance of life without Him but that life is dry.

Synoptic in Matthew, Mark, Luke and John's Gospel

Luke points out that two malefactors where crucified with Christ. In fact, every Gospel has an account of the two thieves.

Luke 23:32 And there were also two other, malefactors, led with him to be put to death.
Luke 23:33 And when they were come to the place, which is called Calvary, there they crucified him, and the malefactors, one on the right hand, and the other on the left.

Jesus made seven statements as He hung on the cross. Matthew and Mark record the same statement, Luke records three and John records three quotes. Each Gospel explains what was said. Luke records the first statement made by Jesus from the cross: This comes as He is being nailed and raised up on the beam of the cross where He is positioned for the first few moments.

Luke 23:34 Then said Jesus, Father, forgive them; for they know not what they do. And they parted his raiment, and cast lots.
Luke 23:35 And the people stood beholding. And the rulers also with them derided _him,_ saying, He saved others; let him save himself, if he be Christ, the chosen of God.
Luke 23:36 And the soldiers also mocked him, coming to him, and offering him vinegar,
Luke 23:37 And saying, If thou be the king of the Jews, save thyself.
Luke 23:38 And a superscription also was written over him in letters of Greek, and Latin, and Hebrew, THIS IS THE KING OF THE JEWS.
Luke 23:39 And one of the malefactors which were hanged railed on him, saying, If thou be Christ, save thyself and us.

Luke 23:40 But the other answering rebuked him, saying, Dost not thou fear God, seeing thou art in the same condemnation?

Luke 23:41 And we indeed justly; for we receive the due reward of our deeds: but this man hath done nothing amiss.

Luke 23:42 And he said unto Jesus, Lord, remember me when thou comest into thy kingdom.

Luke 23:43 And Jesus said unto him, Verily I say unto thee, To day shalt thou be with me in paradise.

Luke 23:44 And it was about the sixth hour, and there was a darkness over all the earth until the ninth hour.

Jesus dies on the cross. His body and spirit separate, and all eternity is marked with the strange things that happen at His death. Now, at the moment of Christ's death, the veil would be torn from top to bottom.

Luke 23:45 And the sun was darkened, and the veil of the temple was rent in the midst.

Luke 23:46 And when Jesus had cried with a loud voice, he said, Father, into thy hands I commend my spirit: and having said thus, he gave up the ghost.

Luke records one of Christs last statements from the cross. The centurion heard this. He then believed and glorified God. What happens when this is heard today? The death, burial, and resurrection of Christ will save today if it is believed by anyone and everyone!

Luke 23:47 Now when the centurion saw what was done, he glorified God, saying, Certainly this was a righteous man.

Luke 23:48 And all the people that came together to that sight, beholding the things which were done, smote their breasts, and returned.

Luke 23:49 And all his acquaintance, and the women that followed him from Galilee, stood afar off, beholding these things.

Luke 23:50 And, behold, *there was* a man named Joseph, a counsellor; *and he was* a good man, and a just:

Luke 23:51 (The same had not consented to the counsel and deed of them;) *he was* of Arimathaea, a city of the Jews: who also himself waited for the kingdom of God.

Luke 23:52 This *man* went unto Pilate, and begged the body of Jesus.

Luke 23:53 And he took it down, and wrapped it in linen, and laid it in a sepulchre that was hewn in stone, wherein never man before was laid.

Luke 23:54 And that day was the preparation, and the sabbath drew on.

Luke 23:55 And the women also, which came with him from Galilee, followed after, and beheld the sepulchre, and how his body was laid.

The body of Christ is being observed. There is very little time to view the body as it was laid in the tomb and the stone could be rolled to seal the tomb at the very end of this day. Now, at 6pm or the start of the high Sabbath, the woman had to get home to honor the high Sabbath of the first day of unleavened bread. This day immediately follows the day that the Passover lamb was killed.

After the high Sabbath of the first day of unleavened bread, the women, Mary Magdalene and Mary the mother of James, and Salome, can go purchase and prepare the spices. I do not know how much work this was, but it was work. They would not be able to do this on the high Sabbath of the first day of unleavened bread or the Saturday Sabbath. Mark says that the women rested on the Sabbath and that a sabbath past before they could buy the spices.

Mark 16:1 And when the sabbath was past, Mary Magdalene, and Mary the *mother* of James, and Salome, had bought sweet spices, that they might come and anoint him.

Three days and three nights now occur. The first day and night is the high Sabbath of the first day of unleavened bread. The second day and night can be a day of work. The spices can now be bought, they can be carried home, and they can be prepared. This means that there must have been a day for work to be done between two Sabbath days. The third day and night are the Saturday Sabbath when the women will have to rest. The following verse says that the women did rest on a Sabbath day according to the

commandment. That would be the fourth commandment which they must follow.

Luke 23:56 And they returned, and prepared spices and ointments; and rested the sabbath day according to the commandment.

At this point in time, the women can rest for a Sabbath. Which Sabbath? This Sabbath is the Sabbath before the first day of the week commonly called the Saturday Sabbath. This Sabbath is after the spices were prepared.

It is not part of the saving Gospel to believe what day Christ died on. It is part of the saving Gospel that HE DID DIE. It is also part of the Gospel that He was buried, and Jesus declared that was for three days and three nights. It is also part of the Gospel that He rose again as Luke explains next and will be discussed in this last chapter to come.

1Co 15:1 Moreover, brethren, I declare unto you the gospel which I preached unto you, which also ye have received, and wherein ye stand;

1Co 15:2 By which also ye are saved, if ye keep in memory what I preached unto you, unless ye have believed in vain.

1Co 15:3 For I delivered unto you first of all that which I also received, how that Christ died for our sins according to the scriptures;

1Co 15:4 And that he was buried, and that he rose again the third day according to the scriptures:

LUKE CHAPTER 24

Highlights:

Chapter twenty-four has Jesus Christ's resurrection. Jesus Christ on the road to Emmaus. Jesus Christ in His spiritual body amongst His disciples. Jesus Christ ascending into heaven.

Main Participants:

Certain women v.1,
Two men (angels) v.4,
The Eleven v.9,
Mary Magdalene v.10,
Joanna v.10,
Mary the mother of James v.10,
Peter v.12,
Two going to Emmaus v.13,
Jesus v,15,
Cleopas, one of the two v.18,
Chief priests and rulers v.20,
Simon Peter, one of the two v.34,

In Brief:

The resurrection of Jesus, the most important event in history. The empty tomb discovered first by woman going to anoint the body of Christ. The disciples, not knowing how to believe that Messiah has gone missing. Jesus appearing first to Mary Magdalene, a sinner, (John 20). He then appears again to

Mary Magdalene and the other Mary (Matthew 21:9). Then Jesus appears to Cleophas and Peter on the road to Emmaus. Then to the eleven the night of Resurrection Sunday. Finally, Jesus ascends into Heaven to be united forevermore with the Father.

Synoptic in Matthew, Mark, Luke and John's Gospel

Luke 24:1 Now upon the first _day_ of the week, very early in the morning, they came unto the sepulchre, bringing the spices which they had prepared, and certain _others_ with them.

Who came to the grave? One of the "certain others" would have been Joanna from Luke 24:10. Another may have been Salome. Salome was with them when they went to purchase the spices on Friday, according to Mark 16:1. All the women did not have to come together. But they had the same thing on their mind. They wanted to care for and anoint the body of Jesus that they expected to see in the tomb. These certain other women come to the grave very early in the morning. They were a little behind Mary Magdalene who was first to see the miracle of the stone rolled away:

Luke 24:2 And they found the stone rolled away from the sepulchre.
Luke 24:3 And they entered in, and found not the body of the Lord Jesus.
Luke 24:4 And it came to pass, as they were much perplexed thereabout, behold, two men stood by them in shining garments:

An angel will appear as a man. This happened all throughout the Bible. To Abraham there appeared two men called angels for the crowd recognized these two as men. The women saw the angels and thought they were men. Even in Hebrews it says that without knowing it we may encounter angels.
Hebrews 13:1 Let brotherly love continue.
Hebrews 13:2 Be not forgetful to entertain strangers: for thereby some have entertained angels unawares.

Angels will also speak as humans do. Angels are different than Cherubim and Seraphim. Nowhere in the Bible does it say that angels have wings. Though it does say that angels can fly. However, wings are not needed to fly, just look at Superman! Only Cherubim and Seraphim have wings in the Bible. Totally different creations of God for His purpose.

Luke 24:5 And as they were afraid, and bowed down *their* faces to the earth, they said unto them, Why seek ye the living among the dead?
Luke 24:6 He is not here, but is risen: remember how he spake unto you when he was yet in Galilee,
Luke 24:7 Saying, The Son of man must be delivered into the hands of sinful men, and be crucified, and the third day rise again.
Luke 24:8 And they remembered his words,

The women have left the tomb. The Apostles did not believe them!

Luke 24:9 And returned from the sepulchre, and told all these things unto the eleven, and to all the rest.
Luke 24:10 It was Mary Magdalene, and Joanna, and Mary *the mother* of James, and other *women that were* with them, which told these things unto the apostles.
Luke 24:11 And their words seemed to them as idle tales, and they believed them not.

Peter now runs to the tomb. There is no indication that he returns to the group where the women went. He joins with Cleopas and heads for Emmaus.

Luke 24:12 Then arose Peter, and ran unto the sepulchre; and stooping down, he beheld the linen clothes laid by themselves, and departed, wondering in himself at that which was come to pass.
Luke 24:13 And, behold, two of them went that same day to a village called Emmaus, which was from Jerusalem *about* threescore furlongs.
Luke 24:14 And they talked together of all these things which had happened.

Luke 24:15 And it came to pass, that, while they communed *together* and reasoned, Jesus himself drew near, and went with them.

This is Jesus Christ's first appearance to a man since His resurrection. He had appeared earlier to Mary Magdalene as John had said:
> John 20:14 And when she had thus said, she turned herself back, and saw Jesus standing, and knew not that it was Jesus.

Then Jesus appears to the group of women as they walked back to where the disciples where:
> Matthew 28:9 And as they went to tell his disciples, behold, Jesus met them, saying, All hail. And they came and held him by the feet, and worshipped him.

> Matthew 28:10 Then said Jesus unto them, Be not afraid: go tell my brethren that they go into Galilee, and there shall they see me.

Now for the first time, Jesus will appear to two men, Peter and Cleopas.

Luke 24:16 But their eyes were holden that they should not know him.
Luke 24:17 And he said unto them, What manner of communications *are* these that ye have one to another, as ye walk, and are sad?
Luke 24:18 And the one of them, whose name was Cleopas, answering said unto him, Art thou only a stranger in Jerusalem, and hast not known the things which are come to pass there in these days?
Luke 24:19 And he said unto them, What things? And they said unto him, Concerning Jesus of Nazareth, which was a prophet mighty in deed and word before God and all the people:
Luke 24:20 And how the chief priests and our rulers delivered him to be condemned to death, and have crucified him.
Luke 24:21 But we trusted that it had been he which should have redeemed Israel: and beside all this, to day is the third day since these things were done.

Since what was done? That is the question. The two men have noticed strange things happening. A crucifixion was not so strange. In fact, there was a hill just for crucifixions to take place

called the place of the skull. This hill was very visible on the road to Damascus. Peter was still remorse from his three-fold denial of Jesus. He knew that the trial of Jesus was set back four days ago from this moment on the first day of the week. But what happened before today being the third day since these very weird things occurred. What was the weirdest thing of all was seeing the chief priests and their rulers acting so strange with the crucifixion of this man. Why just three days ago they had seen the chief priests sealing the tomb of Jesus in desperation as Matthew described.

Matthew 27:62 Now the next day, that followed the day of the preparation, the chief priests and Pharisees came together unto Pilate,

Matthew 27:63 Saying, Sir, we remember that that deceiver said, while he was yet alive, After three days I will rise again.

Matthew 27:64 Command therefore that the sepulchre be made sure until the third day, lest his disciples come by night, and steal him away, and say unto the people, He is risen from the dead: so the last error shall be worse than the first.

Matthew 27:65 Pilate said unto them, Ye have a watch: go your way, make *it* as sure as ye can.

Matthew 27:66 So they went, and made the sepulchre sure, sealing the stone, and setting a watch.

Pilate had ordered the chief priests to go and seal the stone themselves. Imagine the chief priests and scribes mixing mortar to seal the stone at Jesus Christ's tomb. This could only have been done between the two sabbaths. This is hard work and time-consuming work. The Chief Priests, who wanted to look pious to the rest of the people would not do this on either Sabbaths.

Luke 24:22 Yea, and certain women also of our company made us astonished, which were early at the sepulchre;

What could astonish these two men about the women. The fact that this was the third day since they had gone and bought so many spices, went home from the store, prepared the spices and then waited for this morning to anoint the body. With two Sabbaths divided by one day of work being done, this is the only way that the time frame meets all the statements of the Gospels.

The order of events are as follows:
Wednesday 3:00pm Christ dies on the cross.
Wednesday by 6:00pm Christ is in the tomb and the tomb sealed.
Wednesday from 6:00pm to Thursday at 6:00pm- High Sabbath no work to be performed!
First twenty-four-hour period.
Thursday from 6:00pm to Friday at 6:00pm- Day that work could be performed.
Second twenty-four-hour period.
Friday from 6:00pm to Saturday at 6:00pm- Saturday Sabbath, no work to be performed!
Third twenty-four-hour period.
Saturday starting at 6:00pm marks the start of the first day of the week and Jesus can now arise at any time. 72 hours or three days since He was laid in the tomb. The earliest scripture speaks of the resurrection is in the Gospel of John who writes while it was yet dark on the first day of the week, Mary found the empty tomb.

John 20:1 The first *day* of the week cometh Mary Magdalene early, when it was yet dark, unto the sepulchre, and seeth the stone taken away from the sepulchre.

Luke 24:23 And when they found not his body, they came, saying, that they had also seen a vision of angels, which said that he was alive.
Luke 24:24 And certain of them which were with us went to the sepulchre, and found *it* even so as the women had said: but him they saw not.
Luke 24:25 Then he said unto them, O fools, and slow of heart to believe all that the prophets have spoken:

The word for *fool* used here is a unique use of the Greek word *anoētos* (an-o'-ay-tos); and means unintelligent. It is not the

Greek word, *mōros* (mo-ros') meaning stupid or a blockhead as Jesus used in other situations.

Luke 24:26 Ought not Christ to have suffered these things, and to enter into his glory?
Luke 24:27 And beginning at Moses and all the prophets, he expounded unto them in all the scriptures the things concerning himself.

Jesus was with them for three years, explaining to them continually that He was the Messiah and that He came to die. Left to our own strength, no one will ever turn to Jesus Christ and understand the scriptures. The Holy Spirit is needed to open our eyes from being "holden" as stated in verse 16. God does not reveal himself to the unwise (fools) but rather for men to ask for the Spirit of truth. Jesus has gone through the entire Old Testament speaking of those things concerning Him.
The two men arrive in Emmaus and ask Jesus to stay with them.

Luke 24:28 And they drew nigh unto the village, whither they went: and he made as though he would have gone further.
Luke 24:29 But they constrained him, saying, Abide with us: for it is toward evening, and the day is far spent. And he went in to tarry with them.
Luke 24:30 And it came to pass, as he sat at meat with them, he took bread, and blessed *it,* and brake, and gave to them.
Luke 24:31 And their eyes were opened, and they knew him; and he vanished out of their sight.
Luke 24:32 And they said one to another, Did not our heart burn within us, while he talked with us by the way, and while he opened to us the scriptures?

The events of this meal opened Peter's eyes. He sees Jesus doing the same in blessing the bread, breaking it and giving it to him and Cleophas. Their eyes are open, and they realize this is truly the Messiah come back from the dead. Jesus vanishes but in so doing leaves these two men with a burning in their hearts.

Luke 24:33 And they rose up the same hour, and returned to Jerusalem, and found the eleven gathered together, and them that were with them,

Emmaus is a little over 12 kilometers from Jerusalem, sixty furlongs. You can run that in an hour if you are trained. In the days of Peter, all were trained to go on foot faster if needed. By the end of this first day of the week, Resurrection Sunday, Peter and Cleophas are back and telling the eleven that Jesus appeared to Simon who is Peter.

Luke 24:34 Saying, The Lord is risen indeed, and hath appeared to Simon.
Luke 24:35 And they told what things *were done* in the way, and how he was known of them in breaking of bread.

Here is the confirmation of what opened the eyes of Simon, who is Peter, one of the two men and Cleophas. This confirmation was the breaking of bread and the similarities to the Last Supper on Passover. After all, He is the "Bread of Life." Now, Jesus does not leave these two hanging. He appears to them all.

Luke 24:36 And as they thus spake, Jesus himself stood in the midst of them, and saith unto them, Peace *be* unto you.
Luke 24:37 But they were terrified and affrighted, and supposed that they had seen a spirit. Luke 24:38 And he said unto them, Why are ye troubled? and why do thoughts arise in your hearts?
Luke 24:39 Behold my hands and my feet, that it is I myself: handle me, and see; for a spirit hath not flesh and bones, as ye see me have.
Luke 24:40 And when he had thus spoken, he shewed them *his* hands and *his* feet.

This is a view of what our spiritual bodies will be like. A spirit body of flesh and bones. No blood! God gives the reassurance that this is what is in store for us after death.

1John 3:1 Behold, what manner of love the Father hath bestowed upon us, that we should be called the sons of God: therefore the world knoweth us not, because it knew him not.
1John 3:2 Beloved, now are we the sons of God, and it doth not yet appear what we shall be: but we know that, when he shall appear, we shall be like him; for we shall see him as he is.

Luke 24:41 And while they yet believed not for joy, and wondered, he said unto them, Have ye here any meat?
Luke 24:42 And they gave him a piece of a broiled fish, and of an honeycomb.
Luke 24:43 And he took *it,* and did eat before them.

From this it is seen that a spiritual body will have many of the senses and needs of the physical body. It appears the Lord had taste. Along with taste would come smell. Jesus could see and talk and hear and feel. All the senses man has today. And we shall be like Him!

Luke 24:44 And he said unto them, These *are* the words which I spake unto you, while I was yet with you, that all things must be fulfilled, which were written in the law of Moses, and *in* the prophets, and *in* the psalms, concerning me.
Luke 24:45 Then opened he their understanding, that they might understand the scriptures,
Luke 24:46 And said unto them, Thus it is written, and thus it behoved Christ to suffer, and to rise from the dead the third day:
Luke 24:47 And that repentance and remission of sins should be preached in his name among all nations, beginning at Jerusalem.
Luke 24:48 And ye are witnesses of these things.

The understanding of His disciples that were present began to open up. Jesus declared that He fulfilled all the things that were written by Moses. Moses wrote the first five books in the Bible. Jesus had to fulfill all of them.

Matthew 5:17 Think not that I am come to destroy the law, or the prophets: I am not come to destroy, but to fulfil.

Matthew 5:18 For verily I say unto you, Till heaven and earth pass, one jot or one tittle shall in no wise pass from the law, till all be fulfilled.

This is the primary reason He came. His death, burial, and resurrection became the perfect sacrifice that God the Father required.

Luke 24:49 And, behold, I send the promise of my Father upon you: but tarry ye in the city of Jerusalem, until ye be endued with power from on high.

The power from on high came just as Jesus had predicted, exactly fifty days from His resurrection on the feast of Pentecost. Christ's resurrection was on the feast of firstfruits which is celebrated on the first day of the week (Sunday) following the Passover. Fifty days from firstfruits is Pentecost when the disciples, all one-hundred twenty of them were endued with power from on high.

Acts 2:1 And when the day of Pentecost was fully come, they were all with one accord in one place.

Acts 2:2 And suddenly there came a sound from heaven as of a rushing mighty wind, and it filled all the house where they were sitting.

Acts 2:3 And there appeared unto them cloven tongues like as of fire, and it sat upon each of them.

Acts 2:4 And they were all filled with the Holy Ghost, and began to speak with other tongues, as the Spirit gave them utterance.

However, before Pentecost, Jesus had to go to heaven. Jesus was crystal clear when He told His disciples in the Gospel of John the order of events.

John 16:7 Nevertheless I tell you the truth; It is expedient for you that I go away: for if I go not away, the Comforter will not come unto you; but if I depart, I will send him unto you.

Jesus had to leave this earth. Without Him leaving, that is ascending back to heaven, The Holy Ghost could not have come. Later Jesus declares this Comforter to be none other than the Holy Ghost.

John 14:25 These things have I spoken unto you, being *yet* present with you.

John 14:26 But the Comforter, *which is* the Holy Ghost, whom the Father will send in my name, he shall teach you all things, and bring all things to your remembrance, whatsoever I have said unto you.

Luke 24:50 And he led them out as far as to Bethany, and he lifted up his hands, and blessed them.

Luke 24:51 And it came to pass, while he blessed them, he was parted from them, and carried up into heaven.

Luke 24:52 And they worshipped him, and returned to Jerusalem with great joy:

Luke 24:53 And were continually in the temple, praising and blessing God. Amen.

In conclusion, I want to thank you the reader for giving your time to understand more about Jesus Christ. This book is not perfect, in fact, probably a long way from it. But if it gets you to dig into the book that is perfect, that is the Bible, well, my work is done. The ignorance of God's Words is much worse toward the end of my life than it was when I was saved forty-five years ago. Jesus predicted this for the last days. Paul wrote about this also. So did Peter that men would become willingly ignorant of the scriptures. So I leave you with this message that hopefully will not apply to you the reader:

2Peter 3:1 This second epistle, beloved, I now write unto you; in *both* which I stir up your pure minds by way of remembrance:

2Peter 3:2 That ye may be mindful of the words which were spoken before by the holy prophets, and of the commandment of us the apostles of the Lord and Saviour:

2Peter 3:3 Knowing this first, that there shall come in the last days scoffers, walking after their own lusts,

2Peter 3:4 And saying, Where is the promise of his coming? for since the fathers fell asleep, all things continue as *they were* from the beginning of the creation.

2Peter 3:5 For this they willingly are ignorant of, that by the word of God the heavens were of old, and the earth standing out of the water and in the water:

2Peter 3:6 Whereby the world that then was, being overflowed with water, perished:

2Peter 3:7 But the heavens and the earth, which are now, by the same word are kept in store, reserved unto fire against the day of judgment and perdition of ungodly men.

www.ingramcontent.com/pod-product-compliance
Lightning Source LLC
Chambersburg PA
CBHW042137140626

46547CB00038B/744